Philad Dec: 13. 1753

ived your Fav. of the 5th Inst.
our kind Congratulations .
e time since, and sent you
bound Books; the Parcel was
Care of Mr Theyvesandt a
don it is not yet got to hand.
Truth give you a good Acc.t
xcellent Pieces of yours; but where
had, the best Work comes to the
wish the enclos'd were better
me. — I know nothing

The Founding Fathers

B.FRANKLIN LL.D. F.R.S. PRESIDENT OF PENNSYLVANIA, & LATE MINISTER OF THE UNITED STATES OF AMERICA AT THE COURT OF FRANCE. HIS EXCELLENCY

C.W.Peale pinx.t et Fecit 1787

The Founding Fathers

BENJAMIN FRANKLIN

A Biography in His Own Words

VOLUME 1

Edited by
THOMAS FLEMING

With an Introduction by
WHITFIELD J. BELL, Jr.
Librarian, American Philosophical Society

JOAN PATERSON KERR
Picture Editor

NEWSWEEK, New York

Benjamin Franklin, A Biography in His Own Words,
has been produced by the Newsweek Book Division:

Joseph L. Gardner, Editor

Janet Czarnetzki, Art Director

S. Arthur Dembner, Publisher

This book is based on Volumes 1-15 of *The Papers of Benjamin Franklin,*
edited by Leonard W. Labaree (Vols. 1-14) and William B. Willcox (Vol. 15)
and published by Yale University Press.
The texts of documents to be published in forthcoming volumes
of this edition have been supplied by Mr. Willcox, and permission to reproduce
exerpts from these documents has been obtained from their owners.

Contents

Introduction

by Whitfield J. Bell, Jr.
Librarian, American Philosophical Society

In a memorable passage in his famous *Autobiography* Benjamin Franklin tells how he learned to write good English prose. With only two years of formal schooling, he read every book he could find, including works of polemic divinity from his father's collection. An odd volume of *The Spectator* falling into his hands, he was so delighted with it that he took its style for a model. He would outline the major points, then rewrite the essay from the outline; mix up the heads of topics and then reorganize them and compose the essay afresh; and at every stage compare his version with the original. To improve his vocabulary, Franklin tried his hand at ballad-making, cast prose into verse and verse into prose. "Extreamly ambitious" to become "a tolerable English writer," he took every opportunity to practice the art. His surviving commonplace book and drafts of other writings show how carefully he composed even personal letters and routine business correspondence. He was determined that everything he wrote should meet his standards—that it be smooth, clear, and short; in other words, agreeable to the ear, understanding, and patience. That he succeeded in his aim many readers gladly testified. "America has sent us many good things," the Scottish historian and philosopher David Hume told him, "Gold, Silver, Sugar, Tobacco, Indigo, &c.: but you are the first Philosopher, and indeed the first Great Man of Letters for whom we are beholden to her."

From the time when—as a sixteen-year-old apprentice—he had slipped the first Silence Dogood essay under his brother's printing office door, Franklin's skill with a pen was generally recognized. Most of the clubs, societies, and other bodies to which he belonged made him their secretary (and his willingness to discharge the secretary's duties was one of the reasons those groups succeeded). He drafted letters and petitions, wrote notices for the papers, composed bylaws and histories, and was called on for memorial and ceremonial inscriptions. For the Pennsylvania Hospital, for example, Franklin drafted the original petition to the Assembly, the managers' memorial to the Proprietors, the hospital's appeal to the public for financial support, and the regulations for the election of officers. He wrote the managers' business letters, prepared *Some Account of the Pennsylvania Hospital* in 1754, and when the cornerstone of the first building was ready to be laid, he composed the inscription. Not only did he serve the hospital, the American Philosophical Society, the fire company, and the Masonic lodge as author and editor, but he filled the same role in the Pennsylvania Assembly and the First Continental Congress, and as Minister to France—wherever precise thought, logical argument, and a persuasive tone were especially required. "Prose writing has been of great use to me in the course of my life," he reflected, "and was a principal means of my advancement."

As author and publisher, Franklin addressed his writings to the general public. He wrote to inform, instruct, persuade, or entertain, not to gratify himself. But even his personal letters and private literary exercises won him public recognition and fame. His sister-in-law showed around a letter of condolence he wrote her ("a man is not completely born until he be dead: Why then should we grieve that a new child is born among the immortals?"); friends asked for copies; and thus, passing from hand to hand, the letter gave solace and comfort to many beyond the family circle. A similar reputation was earned by a letter Franklin wrote to an officious clergyman whom he had helped cure in an illness, and who undertook to warn his benefactor against taking pride in his achievement. Franklin reminded the clergyman that "real good Works, Works of Kindness, Charity, Mercy, and Publick Spirit" were a more acceptable Christian service than "Holiday-keeping, Sermon-Reading...or making long Prayers, fill'd with Flatteries and Compliments." The epitaph (page 129) Franklin composed for himself in some Junto exercise also achieved popular fame during his lifetime: it was printed and reprinted, and friends sometimes asked for a copy, which he would write out from memory.

Inevitably, selected letters and papers were collected and published during Franklin's lifetime. His reports of electrical experiments sent to Peter Collinson in London were given by Collinson to a printer; and as Franklin made new experiments, they were published as supplements to the original printing. In 1769, when Franklin was in London as the agent for Pennsylvania, a quarto volume of 496 pages was published, which included both the electrical papers and others of a "philosophical" nature and many of general interest. This edition was revised and enlarged five years later. The Continent was no less eager to read Franklin's writings, especially France, where he already had eager admirers and disciples. One of these, the *philosophe* Barbeu Dubourg in 1773 brought out a French translation of the 1769 edition, with the addition of letters Franklin had sent French savants. Not even the American Revolution put a stop to the growing demand. Franklin assisted his young Whig friend Benjamin Vaughan to publish a volume of his *Political, Miscellaneous and Philosophical Pieces* (London, 1779); and Charles Dilly, the London bookseller, in 1787 issued still another collection of letters and papers. None of these volumes, however, nor all of them together, contained more than a fraction of Franklin's writings—and by 1787 he was generally known to be composing an autobiography, which none of his editors had yet seen. But America's patriarch died in 1790 before the book could be either completed or published.

Franklin bequeathed his books and papers to his grandson William Temple Franklin. Temple divided his inheritance, depositing the bulk of it—including thousands of letters to Franklin—in the care of his friend Dr. George Fox of Champlost near Philadelphia, but taking some three thousand letters and papers to London in 1791. From all sides Temple Franklin was called on promptly to publish a comprehensive edition of his grandfather's writings; but Temple proved to be, in the words of a later Franklin scholar, "a slow coach." More than a quarter of a century passed before his *Memoirs of the Life and Writings of Benjamin Franklin* in three volumes appeared in London in 1817–18.

The manuscripts that Dr. Fox received from Temple descended to his son, Charles Pemberton Fox, who eventually stored them in the stable at Champlost—

from which, from time to time, he extracted samples to give his house guests. In 1831 Professor Jared Sparks of Harvard, in Philadelphia to collect materials for his *Writings of George Washington* and other studies of the Revolutionary period, was conducted to the Champlost stable. Fox allowed Sparks to include many of the letters in his ten-volume *Works of Benjamin Franklin,* which appeared in 1836–40. In the latter year, at Sparks's suggestion, Fox gave the entire collection to the American Philosophical Society.

Among the manuscripts that Temple inherited was an autograph draft of his grandfather's *Autobiography.* Begun in 1771 — in the form of a long letter to his son William — then laid aside, it was in Franklin's library when the British occupied Philadelphia in 1777 and requisitioned the house of the archrebel for officers' quarters. In the confusion of the time, the manuscript was thrown out, but rescued from the street by sheerest chance — an old friend of Franklin's saw it lying in a gutter, recognized the handwriting, picked it up, and later returned it to the author. Encouraged by friends who read the manuscript, Franklin resumed writing at Passy in 1784, where he showed portions of it to his French friends, among them M. Le Veillard, mayor of the village. In 1789, in response to his friend's request, Franklin sent Le Veillard a clean copy of the *Autobiography;* he retained the original, on which he continued to work in Philadelphia until within a few months of his death. It took the story forward only as far as Franklin's first mission to England in 1757.

One of Temple Franklin's first acts, after he received his grandfather's legacy, was to ask Le Veillard for the clean copy of the *Autobiography,* in exchange for Franklin's original. Thus, Temple Franklin obtained a fair copy suitable for the printer, while Le Veillard received the working draft of the manuscript with Franklin's last additions and revisions. In 1791 a French translation of Franklin's memoirs appeared, and this was promptly translated into English. At the same time there was published in London, in 1793, a small volume entitled *Works of the late Dr. Benjamin Franklin...together with Essays Humorous, Moral & Literary.* Comprising the *Autobiography,* some letters, bagatelles, and other popular pieces, this work was issued in one edition after another in England, on the Continent, and in America for almost a century after Franklin's death. It fashioned the popular image of Franklin much as Parson Weems's *Life* molded that of Washington; and, like Weems's book, it had a lasting effect on the national character.

The manuscript *Autobiography* that Le Veillard received survived the vicissitudes of the French Revolution, in which Le Veillard was guillotined, and descended to his daughter and her family. Although never willfully concealed, its existence was barely known, and it was almost never seen by any outsider. Not until 1866 was it located and examined. John Bigelow, United States Minister to France, bought the manuscript and in 1868 published for the first time a complete and accurate version of Franklin's own manuscript of the *Autobiography.* This publication, like James Parton's exhaustive *Life and Times of Benjamin Franklin,* published four years earlier, awakened wide popular and scholarly interest in the man.

After his volumes were published, Temple Franklin abandoned the manuscripts he had carried to London, for they were no longer of interest or value to him. About 1840, seventeen years after Temple's death, they were discovered in a London tailor's shop — Temple had lived upstairs, and the tailor, incredibly, had used the papers as patterns for garments he was cutting. They were acquired by "an officer under government," who offered them without success to the British Museum, the British Foreign Office, and several American ministers, until at last the Yankee bookseller in London Henry Stevens of Vermont purchased them in 1851.

In the characteristic spirit of many scholarly booksellers, Stevens made grand plans for the manuscripts, but he was also in debt. He pledged the Franklin papers as collateral, and they disappeared from public sight into a bank vault for nearly thirty years until at last in 1881, after anxious negotiations, they were bought by the United States Government and lodged in the Department of State in Washington. John Bigelow, whose interest in Franklin was unabated after his initial coup of finding the manuscript *Autobiography,* undertook a new edition of Franklin's writings, incorporating material newly acquired in London. The work appeared in ten volumes in 1887–88.

The bicentennial of Franklin's birth in 1906 provided the occasion for yet another edition of Franklin's writings. Albert Henry Smyth, professor of English in Philadelphia's Central High School and the author of several scholarly works on early American literature, undertook the task. Not only could he draw on the great collections of the American Philosophical Society and the Department of State, but, unlike his predecessors, he obtained copies of Franklin's letters in the French Foreign Office and in the possession of descendants and private collectors in the United States, England, and France. The Smyth edition, augmented by I. Minis Hays's *Calendar of the Papers of Benjamin Franklin in the Library of the American Philosophical Society* (1908), was the principal source of authoritative information on Franklin for half a century thereafter.

By 1950, however, the limitations of the Smyth edition and of Hays's *Calendar* were generally recognized. Smyth's volumes contained but a fraction of what was available even in 1906, and Hays's *Calendar* was out of date: in the 1930's and 1940's the American Philosophical Society had acquired several large collections of Franklin's letters. Furthermore, scholars now believed that any edition of collected writings should include letters and papers addressed to the subject. To print only the subject's letters, someone has said, is like listening to one side of a telephone conversation. Besides all this, the existing editions had done little to explicate the text by way of annotation. Clearly what was needed was a new edition of Franklin that should be truly comprehensive and adequately annotated and that should fully meet the canons of twentieth-century scholarship.

That such a scheme was feasible was triumphantly demonstrated in 1950 when the first volume of *The Papers of Thomas Jefferson,* edited by Julian P. Boyd, was published by the Princeton University Press. The Jefferson *Papers* combined financial support, the cooperative efforts of a team of scholars, and modern technology—notably cheap photoduplication—in an imaginative and effective way. In the ensuing few years several scholars privately urged that Franklin's writings should also be published; and Dr. William E. Lingelbach, Librarian of the American Philosophical Society, began to sound out his colleagues and several Franklin scholars on the subject. Before the Society reached a decision, however, there was movement from another quarter.

In the summer of 1952, Bromwell Ault, an alumnus of Yale University, suggested to President A. Whitney Griswold that Yale should undertake an edition like Princeton's Jefferson *Papers.* The proposal was reasonable because Yale had owned since 1936 the magnificent Franklin collection assembled by William Smith Mason—unexcelled in printed works by and about Franklin. From Time Inc., through Henry R. Luce, another Yale alumnus, assurance was obtained of a substantial gift to underwrite the costs. The result was that the two institutions, the American Philosophical Society and Yale, agreed to publish a comprehensive edition of Franklin's writings under their joint auspices. The decision was announced on the anniversary of Franklin's birth in 1954. Meanwhile, Leonard W. Labaree, Farnham professor of history at Yale, had been appointed editor of the new project. During the late winter and spring of 1954 he assembled his staff, and by September of that year work was under way.

The first major task of the new Franklin editors was to locate and copy Franklin's letters in all the places where they were preserved. The American Philosophical Society, the Library of Congress (to which the Department of State's collection had been moved), the Historical Society of Pennsylvania, the University of Pennsylvania, Yale University, and a dozen more institutions accounted for about 85 per cent of the surviving papers; to obtain photocopies of their holdings was not difficult. But the remaining 10 to 15 per cent—some three thousand documents—were, as the search revealed, owned by more than three hundred institutions and private persons. These letters were in one sense the most important, because many were not easily available to scholars and most in fact had never been printed anywhere. In person and by written inquiries the editors searched systematically through libraries and archives where Franklin letters might be expected to be. The Pennsylvania Hospital, which Franklin founded and fostered; the archives of the Pennsylvania Society for Promoting the Abolition of Slavery, which he headed; the Royal Society of London, of which he was a fellow; the Library Company of Philadelphia, which he founded; the Associates of the Late Reverend Dr. Bray, to whom he provided data on the education of Negro children, all yielded manuscripts. Still others were found in such unlikely places as Windsor Castle, the Karl Marx University of Leipzig, and a resort hotel in northern Pennsylvania (which had framed a Franklin letter as a room decoration).

The editors sought out descendants of Franklin—several dozen, although none bore the name of Franklin—who received them cordially, as their parents and grandparents had received Smyth and Sparks, and came away with copies of warmly treasured letters, some of a moving, personal kind. Every owner of a set of autographs of the signers of the Declaration of Independence was solicited for a copy of his Franklin document; and scores of other private collectors were no less willing to cooperate. Perhaps the most unexpected discovery was that of some 150 letters that passed between Franklin, Mrs. Margaret Stevenson, his London landlady, and her daughter Polly, which were owned by descendants of the latter, not twenty minutes from the library of the American Philosophical Society in Philadelphia. All in all, Labaree and his colleagues located and copied some 30,000 manuscripts written by or to Franklin; they represented correspondence with some 4,200 different persons.

When the task of locating was nearly completed—it can never be entirely completed—that of editing began. By checking transcriptions, copy, and proof at every stage against the photocopies, the editors assured a high standard of accuracy; while in their editing they aimed to present Franklin fully and accurately, as his contemporaries saw him. For their annotations, the editors used all the standard works of reference to identify persons and allusions in the text—the dictionaries of national biography, the *Pennsylvania Archives*, for example—and called on some unconventional means as well. Faced with four dated and undated letters from Franklin to his brother John about the latter's bladder complaint, they consulted a urologist, who unhesitatingly diagnosed brother John's trouble and, on the basis of the symptoms described, placed the letters in correct chronological order.

The Benjamin Franklin who has emerged from the volumes thus far published in the new series by the Yale University Press is not remarkably different from the one known through the pages of Temple Franklin, Sparks, Bigelow, and Smyth. Familiar episodes are only drawn in greater detail, and the familiar figure emerges in sharper outline. *The Papers of Benjamin Franklin* have pulled together the story of many single episodes in Franklin's career from many different sources—on American prisoners of war in the Revolution, for example, from the Library of Congress and the American Philosophical Society, the National Maritime Museum at Greenwich, the Public Record Office in London, the Berkshire Record Office in Reading, and the National Library of Scotland. How deeply Franklin was involved in the work of Negro education—to take another example—had not been generally known before; yet no reader is surprised to learn that he was concerned in the matter: this is what one would expect of the man Americans have always known and long admired.

From the published volumes of *The Papers of Benjamin Franklin* and from the much greater mass of papers remaining to be edited, Thomas Fleming has selected and extracted materials for this biography. These selections, explained and annotated by the editor, present Benjamin Franklin largely in his own words. They show him in the many facets of his busy life, public and private; they reveal him in his intense commitment and in his wise reasonableness, moderation, and unfailing good humor.

EDITORIAL NOTE

Most of the Franklin writings reprinted in this biography have been excerpted from the longer original documents being published in their entirety by Yale University Press. Omissions at the beginning or ending of a document are indicated only if the extract begins or ends in the middle of a sentence; however, omissions within a quoted passage are indicated by ellipses. The original spellings in all cases have been retained; editorial insertions are set within square brackets.

Chronology of Franklin and His Times

Benjamin Franklin born in Boston, January 17 (January 6, Old Style)	1706	
	1713	Treaty of Utrecht ends War of Spanish Succession
	1714	Reign of George I of England, 1714–27
Apprenticed to brother James	1718	
First issue of *The New-England Courant*	1721	Robert Walpole, British Prime Minister, 1721–42
Silence Dogood letters published	1722	
Leaves Boston for Philadelphia	1723	
Sails for England with James Ralph	1724	
Returns to America	1726	
Junto organized	1727	George II, King of England, 1727–60
The Pennsylvania Gazette begins publication	1729	
Takes Deborah Read as wife, September 1	1730	
Library Company of Philadelphia founded; son William Franklin born (?)	1731	
Compiles first edition of *Poor Richard*; birth of son Francis Folger Franklin	1732	
	1733	Molasses Act; founding of Colony of Georgia
	1735	John Peter Zenger tried for libel
Union Fire Company formed; death of Francis Folger Franklin	1736	
	1739	War of Jenkins' Ear, 1739–42
	1740	War of the Austrian Succession, 1740–48
Daughter Sarah Franklin born; American Philosophical Society founded	1743	King George's War, American phase of hostilities, 1743–48
"The Speech of Miss Polly Baker" printed; begins experiments with electricity	1747	
Founds Pennsylvania Hospital; elected to Assembly	1751	
Experiments with kite during thunderstorm	1752	
Academy of Philadelphia chartered; description of lightning rod; named joint Deputy Postmaster General with William Hunter of Virginia	1753	French expedition sent to occupy Ohio
Presents Plan of Union at Albany Congress	1754	Americans defeated at Fort Necessity in first action of French and Indian War, 1754–63
Rising dispute between Penns and Quakers	1755	Braddock's campaign
Leads Philadelphia volunteers to western Pennsylvania; elected to Royal Society	1756	Seven Years' War in Europe, 1756–63
Sails to England to negotiate with Proprietors	1757	Coalition ministry of Newcastle and Pitt
Receives degree from St. Andrews; travels to north of England and Scotland	1759	Wolfe defeats Montcalm at Quebec
	1760	Reign of George III of England, 1760–1820
	1761	Ministry of Lord Bute
Receives degree from Oxford; returns to America	1762	William Franklin named Governor of New Jersey
	1763	Pontiac's Uprising; march of Paxton Boys; Ministry of George Grenville, 1763–65

Militia bill; drafts petition for change in government; goes to London as agent for Pennsylvania	1764	Sugar Act; committees of correspondence formed to protest taxation without representation; nonimportation
	1765	Stamp Act; Rockingham ministry, 1765–66
Testifies before House of Commons on Stamp Act	1766	Stamp Act repealed; Chatham ministry, 1766–67
Visits France	1767	Townshend duties; revival of nonimportation; Grafton ministry, 1767–70
Named agent for Georgia	1768	
Becomes agent for New Jersey	1769	
Elected agent for Massachusetts	1770	Boston Massacre; Townshend duties repealed; North Ministry, 1770–82
Begins *Autobiography*; tours Ireland	1771	
Privy Council approves Grand Ohio Company; Hutchinson letters sent to Massachusetts	1772	Committees of correspondence reappear
Discloses part in publication of Hutchinson correspondence	1773	Tea Act passed; Boston Tea Party
Hearing before Privy Council; dismissed as postmaster; Deborah Franklin dies	1774	Punitive Acts; First Continental Congress; Galloway's plan of union; Louis XVI, King of France, 1774–92
Returns to America; named to Second Continental Congress	1775	Battles of Lexington and Concord, Ticonderoga, and Bunker Hill
Signs Declaration of Independence; sails to France as commissioner to negotiate alliance	1776	British evacuate Boston; Americans retreat from Long Island and New York City; Battle of Trenton; Captain James Cook's third voyage to Pacific, 1776–79
Meets Madame Brillon	1777	Battle of Saratoga; Congress agrees to Articles of Confederation
Treaties of alliance and commerce with France; arrival of John Adams	1778	Lord North's conciliation plan; British evacuate Philadelphia; John Paul Jones's raids in *Ranger*
Named minister to French court	1779	Spain declares war on Britain; John Jay named minister to Madrid; *Bonhomme Richard* defeats *Serapis*
Madame Helvetius rejects marriage	1780	Jones sails to America in *Ariel*
Offers resignation; appointed to peace commission	1781	John Laurens mission; Robert Morris named Superintendent of Finance; Battle of Yorktown
Preliminary articles of peace with Britain signed	1782	Rockingham ministry, March–July; Shelburne ministry, July–February, 1783
Definitive treaty of peace proclaimed	1783	British evacuate New York City
	1784	John Jay named Secretary for Foreign Affairs
Returns to America; chosen President of Pennsylvania Executive Council	1785	Adams and Jefferson appointed ministers to Britain and France
	1786	Shays' Rebellion
Attends Constitutional Convention at Philadelphia	1787	
	1788	Constitution ratified; first Federal elections
President of Society for Promoting the Abolition of Slavery	1789	Washington and Adams inaugurated; first Federal Congress; beginning of French Revolution and institution of National Assembly, 1789–91
Benjamin Franklin dies, April 17	1790	Hamilton's First Report on Public Credit; Jefferson takes office as Secretary of State; Louis XVI accepts constitutional monarchy in France

13

Chapter 1

Boston Boy

Benjamin Franklin was born on January 17, 1706, in Boston, Massachusetts. The little Colonial seaport on the edge of the British Empire was still struggling to emerge from the seventeenth century, with its religious obsessions and antagonisms. The Salem witch trials were only fourteen years in the past. Although the Church no longer dominated the State, ministers still wielded considerable secular influence, and a man's religious opinions were considered crucial to his standing in society. But business was already becoming at least as important in Boston's life. Some three hundred merchants and investors depended upon the fortunes of the city's fleet. Wharves, distilleries, and mansions were rising at a rapid rate. The population was edging toward ten thousand, and America's first newspaper, the *Newsletter*, had begun publishing in 1704. Boston was a bustling, growing place, with its own highly developed sense of identity. Unlike the other Founding Fathers, who as a group were rather reticent about their early lives, Franklin wrote a great deal about his boyhood in Boston. Most of these recollections are in his famous *Autobiography*, which he wrote in the form of a letter to his son William in the summer of 1771. After discussing the background of the Franklin family in England—they were small tradesmen with a special interest in blacksmithing in the Northamptonshire village of Ecton—Franklin described the father and mother he remembered from his Boston boyhood.

Autobiography, 1771

Josiah, my Father, married young, and carried his Wife with three Children unto New England, about 1682. The Conventicles having been forbidden by Law, and frequently disturbed, induced some considerable Men of his Acquaintance to remove to that Country, and he was prevail'd with to accompany them thither, where they expected to enjoy their Mode of Religion with Freedom. By the same Wife he had 4 Children more born there, and

The Boston of Franklin's birth and boyhood, from a 1722 map

15

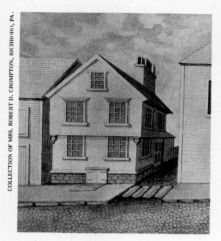

This water color of the Franklin home on Milk Street is a copy of a sketch made on the spot before fire destroyed the house in 1810.

by a second Wife ten more, in all 17, of which I remember 13 sitting at one time at his Table, who all grew up to be Men and Women, and married. I was the youngest Son and the youngest Child but two, and was born in Boston, N. England.

My mother the 2d Wife was Abiah Folger, a Daughter of Peter Folger, one of the first Settlers of New England, of whom honourable mention is made by Cotton Mather, in his Church History of that Country, (entitled Magnalia Christi Americana) as a *godly learned Englishman*, if I remember the words rightly. I have heard that he wrote sundry small occasional Pieces, but only one of them was printed which I saw now many Years since. It was written in 1675, in the homespun Verse of that Time and People, and address'd to those then concern'd in the Government there. It was in favour of Liberty of Conscience, and in behalf of the Baptists, Quakers, and other Sectaries, that had been under Persecution; ascribing the Indian Wars and other Distresses, that had befallen the Country to that Persecution, as so many Judgments of God, to punish so heinous an Offence; and exhorting a Repeal of those uncharitable Laws.

Franklin's only comment of his mother was that she had "an excellent Constitution. She suckled all her 10 Children." His father made a far deeper impression on him, as this description of Josiah Franklin reveals.

Autobiography, 1771

I think you may like to know Something of his Person and Character. He had an excellent Constitution of Body, was of middle Stature, but well set and very strong. He was ingenious, could draw prettily, was skill'd a little in Music and had a clear pleasing Voice, so that when he play'd Psalm Tunes on his Violin and sung withal as he sometimes did in an Evening after the Business of the Day was over, it was extreamly agreable to hear. He had a mechanical Genius too, and on occasion was very handy in the Use of other Tradesmen's Tools. But his great Excellence lay in a sound Understanding, and solid Judgment in prudential Matters, both in private and publick Affairs. In the latter indeed he was never employed, the numerous Family he had to educate and the straitness of his Circumstances, keeping him close to his Trade, but I remember well his being frequently visited by leading People, who consulted him for his Opinion in Affairs of the Town or of the Church he belong'd to and show'd a good deal of Respect for his Judgment and Advice. He was also much consulted by private Persons about their Affairs when any Difficulty occur'd, and frequently chosen an Arbitrator between contending Parties. At his Table he lik'd to have as often as he could, some sensible Friend or Neighbour, to converse with, and always took care to start some ingenious or useful Topic for Discourse, which might tend to improve the Minds of his Children. By this means he turn'd our Attention to what was good, just, and prudent in the Conduct of Life; and little or no Notice was ever taken of what related to the Victuals on the Table, whether it was well or ill drest, in or out of season, of good or bad flavour, preferable or inferior to this or that other thing of the kind; so that I was bro't up in such a perfect Inattention to those Matters as to be quite Indifferent what kind of Food was set before me.

Franklin learned very early about the need for a thick skin to cope with the rough give-and-take of life in a big family. It was an ideal preparation for the political combat of his later years. This recollection is from an essay he wrote in his old age, commonly known as "The Whistle." Typically, he drew a moral from the experience—most of life's troubles, he later decided, came from "giving too much for the whistle."

Passy [France], November 10 1779

When I was a Child of 7 Years old, my Friends on a Holiday fill'd my little Pocket with Halfpence. I went directly to a Shop where they sold Toys for Children; and being charm'd with the Sound of a Whistle, that I met by the way, in the hands of another Boy, I voluntarily offer'd and gave all my Money for it. When I came home, whistling all over the House, much pleased with my Whistle, but disturbing all the Family, my Brothers, Sisters & Cousins, understanding the Bargain I had made, told me I had given four times as much for it as it was worth, put me in mind what good Things I might have bought with the rest of the Money, & laught at me so much for my Folly that I cry'd with Vexation; and the Reflection gave me more Chagrin than the Whistle gave me Pleasure.

Illustration of "The Whistle"
from Holley's Life of Franklin

Growing up in a seaport surrounded by water, with numerous ponds and bays, Franklin "learned early to swim well and to manage boats." In a letter to a French friend, Barbeu Dubourg, written in

17

1773, Franklin recalled some of his aquatic experiments, which foreshadowed, in both their ingenuity and their observation, the scientist of the future.

[London, February–March, 1773]

When a youth, I made two oval pallets, each about ten inches long, and six broad, with a hole for the thumb, in order to retain it fast in the palm of my hand. They much resembled a painter's pallets. In swimming I pushed the edges of these forward, and I struck the water with their flat surfaces as I drew them back. I remember I swam faster by means of these pallets, but they fatigued my wrists. I also fitted to the soles of my feet a kind of sandals, but I was not satisfied with them, because I observed that the stroke is partly given by the inside of the feet and the ancles, and not entirely with the soles of the feet....

I amused myself one day with flying a paper kite; and approaching the bank of a pond, which was near a mile broad, the weather being very warm, I tied the string to a stake, and the kite ascended to a very considerable height above the pond, while I was swimming. In a little time, being desirous of amusing myself with my kite, and enjoying at the same time the pleasure of swimming, I returned; and, loosing from the stake the string with the little stick which was fastened to it, I went again into the water, where I found that lying on my back and holding the stick in my hands, I was drawn along the surface of the water in a very agreeable manner. Having then engaged another boy to carry my clothes round the pond to a place which I pointed out to him on the other side, I began to cross the pond with my kite, which carried me quite over without the least fatigue, and with the greatest pleasure....

The title page illustration in an 1852 book, The Works of Benjamin Franklin, *shows the boy innovator swimming with the aid of a kite.*

In the eighteenth century, most sons of tradesmen had their futures decided for them by their fathers at an early age. A boy could learn a trade only by becoming an apprentice and toiling for many years at extremely low wages. At first, Josiah Franklin envisioned a different future for his son Benjamin. But he was also a realistic man.

Autobiography, 1771

My elder Brothers were all put Apprentices to different Trades. I was put to the Grammar School at Eight Years of Age, my Father intending to devote me as the Tithe of his Sons to the Service of the Church. My early Readiness in learning to read (which must have been very early, as I do not remember when I could not read) and the Opinion of all his Friends that I should certainly make a

*A French engraving shows Franklin
helping his father to make candles.*

good Scholar, encourag'd him in this Purpose of his. My Uncle Benjamin too approv'd of it, and propos'd to give me all his Shorthand Volumes of Sermons I suppose as a Stock to set up with, if I would learn his Character. I continu'd however at the Grammar School not quite one Year, tho' in that time I had risen gradually from the Middle of the Class of that Year to be the Head of it, and farther was remov'd into the next Class above it, in order to go with that into the third at the End of the Year. But my Father in the mean time, from a View of the Expence of a College Education which, having so large a Family, he could not well afford, and the mean Living many so educated were afterwards able to obtain, Reasons that he gave to his Friends in my Hearing, altered his first Intention, took me from the Grammar School, and sent me to a School for Writing and Arithmetic kept by a then famous Man, Mr. Geo. Brownell, very successful in his Profession generally, and that by mild encouraging Methods. Under him I acquired fair Writing pretty soon, but I fail'd in the Arithmetic, and made no Progress in it.

At Ten Years old, I was taken home to assist my Father in his Business, which was that of a Tallow Chandler and Sope-Boiler. A Business he was not bred to, but had assumed on his Arrival in New England and on finding his Dying Trade would not maintain his Family, being in little Request. Accordingly I was employed in cutting Wick for the Candles, filling the Dipping Mold, and the Molds for cast Candles, attending the Shop, going of Errands, &c. I dislik'd the Trade and had a strong Inclination for the Sea; but my Father declar'd against it. . . .

I continu'd thus employ'd in my Father's Business for two Years, that is till I was 12 Years old; and my Brother John, who was bred to that Business having left my Father, married and set up for himself at Rhodeisland, there was all Appearance that I was destin'd to supply his Place and be a Tallow Chandler. But my Dislike to the Trade continuing, my Father was under Apprehensions that if he did not find one for me more agreable, I should break away and get to Sea, as his Son Josiah had done to his great Vexation. He therefore sometimes took me to walk with him, and see Joiners, Bricklayers, Turners, Braziers, &c. at their Work, that he might observe my Inclination, and endeavour to fix it on some Trade or other on Land. . . .

From a Child I was fond of Reading, and all the little
Money that came into my Hands was ever laid out in
Books. . . . This Bookish Inclination at length determin'd
my Father to make me a Printer, tho' he had already one
Son, (James) of that Profession. In 1717 my Brother James
return'd from England with a Press and Letters to set up
his Business in Boston. I lik'd it much better than that of
my Father, but still had a Hankering for the Sea. To prevent the apprehended Effect of such an Inclination, my
Father was impatient to have me bound to my Brother. I
stood out some time, but at last was persuaded and signed
the Indentures, when I was yet but 12 Years old. I was to
serve as an Apprentice till I was 21 Years of Age, only I
was to be allow'd Journeyman's Wages during the last
Year. In a little time I made great Proficiency in the
Business, and became a useful Hand to my Brother.

The printer's apprentice was soon enjoying the greatest
advantage of his trade. He had access to better books than the ones he had
read at home, which consisted mostly of polemic works on religion. Inevitably
this fondness for words led to Franklin's first experiments as a writer. In
this passage he recalled the fate of those experiments, and then moved swiftly
into a discussion of how he taught himself to write good prose. Unfortunately, no copies of his two ballads survive.

Autobiography, 1771

An Acquaintance with the Apprentices of Booksellers,
enabled me sometimes to borrow a small one, which I was
careful to return soon and clean. Often I sat up in my
Room reading the greatest Part of the Night, when the
Book was borrow'd in the Evening and to be return'd
early in the Morning lest it should be miss'd or wanted.
And after some time an ingenious Tradesman Mr.
Matthew Adams who had a pretty Collection of Books,
and who frequented our Printing House, took Notice of
me, invited me to his Library, and very kindly lent me
such Books as I chose to read. I now took a Fancy to
Poetry, and made some little Pieces. My Brother, thinking
it might turn to account encourag'd me, and put me on
composing two occasional Ballads. One was called the
Light House Tragedy, and contain'd an Account of the
drowning of Capt. Worthilake with his Two Daughters;
the other was a Sailor Song on the Taking of *Teach* or
Blackbeard the Pirate. They were wretched Stuff, in the
Grubstreet Ballad Stile, and when they were printed he

sent me about the Town to sell them. The first sold wonderfully, the Event being recent, having made a great Noise. This flatter'd my Vanity. But my Father discourag'd me, by ridiculing my Performances, and telling me Verse-makers were generally Beggars; so I escap'd being a Poet, most probably a very bad one. But as Prose Writing has been of great Use to me in the Course of my Life, and was a principal Means of my Advancement, I shall tell you how in such a Situation I acquir'd what little Ability I have in that Way.

There was another Bookish Lad in the Town, John Collins by Name, with whom I was intimately acquainted. We sometimes disputed, and very fond we were of Argument, and very desirous of confuting one another. Which disputacious Turn, by the way, is apt to become a very bad Habit, making People often extreamly disagreable in Company, by the Contradiction that is necessary to bring it into Practice, and thence, besides souring and spoiling the Conversation, is productive of Disgusts and perhaps Enmities where you may have occasion for Friendship. I had caught it by reading my Father's Books of Dispute about Religion. Persons of good Sense, I have since observ'd, seldom fall into it, except Lawyers, University Men, and Men of all Sorts that have been bred at Edinborough. A Question was once some how or other started between Collins and me, of the Propriety of educating the Female Sex in Learning, and their Abilities for Study. He was of Opinion that it was improper; and that they were naturally unequal to it. I took the contrary Side, perhaps a little for Dispute sake. He was naturally more eloquent, had a ready Plenty of Words, and sometimes as I thought bore me down more by his Fluency than by the Strength of his Reasons. As we parted without settling the Point, and were not to see one another again for some time, I sat down to put my Arguments in Writing, which I copied fair and sent to him. He answer'd and I reply'd. Three or four Letters of a Side had pass'd, when my Father happen'd to find my Papers, and read them. Without entring into the Discussion, he took occasion to talk to me about the Manner of my Writing, observ'd that tho' I had the Advantage of my Antagonist in correct Spelling and pointing (which I ow'd to the Printing House) I fell far short in elegance of Expression, in Method and in Perspicuity, of which he convinc'd me by several In-

An early Life *of Franklin depicts him reading at night.*

21

stances. I saw the Justice of his Remarks, and thence grew more attentive to the *Manner* in Writing, and determin'd to endeavour at Improvement.

About this time I met with an odd Volume of the Spectator. It was the third. I had never before seen any of them. I bought it, read it over and over, and was much delighted with it. I thought the Writing excellent, and wish'd if possible to imitate it. With that View, I took some of the Papers, and making short Hints of the Sentiment in each Sentence, laid them by a few Days, and then without looking at the Book, try'd to compleat the Papers again, by expressing each hinted Sentiment at length and as fully as it had been express'd before, in any suitable Words, that should come to hand.

Then I compar'd my Spectator with the Original, discover'd some of my Faults and corrected them. But I found I wanted a Stock of Words or a Readiness in recollecting and using them, which I thought I should have acquir'd before that time, if I had gone on making Verses, since the continual Occasion for Words of the same Import but of different Length, to suit the Measure, or of different Sound for the Rhyme, would have laid me under a constant Necessity of searching for Variety, and also have tended to fix that Variety in my Mind, and make me Master of it. Therefore I took some of the Tales and turn'd them into Verse: And after a time, when I had pretty well forgotten the Prose, turn'd them back again. I also sometimes jumbled my Collections of Hints into Confusion, and after some Weeks, endeavour'd to reduce them into the best Order, before I began to form the full Sentences, and compleat the Paper. This was to teach me Method in the Arrangement of Thoughts. By comparing my work afterwards with the original, I discover'd many faults and amended them; but I sometimes had the Pleasure of Fancying that in certain Particulars of small Import, I had been lucky enough to improve the Method or the Language and this encourag'd me to think I might possibly in time come to be a tolerable English Writer, of which I was extreamly ambitious.

Franklin also applied his ingenuity to his daily life. He needed more time to read books and practice his exercises in prose style. He gained some time by "evading as much as I could the common Attendance on publick Worship." And he found additional time by reforming his diet.

Autobiography, 1771

When about 16 Years of Age, I happen'd to meet with a Book, written by one Tryon, recommending a Vegetable Diet. I determined to go into it. My Brother being yet unmarried, did not keep House, but boarded himself and his Apprentices in another Family. My refusing to eat Flesh occasioned an Inconveniency, and I was frequently chid for my singularity. I made my self acquainted with Tryon's Manner of preparing some of his Dishes, such as Boiling Potatoes or Rice, making Hasty Pudding, and a few others, and then propos'd to my Brother, that if he would give me Weekly half the Money he paid for my Board I would board my self. He instantly agreed to it, and I presently found that I could save half what he paid me. This was an additional Fund for buying Books: But I had another Advantage in it. My Brother and the rest going from the Printing House to their Meals, I remain'd there alone, and dispatching presently my light Repast, (which often was no more than a Bisket or a Slice of Bread, a Handful of Raisins or a Tart from the Pastry Cook's, and a Glass of Water) had the rest of the Time till their Return, for Study, in which I made the greater Progress from that greater Clearness of Head and quicker Apprehension which usually attend Temperance in Eating and Drinking.

Three years after Benjamin Franklin went to work as an apprentice printer, James Franklin brought out the first issue of *The New-England Courant*. Young Benjamin recalled how "after having work'd in composing the Types and printing off the Sheets I was employ'd to carry the Papers thro' the Streets to the Customers." But the younger Franklin was not satisfied with this laborious side of the newspaper business. He yearned to see some of his own writing in the paper. In this passage from his *Autobiography*, he explained why he felt this way and the method he used to satisfy his desire.

Autobiography, 1771

He had some ingenious Men among his Friends who amus'd themselves by writing little Pieces for this Paper, which gain'd it Credit, and made it more in Demand; and these Gentlemen often visited us. Hearing their Conversations, and their Accounts of the Approbation their Papers were receiv'd with, I was excited to try my Hand among them. But being still a Boy, and suspecting that my Brother would object to printing any Thing of mine in his Paper if he knew it to be mine, I contriv'd to disguise my Hand, and writing an anonymous Paper I put it in at Night under the Door of the Printing House. It was found in the Morning and communicated to his Writing Friends when they call'd in as usual. They read it, commented on it in my Hearing, and I had the exquisite Pleasure, of finding it met with their Approbation, and that in their different Guesses at the Author none were named but Men of some Character among us for Learning and Ingenuity.

Young Benjamin signed his contribution to the paper "Silence Dogood," and then proceeded to create a character to go with the name. Silence described herself as the widow of a country minister, who was "an Enemy to Vice, and a Friend to Vertue. . . . A hearty Lover of the Clergy and all good Men, and a mortal Enemy to arbitrary Government and unlimited Power." She also admitted she had "a natural Inclination to observe and reprove the Faults of others, at which I have an excellent Faculty." Fourteen letters over the signature of Silence came from the sixteen-year-old Franklin's pen between April and October of 1722. Perhaps the best of them was the fourth, in which the apprentice printer took revenge for being denied a college education.

Boston, May 14, 1722

Discoursing the other Day at Dinner with my Reverend Boarder, formerly mention'd, (whom for Distinction sake we will call by the name of Clericus,) concerning the Education of Children, I ask'd his Advice about my young Son William, whether or no I had best bestow upon him Academical Learning, or (as our Phrase is) *bring him up at our College*: He perswaded me to do it by all Means, using many weighty Arguments with me, and answering all the Objections that I could form against it; telling me withal, that he did not doubt but that the Lad would take his Learning very well, and not idle away his Time as too many there now-a-days do. These Words of Clericus gave me a Curiosity to inquire a little more strictly into the present Circumstances of that famous Seminary of Learning; but the Information which he gave me, was neither pleasant, nor such as I expected.

As soon as Dinner was over, I took a solitary Walk into my Orchard, still ruminating on Clericus's Discourse with much Consideration, until I came to my usual Place of Retirement under the *Great Apple-Tree*; where having seated my self, and carelessly laid my Head on a verdant Bank, I fell by Degrees into a soft and undisturbed

Slumber. My waking Thoughts remained with me in my Sleep, and before I awak'd again, I dreamt the following DREAM.

I fancy'd I was travelling over pleasant and delightful Fields and Meadows, and thro' many small Country Towns and Villages; and as I pass'd along, all Places resounded with the Fame of the Temple of LEARNING: Every Peasant, who had wherewithal, was preparing to send one of his Children at least to this famous Place; and in this Case most of them consulted their own Purses instead of their Childrens Capacities: So that I observed, a great many, yea, the most part of those who were travelling thither, were little better than Dunces and Blockheads. Alas! alas!

At length I entred upon a spacious Plain, in the Midst of which was erected a large and stately Edifice: It was to this that a great Company of Youths from all Parts of the Country were going; so stepping in among the Crowd, I passed on with them, and presently arrived at the Gate.

The Passage was kept by two sturdy Porters named *Riches* and *Poverty,* and the latter obstinately refused to give Entrance to any who had not first gain'd the Favour of the former; so that I observed many who came even to the very Gate, were obliged to travel back again as ignorant as they came, for want of this necessary Qualification. However, as a Spectator I gain'd Admittance, and with the rest entred directly into the Temple.

In the Middle of the great Hall stood a stately and magnificent Throne, which was ascended to by two high and difficult Steps. On the Top of it sat LEARNING in awful State; she was apparelled wholly in Black, and surrounded almost on every Side with innumerable Volumes in all Languages. She seem'd very busily employ'd in writing something on half a Sheet of Paper, and upon Enquiry, I understood she was preparing a Paper, call'd *The New-England Courant.* On her Right Hand sat *English,* with a pleasant smiling Countenance, and handsomely attir'd; and on her left were seated several *Antique Figures* with their Faces vail'd. I was considerably puzzl'd to guess who they were, until one informed me, (who stood beside me,) that those Figures on her left Hand were *Latin, Greek, Hebrew,* &c. and that they were very much reserv'd, and seldom or never unvail'd their Faces here, and then to few or none, tho'

A *wood engraving from* Pictorial Life of Benjamin Franklin, *1846, shows Franklin as a printer.*

The lower right-hand column of this 1722 issue of The New-England Courant *bears Franklin's signature above the first appearance of an article signed "Silence Dogood."*

most of those who have in this Place acquir'd so much Learning as to distinguish them from *English,* pretended to an intimate Acquaintance with them. I then enquir'd of him, what could be the Reason why they continued vail'd, in this Place especially: He pointed to the Foot of the Throne, where I saw *Idleness,* attended with *Ignorance,* and these (he informed me) were they, who first vail'd them, and still kept them so.

Now I observed, that the whole Tribe who entred into the Temple with me, began to climb the Throne; but the Work proving troublesome and difficult to most of them, they withdrew their Hands from the Plow, and contented themselves to sit at the Foot, with Madam *Idleness* and her Maid *Ignorance,* until those who were assisted by Diligence and a docible Temper, had well nigh got up the first Step: But the Time drawing nigh in which they could no way avoid ascending, they were fain to crave the Assistance of those who had got up before them, and who, for the Reward perhaps of a *Pint of Milk,* or a *Piece of Plumb-Cake,* lent the Lubbers a helping Hand, and sat them in the Eye of the World, upon a Level with themselves.

The other Step being in the same Manner ascended, and the usual Ceremonies at an End, every Beetle-Scull seem'd well satisfy'd with his own Portion of Learning, tho' perhaps he was *e'en just* as ignorant as ever. And now the Time of their Departure being come, they march'd out of Doors to make Room for another Company, who waited for Entrance: And I, having seen all that was to be seen, quitted the Hall likewise, and went to make my Observations on those who were just gone out before me.

Some I perceiv'd took to Merchandizing, others to Travelling, some to one Thing, some to another, and some to Nothing; and many of them from henceforth, for want of Patrimony, liv'd as poor as Church Mice, being unable to dig, and asham'd to beg, and to live by their Wits it was impossible. But the most Part of the Crowd went along a large beaten Path, which led to a Temple at the further End of the Plain, call'd, *The Temple of Theology.* The Business of those who were employ'd in this Temple being laborious and painful, I wonder'd exceedingly to see so many go towards it; but while I was pondering this Matter in my Mind, I spy'd *Pecunia* behind a Curtain, beckoning to them with her Hand, which Sight immediately satisfy'd me for whose Sake it was, that a great Part of them (I will not say all) travel'd that Road. In this Temple I saw nothing worth mentioning, except the ambitious and fraudulent Contrivances of Plagius, who (notwithstanding he had been severely reprehended for such Practices before) was diligently transcribing some eloquent Paragraphs out of Tillotson's *Works*, &c., to embellish his own.

Now I bethought my self in my Sleep, that it was Time to be at Home, and as I fancy'd I was travelling back thither, I reflected in my Mind on the extream Folly of those Parents, who, blind to their Childrens Dulness, and insensible of the Solidity of their Skulls, because they think their Purses can afford it, will needs send them to the Temple of Learning, where, for want of a suitable Genius, they learn little more than how to carry themselves handsomely, and enter a Room genteely, (which might as well be acquir'd at a Dancing-School,) and from whence they return, after Abundance of Trouble and Charge, as great Blockheads as ever, only more proud and self-conceited.

While I was in the midst of these unpleasant Reflections, Clericus (who with a Book in his Hand was walking under the Trees) accidentally awak'd me; to him I related my Dream with all its Particulars, and he, without much Study, presently interpreted it, assuring me, *That it was a lively Representation of* HARVARD COLLEGE, *Etcetera.* I remain, Sir, Your Humble Servant,

SILENCE DOGOOD

The success of Silence Dogood had an unhappy effect on Franklin's relationship with his brother when the secret of the authorship was at last revealed. James Franklin felt that the attention his friends paid to Benjamin made him "too vain," and this soon led to more serious differences.

Autobiography, 1771

Tho' a Brother, he considered himself as my Master, and me as his Apprentice; and accordingly expected the same Services from me as he would from another; while I thought he demean'd me too much in some he requir'd of me, who from a Brother expected more Indulgence. Our Disputes were often brought before our Father, and I fancy I was either generally in the right, or else a better Pleader, because the Judgment was generally in my favour: But my Brother was passionate and had often beaten me, which I took extreamly amiss; and thinking my Apprenticeship very tedious, I was continually wishing for some Opportunity of shortening it.

Franklin added in a footnote that he believed his brother's "harsh and tyrannical Treatment" created in him "that Aversion to arbitrary Power that has stuck to me thro' my whole Life." Events "in a manner unexpected" gave him a chance to revolt against his brother's rule and say farewell to Boston at the same time.

Autobiography, 1771

One of the Pieces in our News-Paper, on some political Point which I have now forgotten, gave Offence to the Assembly. He was taken up, censur'd and imprison'd for a Month by the Speaker's Warrant, I suppose because he would not discover his Author. I too was taken up and examin'd before the Council; but tho' I did not give them any Satisfaction, they contented themselves with admonishing me, and dismiss'd me; considering me perhaps as an Apprentice who was bound to keep his Master's Secrets. During my Brother's Confinement, which I resented a good deal, notwithstanding our private Differences, I had the Management of the Paper, and I made bold to give our Rulers some Rubs in it, which my Brother took very kindly, while others began to consider me in an unfavourable Light, as a young Genius that had a Turn for Libelling and Satyr. My Brother's Discharge was accompany'd with an Order of the House, (a very odd one) *that James Franklin should no longer print the Paper called the New England Courant.* There was a Consultation held in our Printing House among his Friends what he should do in this Case. Some propos'd to evade the Order by changing the Name of the Paper; but my Brother seeing Inconveniences in that, it was finally concluded on as a better Way, to let it be printed for the future under the Name of *Benjamin Franklin.* And to avoid the Censure of the Assembly that might fall on him, as still printing it by his Apprentice, the Contrivance was, that my old Indenture should be return'd to me with a full Discharge on the Back of it, to be shown on Occasion; but to secure to him the Benefit of my Service I was to sign new Indentures for the Remainder of the Term, which were to be kept private. A very flimsy Scheme it was, but however it was immediately executed, and the Paper went on accordingly under my Name for several Months. At length a fresh Difference arising between my Brother and me, I took upon me to assert my Freedom, presuming that he would not venture to produce the new Indentures. It was not fair in me to take this Advantage, and this I therefore reckon one of the first Errata of my Life: But the Unfairness of it weigh'd little with me, when under the Impressions of Resentment, for the Blows his Passion too often urg'd him to bestow upon me. Tho' he was otherwise not an ill-natur'd Man: Perhaps I was too saucy and provoking.

When he found I would leave him, he took care to prevent my getting Employment in any other Printing-House of the Town, by going round and speaking to every Master, who accordingly refus'd to give me Work. I then thought of going to New York as the nearest Place where there was a Printer: and I was the rather inclin'd to leave Boston, when I reflected that I had already made myself a little obnoxious to the governing Party; and from the arbitrary Proceedings of the Assembly in my Brother's Case it was likely I might if I stay'd soon bring myself into Scrapes; and farther that my indiscrete Disputations about Religion began to make me pointed at with Horror by good People, as an Infidel or Atheist. I determin'd on the Point: but my Father now siding with my Brother, I was sensible that if I attempted to go openly, Means would be used to prevent me. My Friend Collins therefore undertook to manage a little for me. He agreed with the Captain of a New York Sloop for my Passage, under the Notion of my being a young Acquaintance of his that had got a naughty Girl with Child, whose Friends would compel me to marry her, and therefore I could not appear or come away publickly. So I sold some of my Books to raise a little Money, Was taken on board privately, and as we had a fair Wind in three Days I found my self in New York near 300 Miles from home, a Boy of but 17, without the least Recommendation to or Knowledge of any Person in the Place, and with very little Money in my Pocket.

Chapter 2

Footloose Journeyman

In 1723, New York was far from the metropolis it would eventually become. In fact, it was little more than a village, smaller than Boston and Philadelphia, on the lower tip of Manhattan Island. Franklin soon found it had nothing to offer him except an opportunity to become a sailor, which no longer interested him.

Autobiography, 1771

My Inclinations for the Sea, were by this time worne out, or I might now have gratify'd them. But having a Trade, and supposing my self a pretty good Workman, I offer'd my Service to the Printer of the Place, old Mr. Wm. Bradford, (who had been the first Printer in Pensilvania, but remov'd from thence upon the Quarrel of Geo. Keith). He could give me no Employment, having little to do, and Help enough already: But, says he, my Son at Philadelphia has lately lost his principal Hand, Aquila Rose, by Death. If you go thither I believe he may employ you. Philadelphia was 100 Miles farther. I set out, however, in a Boat for Amboy, leaving my Chest and Things to follow me round by Sea. In crossing the Bay we met with a Squall that tore our rotten Sails to pieces, prevented our getting into the Kill, and drove us upon Long Island. In our Way a drunken Dutchman, who was a Passenger too, fell over board; when he was sinking I reach'd thro' the Water to his shock Pate and drew him up so that we got him in again. His Ducking sober'd him a little, and he went to sleep, taking first out of his Pocket a Book which he desir'd I would dry for him. It prov'd to be my old favourite Author Bunyan's Pilgrim's Progress in Dutch, finely printed on good

Paper with copper Cuts, a Dress better than I had ever seen it wear in its own Language....

When we drew near the Island we found it was at a Place where there could be no Landing, there being a great Surff on the stony Beach. So we dropt Anchor and swung round towards the Shore. Some People came down to the Water Edge and hallow'd to us, as we did to them. But the Wind was so high and the Surff so loud, that we could not hear so as to understand each other. There were Canoes on the Shore, and we made Signs and hallow'd that they should fetch us, but they either did not under-stand us, or thought it impracticable. So they went away, and Night coming on, we had no Remedy but to wait till the Wind should abate, and in the mean time the Boatman and I concluded to sleep if we could, and so crouded into the Scuttle with the Dutchman who was still wet, and the Spray beating over the Head of our Boat, leak'd thro' to us, so that we were soon almost as wet as he. In this Manner we lay all Night with very little Rest. But the Wind abating the next Day, we made a Shift to reach Amboy before Night, having been 30 Hours on the Water without Victuals, or any Drink but a Bottle of filthy Rum: The Water we sail'd on being salt.

In the Evening I found my self very feverish, and went in to Bed. But having read somewhere that cold Water drank plentifully was good for a Fever, I follow'd the Prescription, sweat plentifully most of the Night, my Fever left me, and in the Morning crossing the Ferry, I proceeded on my Journey, on foot, having 50 miles to Burlington, where I was told I should find Boats that would carry me the rest of the Way to Philadelphia.

It rain'd very hard all the Day, I was thoroughly soak'd and by Noon a good deal tir'd, so I stopt at a poor Inn, where I staid all Night, beginning now to wish I had never left home. I cut so miserable a Figure too, that I found by the Questions ask'd me I was suspected to be some runaway Servant, and in danger of being taken up on that Suspicion. However I proceeded the next Day, and got in the Evening to an Inn within 8 or 10 Miles of Burlington, kept by one Dr. Brown.

Dr. Brown was an itinerant physician who had wan-dered around most of the countries of Europe. He was an atheist and the young freethinker Franklin got along very well with him. After trudging from his inn to the Delaware, Franklin caught a boat that missed the city in the darkness, and he thus spent another night on the water. Not until nine on Sunday morning did he land at the Market Street wharf. His entry into the city where he was to find fame and wealth was anything but prepossessing.

Autobiography, 1771

I was in my Working Dress, my best Cloaths being to come round by Sea. I was dirty from my Journey; my Pockets were stuff'd out with Shirts and Stockings; I knew no Soul, nor where to look for Lodging. I was fatigu'd with Travelling, Rowing and Want of Rest. I was very hungry, and my whole Stock of Cash consisted of a Dutch Dollar and about a Shilling in Copper. The latter I gave the People of the Boat for my Passage, who at first refus'd it on Account of my Rowing; but I insisted on their taking it, a Man being sometimes more generous when he has but a little Money than when he has plenty, perhaps thro' Fear of being thought to have but little.

Then I walk'd up the Street, gazing about, till near the Market House I met a Boy with Bread. I had made many a Meal on Bread, and inquiring where he got it, I went immediately to the Baker's he directed me to in second Street; and ask'd for Bisket, intending such as we had in Boston, but they it seems were not made in Philadelphia, then I ask'd for a threepenny Loaf, and was told they had none such: so not considering or knowing the Difference of Money and the greater Cheapness nor the Names of his Bread, I bad him give me three penny worth of any sort. He gave me accordingly three great Puffy Rolls. I was surpriz'd at the Quantity, but took it, and having no room in my Pockets, walk'd off, with a Roll under each Arm, and eating the other. Thus I went up Market Street as far as fourth Street, passing by the Door of Mr. Read, my future Wife's Father, when she standing at the Door saw me, and thought I made as I certainly did a most awkward ridiculous Appearance. Then I turn'd and went down Chestnut Street and part of Walnut Street, eating my Roll all the Way, and coming round found my self again at Market Street Wharff, near the Boat I came in, to which I went for a Draught of the River Water, and being fill'd with one of my Rolls, gave the other two to a Woman and her Child that came down the River in the Boat with us and were waiting to go farther. Thus refresh'd I walk'd again up the Street,

Two nineteenth-century books on Franklin's life show him passing by Miss Read's door and giving away his rolls to a woman at the wharf.

An illustrated Autobiography *from 1849 included numerous "designs" by J. G. Chapman, such as Franklin asleep in meeting.*

which by this time had many clean dress'd People in it who were all walking the same Way; I join'd them, and thereby was led into the great Meeting House of the Quakers near the Market. I sat down among them, and after looking round a while and hearing nothing said, being very drowzy thro' Labour and want of Rest the preceding Night, I fell fast asleep, and continu'd so till the Meeting broke up, when one was kind enough to rouse me. This was therefore the first House I was in or slept in, in Philadelphia.

Walking again down towards the River, and looking in the Faces of People, I met a young Quaker Man whose Countenance I lik'd, and accosting him requested he would tell me where a Stranger could get Lodging. We were then near the Sign of the Three Mariners. Here, says he, is one Place that entertains Strangers, but it is not a reputable House; if thee wilt walk with me, I'll show thee a better. He brought me to the Crooked Billet in Water-Street. Here I got a Dinner. And while I was eating it, several sly Questions were ask'd me, as it seem'd to be suspected from my youth and Appearance, that I might be some Runaway. After Dinner my Sleepiness return'd: and being shown to a Bed, I lay down without undressing, and slept till Six in the Evening; was call'd to Supper; went to Bed again very early and slept soundly till the next Morning.

Philadelphia did not offer Franklin much in the way of work—there were but two printers in the place. But he was fortunate to find employment with one.

Autobiography, 1771

I made my self as tidy as I could and went to Andrew Bradford the Printer's. I found in the Shop the old Man his Father, whom I had seen at New York, and who travelling on horse back had got to Philadelphia before me. He introduc'd me to his Son, who receiv'd me civilly, gave me a Breakfast, but told me he did not at present want a Hand, being lately supply'd with one. But there was another Printer in town lately set up, one Keimer, who perhaps might employ me; if not, I would be welcome to lodge at his House, and he would give me a little Work to do now and then till fuller Business should offer.

The old Gentleman said, he would go with me to the new Printer: And when we found him, Neighbour, says

Bradford, I have brought to see you a young Man of your Business, perhaps you may want such a One. He ask'd me a few Questions, put a Composing Stick in my Hand to see how I work'd, and then said he would employ me soon, tho' he had just then nothing for me to do....

Keimer's Printing House I found, consisted of an old shatter'd Press, and one small worn-out Fount of English, which he was then using himself, composing in it an Elegy on Aquila Rose before-mentioned, an ingenious young Man of excellent Character much respected in the Town, Clerk of the Assembly, and a pretty Poet. Keimer made Verses, too, but very indifferently. He could not be said to write them, for his Manner was to compose them in the Types directly out of his Head; so there being no Copy, but one Pair of Cases, and the Elegy likely to require all the Letter, no one could help him. I endeavour'd to put his Press (which he had not yet us'd, and of which he understood nothing) into Order fit to be work'd with; and promising to come and print off his Elegy as soon as he should have got it ready, I return'd to Bradford's who gave me a little Job to do for the present, and there I lodged and dieted. A few Days after Keimer sent for me to print off the Elegy. And now he had got another Pair of Cases, and a Pamphlet to reprint, on which he set me to work.

These two Printers I found poorly qualified for their Business. Bradford had not been bred to it, and was very illiterate; and Keimer tho' something of a Scholar, was a mere Compositor, knowing nothing of Presswork. He had been one of the French Prophets and could act their enthusiastic Agitations. At this time he did not profess any particular Religion, but something of all on occasion; was very ignorant of the World, and had, as I afterwards found, a good deal of the Knave in his Composition. He did not like my Lodging at Bradford's while I work'd with him. He had a House indeed, but without Furniture, so he could not lodge me: But he got me a Lodging at Mr. Read's before-mentioned, who was the Owner of his House. And my Chest and Clothes being come by this time, I made rather a more respectable Appearance in the Eyes of Miss Read, than I had done when she first happen'd to see me eating my Roll in the Street.

I began now to have some Acquaintance among the young People of the Town, that were Lovers of Reading

Franklin courting Deborah Read

with whom I spent my Evenings very pleasantly and gaining Money by my Industry and Frugality, I lived very agreably, forgetting Boston as much as I could, and not desiring that any there should know where I resided, except my Friend Collins who was in my Secret, and kept it when I wrote to him. At length an Incident happened that sent me back again much sooner than I had intended.

Franklin's brother-in-law Robert Homes, husband of his sister Mary, was captain of a sloop that traded between Boston and Delaware. Homes heard that young Ben was in Philadelphia and wrote him a letter, urging him to come home. Franklin wrote him a stiff reply, making it clear that there was not much hope of his returning to Boston, or finding reconciliation there. Homes showed the letter to Sir William Keith, Governor of Pennsylvania, who happened to be visiting "the Lower Counties," as Delaware was then called. Apparently Homes hoped that the Governor would force or persuade Ben to return to his family. Instead, young Franklin's well-written letter set off a totally unexpected chain reaction.

Autobiography, 1771

The Governor read it, and seem'd surpriz'd when he was told my Age. He said I appear'd a young Man of promising Parts, and therefore should be encouraged: The Printers at Philadelphia were wretched ones, and if I would set up there, he made no doubt I should succeed; for his Part, he would procure me the publick Business, and do me every other Service in his Power. This my Brother-in-Law afterwards told me in Boston. But I knew as yet nothing of it; when one Day Keimer and I being at Work together near the Window, we saw the Governor and another Gentleman (which prov'd to be Col. French, of New Castle) finely dress'd, come directly across the Street to our House, and heard them at the Door. Keimer ran down immediately, thinking it a Visit to him. But the Governor enquir'd for me, came up, and with a Condescension and Politeness I had been quite unus'd to, made me many Compliments, desired to be acquainted with me, blam'd me kindly for not having made my self known to him when I first came to the Place, and would have me away with him to the Tavern where he was going with Col. French to taste as he said some excellent Madeira. I was not a little surpriz'd, and Keimer star'd like a Pig poison'd. I went however with the Governor and Col. French, to a Tavern the Corner of Third Street, and over the Madeira he propos'd my Setting up my

Governor Keith and Colonel French pay a visit to Franklin at Keimer's.

Sir William Keith

Business, laid before me the Probabilities of Success, and both he and Col. French assur'd me I should have their Interest and Influence in procuring the Publick Business of both Governments. On my doubting whether my Father would assist me in it, Sir William said he would give me a Letter to him, in which he would state the Advantages, and he did not doubt of prevailing with him. So it was concluded I should return to Boston in the first Vessel with the Governor's Letter recommending me to my Father. In the mean time the Intention was to be kept secret, and I went on working with Keimer as usual, the Governor sending for me now and then to dine with him, a very great Honour I thought it, and conversing with me in the most affable, familiar, and friendly manner imaginable.

Toward the end of April, 1724, young Ben returned to Boston with a letter from Governor Keith to Josiah Franklin, "saying many flattering things of me . . . and strongly recommending the Project of my setting up at Philadelphia, as a Thing that must make my Fortune." Although his father and mother greeted Ben affectionately, Josiah Franklin was not especially impressed with Governor Keith's letter.

Autobiography, 1771

When Capt. Homes returning, he show'd it to him, ask'd if he knew Keith, and what kind of a Man he was: Adding his Opinion that he must be of small Discretion, to think of setting a Boy up in Business who wanted yet 3 Years of being at Man's Estate. Homes said what he could in favour of the Project; but my Father was clear in the Impropriety of it; and at last gave a flat Denial to it. Then he wrote a civil Letter to Sir William thanking him for the Patronage he had so kindly offered me, but declining to assist me as yet in Setting up, I being in his Opinion too young to be trusted with the Management of a Business so important, and for which the Preparation must be so expensive. . . .

My Father, tho' he did not approve Sir William's Proposition was yet pleas'd that I had been able to obtain so advantageous a Character from a Person of such Note where I had resided, and that I had been so industrious and careful as to equip my self so handsomely in so short a time: therefore seeing no Prospect of an Accommodation between my Brother and me, he gave his Consent to my Returning again to Philadelphia, advis'd me to behave respectfully to the People there, endeavour to obtain the general Esteem, and avoid lampooning and libelling to which he thought I had too much Inclination; telling me, that by steady Industry and a prudent Parsimony, I might save enough by the time I was One and Twenty to set me up, and that if I came near the Matter he would help me out with the rest. This was all I could obtain, except some small Gifts as Tokens of his and my Mother's Love, when I embark'd again for New-York, now with their Approbation and their Blessing.

Franklin's best friend in Boston, John Collins, decided to return to Philadelphia with him. He went overland to New York, while Ben took a sloop that put in at Newport, Rhode Island, enabling him to visit his brother John, who had been living there for some years. Samuel Vernon, a merchant friend of John's, asked Franklin to collect some thirty-five pounds due to him in Pennsylvania, and gave him an order for that sum. This was the usual way that merchants collected debts in other Colonies. In New York, Franklin found his friend Collins had become a very different person from the young man he had known in Boston.

Autobiography, 1771

We had been intimate from Children, and had read the same Books together. But he had the Advantage of more time for reading, and Studying and a wonderful Genius for Mathematical Learning in which he far outstript me. While I liv'd in Boston most of my Hours of Leisure for Conversation were spent with him, and he continu'd a sober as well as an industrious Lad; was much respected for his Learning by several of the Clergy and other Gentlemen, and seem'd to promise making a good Figure in Life: but during my Absence he had acquir'd a Habit of Sotting with Brandy; and I found by his own Account and what I heard from others, that he had been drunk every day since his Arrival at New York, and behav'd very oddly. He had gam'd too and lost his Money, so that I was oblig'd to discharge his Lodgings, and defray his Expences to and at Philadelphia: Which prov'd extreamly inconvenient to me. The then Governor of N York, Burnet, Son of Bishop Burnet hearing from the Captain that a young Man, one of his Passengers, had a great many Books, desired he would bring me to see him. I waited upon him accordingly, and should have taken Collins with me but that he was not sober. The Governor treated me with great Civility, show'd me his

Library, which was a very large one, and we had a good deal of Conversation about Books and Authors. This was the second Governor who had done me the Honour to take Notice of me, which to a poor Boy like me was very pleasing.

We proceeded to Philadelphia. I received on the Way Vernon's Money, without which we could hardly have finish'd our Journey. Collins wish'd to be employ'd in some Counting House; but whether they discover'd his Dramming by his Breath, or by his Behaviour, tho' he had some Recommendations, he met with no Success in any Application, and continu'd Lodging and Boarding at the same House with me and at my Expence. Knowing I had that Money of Vernon's he was continually borrowing of me, still promising Repayment as soon as he should be in Business. At length he had got so much of it, that I was distress'd to think what I should do, in case of being call'd on to remit it. His Drinking continu'd about which we sometimes quarrel'd, for when a little intoxicated he was very fractious.

Franklin felt that using Vernon's money to support himself and Collins—who eventually departed for Barbados without reimbursing his friend—was "the first great errata of my life." His carelessness with this money convinced him that "my Father was not much out in his Judgment when he suppos'd me too young to manage Business of Importance." He gave his father's letter to Governor Keith, and abandoned his dreams of economic independence. But the Governor had different ideas.

Autobiography, 1771

Sir William, on reading his Letter, said he was too prudent. There was great Difference in Persons, and Discretion did not always accompany Years, nor was Youth always without it. And since he will not set you up, says he, I will do it my self. Give me an Inventory of the Things necessary to be had from England, and I will send for them. You shall repay me when you are able; I am resolv'd to have a good Printer here, and I am sure you must succeed. This was spoken with such an Appearance of Cordiality, that I had not the least doubt of his meaning what he said. I had hitherto kept the Proposition of my Setting up a Secret in Philadelphia, and I still kept it. Had it been known that I depended on the Governor, probably some Friend that knew him better would have advis'd me not to rely on him, as I afterwards heard it as his known Character to be liberal of Promises which he never meant to keep. . . .

I presented him an Inventory of a little Printing House, amounting by my Computation to about £100 Sterling. He lik'd it, but ask'd me if my being on the Spot in England to chuse the Types and see that every thing was good of the kind, might not be of some Advantage. Then, says he, when there, you may make Acquaintances and establish Correspondencies in the Bookselling and Stationary Way. I agreed that this might be advantageous. Then says he, get yourself ready to go with Annis; which was the annual Ship, and the only one at that Time usually passing between London and Philadelphia. But it would be some Months before Annis sail'd, so I continu'd working with Keimer, fretting about the Money Collins had got from me, and in daily Apprehensions of being call'd upon by Vernon, which however did not happen for some Years after.

While he was waiting for the ship that would take him to England, Franklin had a good time. Keimer provided a sideshow all by himself. He was one of those men who loved to argue about religion and display his wide but erratic reading. He soon found young Franklin was more than a match for him.

Autobiography, 1771

I us'd to work him so with my Socratic Method, and had trapann'd him so often by Questions apparently so distant from any Point we had in hand, and yet by degrees led to the Point, and brought him into Difficulties and Contradictions that at last he grew ridiculously cautious, and would hardly answer me the most common Question, without asking first, *What do you intend to infer from that?* However it gave him so high an Opinion of my Abilities in the Confuting Way, that he seriously propos'd my being his Colleague in a Project he had of setting up a new Sect. He was to preach the Doctrines, and I was to confound all Opponents. When he came to explain with me upon the Doctrines, I found several Conundrums which I objected to unless I might have my Way a little too, and introduce some of mine. Keimer wore his Beard at full Length, because somewhere in the Mosaic Law it is said, *thou shalt not mar the Corners of thy Beard.* He likewise kept the seventh day Sabbath; and these two Points were Essentials with him. I dislik'd both, but agreed to admit them upon Condition of his adopting the Doctrine of using no animal Food. I doubt, says he, my Constitution will not bear that. I assur'd him it would, and that he would be the better for it. He was usually a great Glutton, and I promis'd my self some Diversion in half-starving him. He agreed to try the Practice if I would keep him Company. I did so and we held it for three Months. We had our Victuals dress'd and brought to us regularly by a Woman in the Neighbourhood, who had from me a List of 40 Dishes to be prepar'd for us at different times, in all which there was neither Fish Flesh nor Fowl, and the whim suited me the better at this time from the Cheapness of it, not costing us above 18d. Sterling each, per Week. I have since kept several Lents most strictly, Leaving the common Diet for that, and that for the common, abruptly, without the least Inconvenience: So that I think there is little in the Advice of making those Changes by easy Gradations. I went on pleasantly, but poor Keimer suffer'd grievously, tir'd of the Project, long'd for the Flesh Pots of Egypt, and order'd a roast Pig. He invited me and two Women Friends to dine with him, but it being brought too soon upon table, he could not resist the Temptation, and ate it all up before we came.

Franklin also made friends with young men his own age, "All Lovers of Reading." Inadvertently, he encouraged one of them, James Ralph, to become America's first professional writer.

Autobiography, 1771

My chief Acquaintances at this time were, Charles Osborne, Joseph Watson, and James Ralph; All Lovers of Reading. . . . Many pleasant Walks we four had together on Sundays into the Woods near Skuylkill, where we read to one another and conferr'd on what we read.

Ralph was inclin'd to pursue the Study of Poetry, not doubting but he might become eminent in it and make his Fortune by it, alledging that the best Poets must when they first began to write, make as many Faults as he did. Osborne dissuaded him, assur'd him he had no Genius for Poetry, and advis'd him to think of nothing beyond the Business he was bred to; that in the mercantile way tho' he had no Stock, he might by his Diligence and Punctuality recommend himself to Employment as a Factor, and in time acquire wherewith to trade on his own Account. I

*Franklin departs for London aboard
the* Annis *in 1724.*

approv'd the amusing one's self with Poetry now and then,
so far as to improve one's Language, but no farther. On
this it was propos'd that we should each of us at our next
Meeting produce a Piece of our own Composing, in order
to improve by our mutual Observations, Criticisms and
Corrections. As Language and Expression was what we
had in View, we excluded all Considerations of Invention, by agreeing that the Task should be a Version of
the 18th Psalm, which describes the Descent of a
Deity. When the Time of our Meeting drew nigh, Ralph
call'd on me first, and let me know his Piece was ready.
I told him I had been busy, and having little Inclination
had done nothing. He then show'd me his Piece for my
Opinion; and I much approv'd it, as it appear'd to me
to have great Merit. Now, says he, Osborne never will
allow the least Merit in any thing of mine, but makes
1000 Criticisms out of mere Envy. He is not so jealous
of you. I wish therefore you would take this Piece, and
produce it as yours. I will pretend not to have had time,
and so produce nothing: We shall then see what he will
say to it. It was agreed, and I immediately transcrib'd it
that it might appear in my own hand. We met. Watson's
Performance was read: there were some Beauties in it:
but many Defects. Osborne's was read: It was much
better. Ralph did it Justice, remark'd some Faults, but
applauded the Beauties. He himself had nothing to produce. I was backward, seem'd desirous of being excus'd,
had not had sufficient Time to correct; &c. but no Excuse
could be admitted, produce I must. It was read and re-
peated; Watson and Osborne gave up the Contest; and
join'd in applauding it immoderately. Ralph only made
some Criticisms and propos'd some Amendments, but I
defended my Text. Osborne was against Ralph, and told
him he was no better a Critic than Poet; so he dropt
the Argument. As they two went home together,
Osborne express'd himself still more strongly in favour
of what he thought my Production, having restrain'd
himself before as he said, lest I should think it Flat-
tery. But who would have imagin'd, says he, that
Franklin had been capable of such a Performance;
such Painting, such Force! such Fire! he has even improv'd the Original! In his common Conversation, he
seems to have no Choice of Words; he hesitates and
blunders; and yet, good God, how he writes! When we

next met, Ralph discover'd the Trick, we had plaid him, and Osborne was a little laught at. This Transaction fix'd Ralph in his Resolution of becoming a Poet.

Although he was married and had one child, Ralph decided to accompany Franklin to London in the fall of 1724. Franklin did not realize it at the time, but his friend, filled with dreams of literary glory, had no intention of returning. Franklin had a pressing personal matter of his own on his mind. For some time he had "made some Courtship" to Deborah Read, the young girl who had gazed in astonishment at his disheveled appearance on his first day in Philadelphia. He had proposed marriage, but her mother pointed out that they were both only eighteen, and Franklin was going on a long voyage. Perhaps it would be better to wait until he returned. So Deborah and Benjamin "interchang'd some Promises" and Franklin went aboard the *Annis*. When the man carrying Governor Keith's dispatches came aboard, Franklin asked for the Governor's letters of credit and introduction. He was told that they were all in the dispatch bag and when they landed in England the bag would be opened and he could pick out the ones that belonged to him. Satisfied, Franklin settled down to a long stormy voyage. He became very friendly with a Quaker merchant named Thomas Denham. But not even to him did Franklin reveal the purpose of his voyage. He soon found himself wishing that he had told his secret before he sailed.

Autobiography, 1771

When we came into the Channel, the Captain kept his Word with me, and gave me an Opportunity of examining the Bag for the Governor's Letters. I found none upon which my Name was put, as under my Care; I pick'd out 6 or 7 that by the Hand writing I thought might be the promis'd Letters, especially as one of them was directed to Basket the King's Printer, and another to some Stationer. We arriv'd in London the 24th of December, 1724. I waited upon the Stationer who came first in my Way, delivering the Letter as from Gov. Keith. I don't know such a Person, says he: but opening the Letter, O, this is from Riddlesden; I have lately found him to be a compleat Rascal, and I will have nothing to do with him, nor receive any Letters from him. So putting the Letter into my Hand, he turn'd on his Heel and left me to serve some Customer. I was surprized to find these were not the Governor's Letters. And after recollecting and comparing Circumstances, I began to doubt his Sincerity. I found my Friend Denham, and opened the whole Affair to him. He let me into Keith's Character, told me there was not the least Probability that he had written any Letters for me, that no one who knew him had the smallest Dependance on him, and he laught at the Notion of the Governor's giving me a Letter of Credit, having as he said no Credit to give.

In his later years, Franklin told friends in Paris that he was panicked by the thought of surviving on his own in London. He credited much of his survival to the friendship of a Boston physician, Zabdiel Boylston, who lent him twenty guineas and gave him advice and encouragement. Fortunately, Franklin also had his trade to support him and he soon found work at a large London printing house. For company, Franklin relied largely on Ralph, who was something of a problem.

Autobiography, 1771

Ralph and I were inseparable Companions. We took Lodgings together in Little Britain at 3*s*. 6*d*. per Week, as much as we could then afford. He found some Relations, but they were poor and unable to assist him. He now let me know his Intentions of remaining in London, and that he never meant to return to Philadelphia. He had brought no Money with him, the whole he could muster having been expended in paying his Passage. I had 15 Pistoles: So he borrowed occasionally of me, to subsist while he was looking out for Business. He first endeavoured to get into the Playhouse, believing himself qualify'd for an Actor; but Wilkes, to whom he apply'd, advis'd him candidly not to think of that, Employment, as it was impossible he should succeed in it. Then he propos'd to Roberts, a Publisher in Paternoster Row, to write for him a Weekly Paper like the Spectator, on certain Conditions, which Roberts did not approve. Then he endeavour'd to get Employment as a Hackney Writer to copy for the Stationers and Lawyers about the Temple: but could find no Vacancy.

I immediately got into Work at Palmer's then a famous Printing House in Bartholomew Close; and here I continu'd near a Year. I was pretty diligent; but spent with Ralph a good deal of my Earnings in going to Plays and other Places of Amusement. We had together consum'd all my Pistoles, and now just rubb'd on from hand to mouth. He seem'd quite to forget his Wife and Child, and I by degrees my Engagements with Miss Read, to whom I never wrote more than one Letter, and that was to let her know I was not likely soon to return. This was

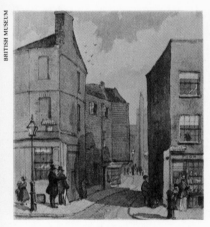

Franklin's lodgings were here in London's "Little Britain."

another of the great Errata of my Life, which I should wish to correct if I were to live it over again.

Having run short of money, young Franklin decided to sell a few odd items he had brought with him from America. He wrote the following letter to Sir Hans Sloane, physician to the King and a prominent member of the Royal Society, well known as a collector of natural history specimens. Later, in his *Autobiography*, Franklin turned this story inside out, saying Sloane "heard of" his curiosities and "persuaded" him to add them to his collection.

[London] June 2, 1725

Having lately been in the Nothern Parts of America, I have brought from thence a Purse made of the Stone Asbestus, a Piece of the Stone, and a Piece of Wood, the Pithy Part of which is of the same Nature, and call'd by the Inhabitants, Salamander Cotton. As you are noted to be a Lover of Curiosities, I have inform'd you of these; and if you have any Inclination to purchase them, or see 'em, let me know your Pleasure by a Line directed for me at the Golden Fan in Little Britain, and I will wait upon you with them.

Franklin also attracted some attention at this time by writing a religious pamphlet, entitled *A Dissertation on Liberty and Necessity, Pleasure and Pain.* Perhaps the best commentary on it was written by Franklin himself, fifty years later, in a letter to a British friend, Benjamin Vaughan.

Passy Nov. 9. 1779.

It was addres'd to Mr. J. R., that is James Ralph, then a Youth of about my age, and my intimate friend, afterwards a Political Writer and Historian. The Purport of it was to prove the Doctrine of fate, from the suppos'd attributes of God; in some such manner as this, that in creating and governing the World, as he was infinitely wise he knew what would be best; infinitely good, he must be disposed, and infinitely powerful, he must be able to execute it. Consequently *all is right*. There were only an hundred Copies printed, of which I gave a few to friends, and afterwards disliking the Piece, as conceiving it might have an ill Tendency, I burnt the rest except one Copy the Margin of which was filled with manuscript Notes by Lyons, author of the *Infallibility of Human Judgment*, who was at that time another of my Acquaintance in London. I was not 19 Years of age when

An old cut of Palmer's printing house during Franklin's day

St. Bartholomew's Lady Chapel in London was once occupied by Palmer's printing house.

it was written. In 1730 I wrote a Piece on the other side of the Question, which began with laying for its foundation this fact, *that almost all men in all ages and Country's, have at times made use of Prayer:* Thence I reasoned, that if all things are ordain'd, prayer must among the rest be ordain'd. But as prayer can produce no Change in Things that are ordain'd, Praying must then be useless and an absurdity. God would therefore not ordain Praying if everything else was ordain'd. But Praying exists, therefore all Things are not ordain'd &c. This Pamphlet was never printed, and the manuscript has been long lost. The great uncertainty I found in metaphysical reasonings disgusted me, and I quitted that kind of reading and study for others more satisfactory.

The master printer Samuel Palmer was impressed by the essay, although he told Franklin that the principles were "abominable." Through the attention it won, Franklin met several minor writers in local coffeehouses. Meanwhile, he and Ralph cane to a parting of the ways, and Franklin went to work for another printer, named Watts. At Watts's, Franklin drew on his Boston experience to save money and time. But his unorthodox ways clashed with the customs of the English printers.

Autobiography, 1771

At my first Admission into this Printing House, I took to working at Press, imagining I felt a Want of the Bodily Exercise I had been us'd to in America, where Presswork is mix'd with Composing. I drank only Water; the other Workmen, near 50 in Number, were great Guzzlers of Beer. On occasion I carried up and down Stairs a large Form of Types in each hand, when others carried but one in both Hands. They wonder'd to see from this and several Instances that the Water-American as they call'd me was *stronger* than themselves who drank *strong* Beer. We had an Alehouse Boy who attended always in the House to supply the Workmen. My Companion at the Press, drank every day a Pint before Breakfast, a Pint at Breakfast with his Bread and Cheese; a Pint between Breakfast and Dinner; a Pint at Dinner; a Pint in the Afternoon about Six o'Clock, and another when he had done his Day's-Work. I thought it a detestable Custom. But it was necessary, he suppos'd, to drink *strong* Beer that he might be *strong* to labour. I endeavour'd to convince him that the Bodily Strength afforded by Beer could only be in proportion to the Grain or Flour of the

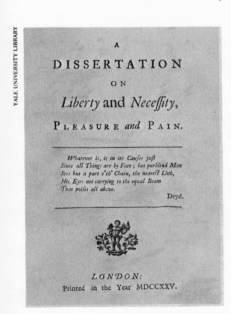

A

DISSERTATION
ON
Liberty and *Necessity,*
PLEASURE *and* PAIN.

*Whatever is, is in its Causes just
Since all Things are by Fate; but purblind Man
Sees but a part o'th' Chain, the nearest Link,
His Eyes not carrying to the equal Beam
That poises all above.*

Dryd.

LONDON:
Printed in the Year MDCCXXV.

Franklin both wrote and printed this pamphlet while he was working at Palmer's in 1725.

*Franklin and printers supping
on "hot Water-gruel" and bread*

*Pay table on Saturday nights;
both from Holley's* Franklin

Barley dissolved in the Water of which it was made; that there was more Flour in a Penny-worth of Bread, and therefore if he would eat that with a Pint of Water, it would give him more Strength than a Quart of Beer. He drank on however, and had 4 or 5 Shillings to pay out of his Wages every Saturday Night for that muddling Liquor; an Expence I was free from. And thus these poor Devils keep themselves always under.

Watts after some Weeks desiring to have me in the Composing Room, I left the Pressmen. A new *Bienvenu* or Sum for Drink, being 5 *s.*, was demanded of me by the Compositors. I thought it an Imposition, as I had paid below. The Master thought so too, and forbad my Paying it. I stood out two or three Weeks, was accordingly considered as an Excommunicate, and had so many little Pieces of private Mischief done me, by mixing my Sorts, transposing my Pages, breaking my Matter, &c. &c. if I were ever so little out of the Room, and all ascrib'd to the Chapel Ghost, which they said ever haunted those not regularly admitted, that notwithstanding the Master's Protection, I found myself oblig'd to comply and pay the Money; convinc'd of the Folly of being on ill Terms with those one is to live with continually. I was now on a fair Footing with them, and soon acquir'd considerable Influence. I propos'd some reasonable Alterations in their Chapel Laws, and carried them against all Opposition. From my Example a great Part of them, left their muddling Breakfast of Beer and Bread and Cheese, finding they could with me be supply'd from a neighbouring House with a large Porringer of hot Water-gruel, sprinkled with Pepper, crumb'd with Bread, and a Bit of Butter in it, for the Price of a Pint of Beer, viz, three halfpence. This was a more comfortable as well as cheaper Breakfast, and kept their Heads clearer. Those who continu'd sotting with Beer all day, were often, by not paying, out of Credit at the Alehouse, and us'd to make Interest with me to get Beer, *their Light*, as they phras'd it, *being out*. I watch'd the Pay table on Saturday Night, and collected what I stood engag'd for them, having to pay some times near Thirty Shillings a Week on their Accounts. This, and my being esteem'd a pretty good Riggite, that is a jocular verbal Satyrist, supported my Consequence in the Society. My constant Attendance, (I never making a St. Monday), recommended me to the

Master; and my uncommon Quickness at Composing, occasion'd my being put upon all Work of Dispatch which was generally better paid. So I went on now very agreably.

At Watts's Printing House, Franklin made another friend, a youth named Wygate, who, like most of Franklin's friends, "lov'd Reading" and, unlike most printers, had a good education. He was, Franklin said, "a tolerable Latinist, spoke French." But Franklin's relationship with him took a strange turn when he taught him how to swim.

Autobiography, 1771

I taught him, and a Friend of his, to swim, at twice going into the River, and they soon became good Swimmers. They introduc'd me to some Gentlemen from the Country who went to Chelsea by Water to see the College and Don Saltero's Curiosities. In our Return, at the Request of the Company, whose Curiosity Wygate had excited, I stript and leapt into the River, and swam from near Chelsea to Blackfryars, performing on the Way many Feats of Activity both upon and under Water, that surpriz'd and pleas'd those to whom they were Novelties. I had from a Child been ever delighted with this Exercise, had studied and practis'd all Thevenot's Motions and Positions, added some of my own, aiming at the graceful and easy, as well as the Useful. All these I took this Occasion of exhibiting to the Company, and was much flatter'd by their Admiration. And Wygate, who was desirous of becoming a Master, grew more and more attach'd to me, on that account, as well as from the Similarity of our Studies. He at length propos'd to me travelling all over Europe together, supporting ourselves everywhere by working at our Business. I was once inclin'd to it. But mentioning it to my good Friend Mr. Denham, with whom I often spent an Hour, when I had Leisure. He dissuaded me from it, advising me to think only of returning to Pensilvania, which he was now about to do. . . .

He now told me he . . . should carry over a great Quantity of Goods in order to open a Store there: He propos'd to take me over as his Clerk, to keep his Books (in which he would instruct me) copy his Letters, and attend the Store. He added, that as soon as I should be acquainted with mercantile Business he would promote me by sending me with a Cargo of Flour and Bread &c. to the West Indies, and procure me Commissions from others; which would be profitable, and if I manag'd well, would establish me

Illustrations from the Art of Swimming, *including how to cut your toenails under water*

handsomely. The Thing pleas'd me, for I was grown tired of London, remember'd with Pleasure the happy Months I had spent in Pennsylvania, and wish'd again to see it. Therefore I immediately agreed, on the Terms of Fifty Pounds a Year, Pensylvania Money; less indeed than my present Gettings as a Compostor, but affording a better Prospect.

I now took Leave of Printing, as I thought for ever, and was daily employ'd in my new Business; going about with Mr. Denham among the Tradesmen, to purchase various Articles, and seeing them pack'd up, doing Errands, calling upon Workmen to dispatch, &c. and when all was on board, I had a few Days Leisure. On one of these Days I was to my Surprize sent for by a great Man I knew only by Name, a Sir William Wyndham and I waited upon him. He had heard by some means or other of my Swimming from Chelsey to Blackfryars, and of my teaching Wygate and another young Man to swim in a few Hours. He had two Sons about to set out on their Travels; he wish'd to have them first taught Swimming; and propos'd to gratify me handsomely if I would teach them. They were not yet come to Town and my Stay was uncertain, so I could not undertake it. But from this Incident I thought it likely, that if I were to remain in England and open a Swimming School, I might get a good deal of Money. And it struck me so strongly, that had the Overture been sooner made me, probably I should not so soon have returned to America.

Old engraving of the interior of an eighteenth-century printing house

On the voyage back to America in the summer of 1726, Franklin began the habit of keeping a journal. This fascinating document has come down to us, and it gives us a vivid picture of Franklin's interests at twenty. Already his inquiring mind was turning from religion to science. The following passages display both his acute observation and his inclination to experiment to prove a theory.

Friday, September 2 [1726]

This morning the wind changed, a little fair. We caught a couple of dolphins, and fried them for dinner. They tasted tolerably well. These fish make a glorious appearance in the water: their bodies are of a bright green, mixed with a silver colour, and their tails of a shining golden yellow; but all this vanishes presently after they are taken out of their element, and they change all over to a light grey. I observed that cutting off pieces of a just-caught living dolphin for baits, those pieces did not lose their lustre and fine colours when the dolphin died, but retained them perfectly. Every one takes notice of that vulgar error of the painters, who always represent this fish monstrously crooked and deformed, when it is in reality as beautiful and well shaped a fish as any that swims. I cannot think what should be the original of this chimera of theirs, (since there is not a creature in nature that in the least resembles their dolphin) unless it proceeded at first from a false imitation of a fish in the posture of leaping, which they have since improved into a crooked monster with a head and eyes like a bull, a hog's snout, and a tail like a blown tulip. But the sailors give me another reason, though a whimsical one, viz. that as this most beautiful fish is only to be caught at sea, and that very far to the Southward, they say the painters wilfully deform it in their representations, lest pregnant women should long for what it is impossible to procure for them. . . .

Wednesday, September 28

We had very variable winds and weather last night, accompanied with abundance of rain; and now the wind is come about westerly again, but we must bear it with patience. This afternoon we took up several branches of gulf weed (with which the sea is spread all over from the Western Isles to the coast of America); but one of these branches had something peculiar in it. In common with the rest it had a leaf about three quarters of an inch long, indented like a saw, and small yellow berry filled with nothing but wind; besides which it bore a fruit of the animal kind, very surprising to see. It was a small shellfish like a heart, the stalk by which it proceeded from the branch being partly of a gristly kind. Upon this one branch of the weed there were near forty of these vegetable animals; the smallest of them near the end contained a substance somewhat like an oyster, but the larger were visibly animated, opening their shells every moment, and thrusting out a set of unformed claws, not unlike those of a crab; but the inner part was still a kind of soft jelly. Observing the weed more narrowly, I spied a very small crab crawling among it, about as big as the head of a ten-penny nail, and of a yellowish colour, like the weed itself. This gave me some reason to think that he was a native of the branch, that he had not long since been in the same condition with the rest of those little embrios that appeared in the shells, this being the method of their generation; and that consequently all the rest of this odd kind of fruit might be crabs in due time. To strengthen my conjecture, I have resolved to keep the weed in salt water, renewing it every day till we come on shore, by this experiment to see whether any more crabs will be produced or not in this manner....

Thursday, September 29

Upon shifting the water in which I had put the weed yesterday, I found another crab, much smaller than the former, who seemed to have newly left his habitation. But the weed begins to wither, and the rest of the embrios are dead. This new comer fully convinces me, that at least this sort of crabs are generated in this manner.

Friday, September 30

I took in some more gulf-weed to-day with the boat-hook, with shells upon it like that before mentioned, and three living perfect crabs, each less than the nail of my little finger. One of them had something particularly observable, to wit, a thin piece of the white shell which I before noticed as their covering while they remained in the condition of embrios, sticking close to his natural shell upon his back. This sufficiently confirms me in my opinion of the manner of their generation....

The long hours at sea also gave Franklin time to reflect on his life thus far. He drew up a plan to guide his future conduct. The manuscript has been lost. Only four points—but very important ones—survive.

[1726]

Those who write of the art of poetry teach us that if we would write what may be worth the reading, we ought always, before we begin, to form a regular plan and design of our piece: otherwise, we shall be in danger of incongruity. I am apt to think it is the same as to life. I have never fixed a regular design in life; by which means it has been a confused variety of different scenes. I am now entering upon a new one: let me, therefore, make some resolutions, and form some scheme of action, that, henceforth, I may live in all respects like a rational creature.

1. It is necessary for me to be extremely frugal for some time, till I have paid what I owe.

2. To endeavour to speak truth in every instance; to

give nobody expectations that are not likely to be answered, but aim at sincerity in every word and action—the most amiable excellence in a rational being.

3.   To apply myself industriously to whatever business I take in hand, and not divert my mind from my business by any foolish project of growing suddenly rich; for industry and patience are the surest means of plenty.

4.   I resolve to speak ill of no man whatever, not even in a matter of truth; but rather by some means excuse the faults I hear charged upon others, and upon proper occasions speak all the good I know of every body.

In the *Autobiography*, Franklin told how he also examined his religious beliefs, using a highly experimental approach—testing the effect of his skepticism on himself and his friends.

Autobiography, 1771

My Arguments perverted some others, particularly Collins and Ralph: but each of them having afterwards wrong'd me greatly without the least Compunction and recollecting Keith's Conduct towards me, (who was another Freethinker) and my own towards Vernon and Miss Read which at Times gave me great Trouble, I began to suspect that this Doctrine tho' it might be true, was not very useful....

...I grew convinc'd that *Truth, Sincerity and Integrity* in Dealings between Man and Man, were of the utmost Importance to the Felicity of Life, and I form'd written Resolutions, (which still remain in my Journal Book) to practice them ever while I lived. Revelation had indeed no weight with me as such; but I entertain'd an Opinion, that tho' certain Actions might not be bad *because* they were forbidden by it, or good *because* it commanded them; yet probably those Actions might be forbidden *because* they were bad for us, or commanded *because* they were beneficial to us, in their own Natures, all the Circumstances of things considered. And this Persuasion, with the kind hand of Providence, or some guardian Angel, or accidental favourable Circumstances and Situations, or all together, preserved me (thro' this dangerous Time of Youth and the hazardous Situations I was sometimes in among Strangers, remote from the Eye and Advice of my Father) without any *wilful* gross Immorality or Injustice that might have been expected from my Want of Religion. I say *wilful*, because the Instances I have mentioned, had something of *Necessity* in them, from my Youth, Inexperience, and the Knavery of others. I had therefore a tolerable Character to begin the World with, I valued it properly, and determin'd to preserve it.

Another explanation for Franklin's swing back to a religious attitude, if not orthodox convictions, was his brush with death and economic disaster soon after he landed in Philadelphia.

Autobiography, 1771

Mr. Denham took a Store in Water Street, where we open'd our Goods. I attended the Business diligently, studied Accounts, and grew in a little Time expert at selling. We lodg'd and boarded together, he counsell'd me as a Father, having a sincere Regard for me: I respected and lov'd him: and we might have gone on together very happily: But in the Beginning of Feby. 1726/7 when I had just pass'd my 21st Year, we both were taken ill. My Distemper was a Pleurisy, which very nearly carried me off: I suffered a good deal, gave up the Point in my own mind, and was rather disappointed when I found my Self recovering; regretting in some degree that I must now some time or other have all that disagreable Work to do over again. I forget what his Distemper was. It held him a long time, and at length carried him off. He left me a small Legacy in a nuncupative [oral] Will, as a Token of his Kindness for me, and he left me once more to the wide World. For the Store was taken into the Care of his Executors, and my Employment under him ended: My Brother-in-law Homes, being now at Philadelphia, advis'd my Return to my Business. And Keimer tempted me with an Offer of large Wages by the Year to come and take the Management of his Printing-House, that he might better attend his Stationer's Shop. . . . I try'd for farther Employment as a Merchant's Clerk; but not readily meeting with any, I clos'd again with Keimer.

Thus this second phase of Franklin's career came to a close with the young man seemingly back where he started when he first came to Philadelphia. He was working for Keimer again as a journeyman printer. But there were subtle, enormously important differences. The naïve runaway had become a man of the world. He had survived cynicism, atheism, the temptations of London, and the dangers of the Atlantic. Benjamin Franklin knew who he was now and a little, at least, of where he wanted to go.

Chapter 3

A Man of Business

Franklin was much too talented and too intelligent to remain an employee of a fool like Keimer for long. The master sensed this, and as soon as Franklin had put the print shop in order and trained the raw hands, Keimer invented a quarrel with Franklin and fired him. But one of the hands, Hugh Meredith, had in the meantime become a strong Franklin admirer. Meredith persuaded his father to put up the money so that he and Franklin could go into the printing business in a shop of their own, as partners. The business prospered. The elder Meredith sent customers to them, but most of their progress was due to Franklin's remarkable energy. In this passage from the *Autobiography* he recalls how hard he worked in those days when he was establishing himself in business.

Autobiography, 1771

Brientnal particulary procur'd us from the Quakers, the Printing 40 Sheets of their History, the rest being to be done by Keimer: and upon this we work'd exceeding hard, for the Price was low. It was a Folio, Pro Patria Size, in Pica with Long Primer Notes. I compos'd of it a Sheet a Day, and Meredith work'd it off at Press. It was often 11 at Night and sometimes later, before I had finish'd my Distribution for the next days Work: For the little Jobbs sent in by our other Friends now and then put us back. But so determin'd I was to continue doing a Sheet a Day of the Folio, that one Night when having impos'd my Forms, I thought my Days Work over, one of them by accident was broken and two Pages reduc'd to Pie, I immediately distributed and compos'd it over again before I went to bed. And this Industry visible to our Neighbours began to give us Character and Credit; particularly I was told, that mention being made of the new Printing Office at the Merchants every-night-Club, the general Opinion was that it must fail, there being already two Printers in the Place, Keimer and Bradford; but Doctor Baird . . . gave a contrary Opinion; for the Industry of that Franklin, says he, is superior to any thing I ever saw of the kind: I see him still at work when I go home from Club; and he is at Work again before his Neighbours are out of bed.

With James Franklin's experience as a guide, Franklin laid plans to found a newspaper. But the path to this turning point in his career proved by no means smooth. He told how he dealt with the obstacles that confronted him in this passage from the *Autobiography*.

Autobiography, 1771

George Webb, who had found a Female Friend that lent him wherewith to purchase his Time of Keimer, now came to offer himself as a Journeyman to us. We could not then imploy him, but I foolishly let him know, as a Secret, that I soon intended to begin a Newspaper, and might then have Work for him. My Hopes of Success as I told him were founded on this, that the then only Newspaper, printed by Bradford was a paltry thing, wretchedly manag'd, and no way entertaining; and yet was profitable to him. I therefore thought a good Paper could scarcely fail of good Encouragement. I requested Webb not to mention it, but he told it to Keimer, who immediately, to be beforehand with me, published Proposals for Printing one himself, on which Webb was to be employ'd. I resented this, and to counteract them, as I could not yet begin our Paper, I wrote several Pieces of Entertainment for Bradford's Paper, under the Title of the Busy Body which Brientnal continu'd some Months. By this means the Attention of the Publick was fix'd on that Paper, and Keimers Proposals which we burlesqu'd and ridicul'd, were disregarded. He began his Paper however, and after carrying it on three Quarters of a Year, with at most only 90 Subscribers, he offer'd it to me for a Trifle, and I having been ready some time to go on with it, took it in hand directly.

Franklin trundled the papers himself.

Keimer called his paper *The Universal Instructor in All Arts and Sciences: and Pennsylvania Gazette.* Franklin and Meredith shortened the title to *The Pennsylvania Gazette,* and thanks to Franklin's talent as a writer and printer, it swiftly became "extreamly profitable." The thorough professionalism of Franklin's approach is evident in this statement of policy, which appeared in the first issue under his editorship.

First issue of The Pennsylvania Gazette *under Franklin's aegis*

The Pennsylvania Gazette,
October 2, 1729

There are many who have long desired to see a good News-Paper in Pennsylvania; and we hope those Gentlemen who are able, will contribute towards the making This such. We ask Assistance, because we are fully sensible, that to publish a good News-Paper is not so easy an Undertaking as many People imagine it to be. The Author of a Gazette (in the Opinion of the Learned) ought to be qualified with an extensive Acquaintance with Languages, a great Easiness and Command of Writing and Relating Things cleanly and intelligibly, and in few Words; he should be able to speak of War both by Land and Sea; be well acquainted with Geography, with the History of the Time, with the several Interests of Princes and States, the Secrets of Courts, and the Manners and Customs of all Nations. Men thus accomplish'd are very rare in this remote Part of the World; and it would be well if the Writer of these Papers could make up among his Friends what is wanting in himself.

Upon the Whole, we may assure the Publick, that as far as the Encouragement we meet with will enable us, no Care and Pains shall be omitted, that may make the *Pennsylvania Gazette* as agreeable and useful an Entertainment as the Nature of the Thing will allow.

From the beginning, *The Pennsylvania Gazette* reflected Franklin's fundamental interests. He took up the clash between Governor William Burnet and the Massachusetts Assembly in a style that "struck the principal People, occasion'd the Paper and Manager of it to be much talk'd of, and in a few weeks brought them all to be our Subscribers." Here in Franklin's forthright prose is the story that started him on his way to success.

The Pennsylvania Gazette,
October 9, 1729

His Excellency Governor Burnet died unexpectedly. . . . And it was thought the Dispute would have ended with him, or at least have lain dormant till the Arrival of a new Governor from England, who possibly might, or might not be inclin'd to enter too rigorously into the Measures of his Predecessor. But our last Advices by the Post acquaint us, that his Honour the Lieutenant Governour (on whom the Government immediately devolves upon the Death or Absence of the Commander in Chief) has vigorously renew'd the Struggle on his own Account; of

For *BARBADOS* directly,
The S H I P
I N D U S T R Y,
William Rankin,
Commander ;
Will fail with all ex-
pedition.
For freight or paſſage, ap-
ply to ſaid commander on
board, or John Erwin, in
Strawberry Alley.

*Franklin greatly increased the
number of ads in the* Gazette; *this is
a notice of a ship sailing.*

which the Particulars will be seen in our Next.

Perhaps some of our Readers may not fully understand the Original or Ground of this warm Contest between the Governour and Assembly. It seems, that People have for these Hundred Years past, enjoyed the Privilege of Rewarding the Governour for the Time being, according to *their Sense* of his Merit and Services; and few or none of their Governors have hitherto complain'd, or had Reason to complain, of a too scanty Allowance. But the late Gov. Burnet brought with him Instructions to demand a *settled Salary* of £1000 *per Annum,* Sterling, on him and all his Successors, and the Assembly were required to fix it immediately. He insisted on it strenuously to the last, and they as constantly refused it. It appears by their Votes and Proceedings, that they thought it an Imposition, contrary to their own Charter, and to *Magna Charta;* and they judg'd that by the Dictates of Reason there should be a mutual Dependence between the *Governor* and the *Governed*, and that to make any Governour independent on his People, would be dangerous, and destructive of their Liberties, and the ready Way to establish Tyranny: They thought likewise, that the Province was not the less dependent on the Crown of Great-Britain, by the Governour's depending immediately on them and his own good Conduct for an ample Support, because all Acts and Laws which he might be induc'd to pass, must nevertheless be constantly sent Home for Approbation in Order to continue in Force. Many other Reasons were given and Arguments us'd in the Course of the Controversy, needless to particularize here, because all the material Papers relating to it, have been inserted already in our Publick news.

Much deserved Praise has the deceas'd Governour received, for his steady Integrity in adhering to his Instructions, notwithstanding the great Difficulty and Opposition he met with, and the strong Temptations offer'd from time to time to induce him to give up the Point. And yet perhaps something is due to the Assembly (as the Love and Zeal of that Country for the present Establishment is too well known to suffer any Suspicion of Want of Loyalty) who continue thus resolutely to Abide by what *they Think* their Right, and that of the People they represent, maugre all the Arts and Menaces of a Governour fam'd for his Cunning and Politicks, back'd with Instructions from

Home, and powerfully aided by the great Advantage such an Officer always has of engaging the principal Men of a Place in his Party, by conferring where he pleases so many Posts of Profit and Honour. Their happy Mother Country will perhaps observe with Pleasure, that tho' her gallant Cocks and matchless Dogs abate their native Fire and Intrepidity when transported to a Foreign Clime (as the common Notion is) yet her Sons in the remotest Part of the Earth, and even to the third and fourth Descent, still retain that ardent Spirit of Liberty, and that undaunted Courage in the Defence of it, which has in every Age so gloriously distinguished Britons and English-men from all the Rest of Mankind.

At the same time, Franklin did not forget his family and friends in Massachusetts. The only surviving letter from this period is the one that follows, to his younger sister Jane. Captain Freeman, whom Franklin mentions in the first line, was a Boston friend of the family.

Philadelphia, January 6 [1727]

Dear Sister,

I am highly pleased with the account captain Freeman gives me of you. I always judged by your behaviour when a child that you would make a good, agreeable woman, and you know you were ever my peculiar favourite. I have been thinking what would be a suitable present for me to make, and for you to receive, as I hear you are grown a celebrated beauty. I had almost determined on a tea table, but when I considered that the character of a good housewife was far preferable to that of being only a pretty gentlewoman, I concluded to send you a *spinning wheel*, which I hope you will accept as a small token of my sincere love and affection.

Sister, farewell, and remember that modesty, as it makes the most homely virgin amiable and charming, so the want of it infallibly renders the most perfect beauty disagreeable and odious. But when that brightest of female virtues shines among other perfections of body and mind in the same person, it makes the woman more lovely than an angel. Excuse this freedom, and use the same with me. I am, dear Jenny, your loving brother,

B. Franklin

Sex was very much on Franklin's mind at this time. At first he tried to find a wife with a dowry large enough to pay off the debts he owed on his printing house. But he soon discovered that no dowries were forthcoming from parents of available girls. He then decided to correct one of the great errata of his life. While he was in England, Deborah Read, perhaps suffering from a broken heart, had married a ne'er-do-well named John Rogers, who soon revealed he had "a preceding Wife" in England and then, after running up a string of debts, absconded to the West Indies. This left Deborah a grass widow, an extremely unpleasant situation for a young woman in the eighteenth century. Franklin's solution was a common-law marriage.

Autobiography, 1771

... having turn'd my Thoughts to Marriage, I look'd round me, and made Overtures of Acquaintance in other Places; but soon found that the Business of a Printer being generally thought a poor one, I was not to expect Money with a Wife unless with such a one, as I should not otherwise think agreable. In the mean time, that hard-to-be-govern'd Passion of Youth, had hurried me frequently into Intrigues with low Women that fell in my Way, which were attended with some Expence and great Inconvenience, besides a continual Risque to my Health by a Distemper which of all Things I dreaded, tho' by great good Luck I escaped it.

A friendly Correspondence as Neighbours and old Acquaintances, had continued between me and Mrs. Read's Family, who all had a Regard for me from the time of my first Lodging in their House. I was often invited there and consulted in their Affairs, wherein I sometimes was of service. I pity'd poor Miss Read's unfortunate Situation, who was generally dejected, seldom chearful, and avoided Company. I consider'd my Giddiness and Inconstancy when in London as in a great degree the Cause of her Unhappiness; tho' the Mother was good enough to think the Fault more her own than mine, as she had prevented our Marrying before I went thither, and persuaded the other Match in my Absence. Our mutual Affection was revived, but there were now great Objections to our Union. That Match was indeed look'd upon as invalid, a preceding Wife being said to be living in England; but this could not easily be prov'd, because of the Distance. And tho' there was a Report of his Death, it was not certain. Then tho' it should be true, he had left many Debts which his Successor might be call'd on to pay. We ventured however, over all these Difficulties, and I [took] her to Wife Sept. 1. 1730. None of the

Inconveniences happened that we had apprehended, she prov'd a good and faithful Helpmate, assisted me much by attending the Shop, we throve together, and have ever mutually endeavour'd to make each other happy.

Not long after his marriage, Franklin brought home one of the results of his intrigues with low women that he did not mention in his *Autobiography* (except indirectly, where he alludes to "sinister events" in his life that he regretted). His illegitimate son, William, had been born about six months after his marriage. Franklin took the baby into his house and made him part of the family—a decision that caused no little inner turmoil in his wife. Otherwise, however, the marriage was happy. One reason was Franklin's policy of letting Deborah have her own way, recalled in this ironic passage from the second part of his *Autobiography*, composed in France in 1784.

Autobiography, 1784

We have an English Proverb that says,

He that would thrive

Must ask his Wife;

Deborah stitching pamphlets

it was lucky for me that I had one as much dispos'd to Industry and Frugality as my self. She assisted me chearfully in my Business, folding and stitching Pamphlets, tending Shop, purchasing old Linen Rags for the Papermakers, &c. &c. We kept no idle Servants, our Table was plain and simple, our Furniture of the cheapest. For instance my Breakfast was a long time Bread and Milk, (no Tea) and I ate it out of a twopenny earthen Porringer with a Pewter Spoon. But mark how Luxury will enter Families, and make a Progress, in Spite of Principle. Being call'd one Morning to Breakfast, I found it in a China Bowl with a Spoon of Silver. They had been bought for me without my Knowledge by my Wife, and had cost her the enormous Sum of three and twenty Shillings, for which she had no other Excuse or Apology to make, but that she thought *her* Husband deserv'd a Silver Spoon and China Bowl as well as any of his Neighbours.

In the fall of 1727, while he still was working as Keimer's chief assistant, Franklin organized the Junto. It was a club "formed of my ingenious acquaintances...for mutual improvement." Franklin found the idea in a book he had read in Boston, *Essays to Do Good*, by Cotton Mather. The Puritan minister's goal had been to promote religion and morality. Franklin's club was aimed at the betterment of its members, and of the city and Colony in which they lived. As its members rose to influence and wealth in Philadelphia, the Junto became a political powerhouse. With the help of the Junto, Franklin launched his "first Project of a public Nature," the creation of the first subscription library in North America. He told the story and the lessons he learned from it in his *Autobiography*.

Autobiography, 1784

At the time I establish'd my self in Pensylvania, there was not a good Bookseller's Shop in any of the Colonies to the Southward of Boston. In New-York and Philadelphia the Printers were indeed Stationers, they sold only Paper, &c., Almanacks, Ballads, and a few common School Books. Those who lov'd Reading were oblig'd to send for their Books from England. The Members of the Junto had each a few. We had left the Alehouse where we first met, and hired a Room to hold our Club in. I propos'd that we should all of us bring our Books to that Room, where they would not only be ready to consult in our Conferences, but become a common Benefit, each of us being at Liberty to borrow such as he wish'd to read at home. This was accordingly done, and for some time contented us. Finding the Advantage of this little Collection, I propos'd to render the Benefit from Books more common by commencing a Public Subscription Library. I drew a Sketch of the Plan and Rules that would be necessary, and got a skilful Conveyancer, Mr. Charles Brockden to put the whole in Form of Articles of Agreement to be subscribed; by which each Subscriber engag'd to pay a certain Sum down for the first Purchase of Books and an annual Contribution for encreasing them. So few were the Readers at that time in Philadelphia, and the Majority of us so poor, that I was not able with great Industry to find more than Fifty Persons, mostly young Tradesmen, willing to pay down for this purpose Forty shillings each, and Ten Shillings per Annum. On this little Fund we began. The Books were imported. The Library was open one Day in the Week for lending them to the Subscribers, on their Promisory Notes to pay Double the Value if not duly returned. The Institution soon manifested its Utility, was imitated by other Towns and in other Provinces, the Librarys were augmented by Donations, Reading became fashionable, and our People having no publick Amusements to divert their Attention from Study became better acquainted with Books, and in a few Years were observ'd by Strangers to be better instructed and more intelligent than People of the same Rank generally are in other Countries....

This Library afforded me the means of Improvement

‡Belonging to the *Library Company of Philadelphia*.‡
Communiter bona profundere deſim eſt.

Book labels for the Library Company were printed on Franklin's presses, and he also composed the inscription for the building's cornerstone.

Be it remembered,
In Honor of the Philadelphian Youth,
(Then chiefly Artificers)
That in MDCCXXXI
They cheerfully,
At the Inſtance of BENJAMIN FRANKLIN,
One of their Number,
INSTITUTED THE PHILADELPHIA LIBRARY,
Which, though ſmall at firſt,
Is become highly valuable,
And extenſively uſeful;
And which the Walls of this Edifice
Are now deſtined to contain and preſerve:
The FIRST STONE of whoſe FOUNDATION,
Was here placed
The thirty-firſt Day of AUGUST,
Anno Domini, MDCCLXXXIX,

1 Benjamin Gibbs,
2 Joſiah Hewes,
3 John Kaighn,
4 Mordecai Lewis,
5 Thomas Morris,
Thomas Parke,
Joſeph Paſchall,
Benjamin Poultney,
Richard Wells,
Richard Wiſtar,

then being Directors.

Samuel Coates, Treaſurer,
William Rawle, Secretary,
Zachariah Poulſon, junʳ Librarian

by constant Study, for which I set apart an Hour or two each Day; and thus repair'd in some Degree the Loss of the Learned Education my Father once intended for me.

Meanwhile, *The Pennsylvania Gazette* thrived. Within a year friends advanced Franklin enough money to buy out his partner Meredith, who decided he would rather be a farmer than a printer. The *Gazette's* success was due not only to Franklin's boldness in politics; he also exercised in its pages his talent for humor—under a number of pseudonyms. Among the *Gazette* correspondents were several descendants of Silence Dogood. Anthony Afterwit told how his wife spent him into bankruptcy. Celia Single was a born shrew who lectured the editor in scorching terms because of his partiality to men. Perhaps best of all was Alice Addertongue, who announced that she was organizing a kind of stock exchange for the sale and transfer of calumnies, slanders, and other reputation-wrecking pastimes of the gentler sex.

The Pennsylvania Gazette,
September 12, 1732

Mr. Gazetteer,

. . . I am a young Girl of about thirty-five, and live at present with my Mother. I have no Care upon my Head of getting a Living, and therefore find it my Duty as well as Inclination, to exercise my Talent at CENSURE, for the Good of my Country folks. There was, I am told, a certain generous Emperor, who if a Day had passed over his Head, in which he had conferred no Benefit on any Man, used to say to his Friends, in Latin, *Diem perdidi*, that is, it seems, *I have lost a Day*. I believe I should make use of the same Expression, if it were possible for a Day to pass in which I had not, or miss'd, an Opportunity to scandalize somebody: But, Thanks be praised, no such Misfortune has befel me these dozen Years.

Yet, whatever Good I may do, I cannot pretend that I first entred into the Practice of this Virtue from a Principle of Publick Spirit; for I remember that when a Child, I had a violent Inclination to be ever talking in my own Praise, and being continually told that it was ill Manners, and once severely whipt for it, the confin'd Stream form'd itself a new Channel, and I began to speak for the future in the Disprise of others. This I find more agreable to Company, and almost as much so to my self: For what great Difference can there be, between putting your self up, or putting your Neighbour down? *Scandal*, like other Virtues, is in part its own Reward, as it gives us

*Home of the Library Company
of Philadelphia, completed in 1790*

the Satisfaction of making our selves appear better than others, or others no better than ourselves....

By Industry and Application, I have made my self the Center of all the *Scandal* in the Province, there is little stirring but I hear of it. I began the World with this Maxim, *That no Trade can subsist without Returns*; and accordingly, whenever I receiv'd a good story, I endeavour'd to give two or a better in the Room of it. My Punctuality in this Way of Dealing gave such Encouragement, that it has procur'd me an incredible deal of Business, which without Diligence and good Method it would be impossible for me to go through. For besides the Stock of Defamation thus naturally flowing in upon me, I practice an Art by which I can pump Scandal out of People that are the least enclin'd that way. Shall I discover my Secret? Yes; to let it die with me would be inhuman. If I have never heard ill of some Person, I always impute it to defective Intelligence; *for there are none without their Faults, no not one.* If she is a Woman, I take the first Opportunity to let all her Acquaintance know I have heard that one of the handsomest or best Men in Town has said something in Praise either of her Beauty, her Wit, her Virtue, or her good Management. If you know any thing of Humane Nature, you perceive that this naturally introduces a Conversation turning upon all her Failings, past, present, and to come. To the same purpose, and with the same Success, I cause every Man of Reputation to be praised before his Competitors in Love, Business, or Esteem on Account of any particular Qualification. Near the Times of *Election*, if I find it necessary, I commend every Candidate before some of the opposite Party, listning attentively to what is said of him in answer: (But Commendations in this latter Case are not always necessary, and should be used judiciously;) of late Years I needed only observe what they said of one another freely; and having for the Help of Memory taken Account of all Informations and Accusations received, whoever peruses my Writings after my Death, may happen to think, that during a certain Term, the People of Pennsylvania chose into all their Offices of Honour and Trust, the veriest Knaves, Fools and Rascals in the whole Province....

I mention'd above, that without good Method I could not go thro' my Business: In my Father's Life-time I had some Instruction in Accompts, which I now apply with Advantage to my own Affairs. I keep a regular Set of Books, and can tell at an Hour's Warning how it stands between me and the World. In my *Daybook* I enter every Article of Defamation as it is transacted; for Scandals *receiv'd in*, I give Credit; and when I pay them out again, I make the Persons to whom they respectively relate *Debtor*. In my *Journal*, I add to each Story by Way of Improvement, such probable Circumstances as I think it will bear, and in my *Ledger* the whole is regularly posted.

I suppose the Reader already condemns me in his Heart, for this particular of *adding Circumstances*; but I justify that part of my Practice thus. 'Tis a Principle with me, that none ought to have a greater Share of Reputation than they really deserve; if they have, 'tis an Imposition upon the Publick: I know it is every one's Interest, and therefore believe they endeavour, to conceal *all* their Vices and Follies; and I hold, that those People are *extraordinary* foolish or careless who suffer a *Fourth* of their Failings to come to publick Knowledge: Taking then the common Prudence and Imprudence of Mankind in a Lump, I suppose none suffer above *one Fifth* to be discovered: Therefore when I hear of any Person's Misdoing, I think I keep within Bounds if in relating it I only make it *three times* worse than it is; and I reserve to my self the Privilege of charging them with one Fault in four, which, for aught I know, they may be entirely innocent of. You see there are but few so careful of doing Justice as my self; what Reason then have Mankind to complain of *Scandal*? In a general way, the worst that is said of us is only half of what *might* be said, if all our Faults were seen.

But alas, two great Evils have lately befaln me at the same time; an extream Cold that I can scarce speak, and a most terrible Toothach that I dare hardly open my Mouth: For some Days past I have receiv'd ten Stories for one I have paid; and I am not able to ballance my Accounts without your Assistance. I have long thought that if you would make your Paper a Vehicle of Scandal, you would double the Number of your Subscribers. I send you herewith Account of *4 Knavish Tricks, 2 crackt M——n—ds, 5 Cu——ld–ms, 3 drub'd Wives,* and *4 Hen-peck'd Husbands*, all within this Fortnight; which you

Eighteenth-century type case used by printers, from the renowned Diderot Encyclopedia

may, as Articles of News, deliver to the Publick; and if my Toothach continues, shall send you more; being, in the mean time, Your constant Reader,

ALICE ADDERTONGUE

Franklin also utilized letters to the editor to shoot holes in his chief competition, Andrew Bradford's *The American Weekly Mercury.* Here is a sample of this tactic.

The Pennsylvania Gazette,
November 9, 1732

To the Printer of the *Gazette.*

As you sometimes take upon you to correct the Publick, you ought in your Turn patiently to receive publick Correction. My Quarrel against you is, your Practice of publishing under the Notion of News, old Transactions which I suppose you hope we have forgot. For Instance, in your Numb. 669, you tell us from London of July 20. That the Losses of our Merchants are laid before the Congress of Soissons, by Mr. Stanhope, &c. and that Admiral Hopson died the 8th of May last. Whereas 'tis certain, there has been no Congress at Soissons nor any where else these three Years at least; nor could Admiral Hopson possibly die in May last, unless he has made a Resurrection since his Death in 1728. And in your Numb. 670. among other Articles of equal Antiquity, you tell us a long Story of a Murder and Robbery perpetrated on the Person of Mr. Nath. Bostock, which I have read Word for Word not less than four Years since in your own Paper. Are these your *freshest Advices foreign and domestick?* I insist that you insert this in your next, and let us see how you justify yourself.

MEMORY

I need not say more in Vindication of my self against this Charge, than that the Letter is evidently wrong directed, and should have been *To the Publisher of the Mercury*: Inasmuch as the Numb. of my Paper is not yet amounted to 669, nor are those old Articles any where to be found in the *Gazette*, but in the *Mercury* of the two last Weeks.

But some of the correspondence was for the amusement of Franklin and his readers, and nothing else. The following exchange with the pretty creatures of Pennsylvania is definitely in this category.

The Pennsylvania Gazette,
November 20 and
November 27, 1735

Mr. Franklin,

Pray let the prettiest Creature in this Place know, (by publishing this) That if it was not for her Affectation, she would be absolutely irresistible.

The little Epistle in our last, has produced no less than six, which follow in the order we receiv'd 'em.

Mr. Franklin,

I cannot conceive who your Correspondent means by *the prettiest Creature* in this Place; but I can assure either him or her, that she who is truly so, has no Affectation at all.

Sir,

Since your last Week's Paper I have look'd in my Glass a thousand Times, I believe, in one Day; and if it was not for the Charge of Affectation I might, without Partiality, believe myself the Person meant.

Mr. Franklin,

I must own that several have told me, I am the prettiest Creature in this Place; but I believe I should not have been tax'd with Affectation if I could have thought as well of them as they do of themselves.

Sir,

Your Sex calls me pretty; my own affected. Is it from Judgment in the one, or Envy in the other?

Mr. Franklin,

They that call me affected are greatly mistaken; for I don't know that I ever refus'd a Kiss to any Body but a Fool.

Friend Benjamin,

I am not at all displeased at being charged with Affectation. Thou know'st the vain People call Decency of Behaviour by that Name.

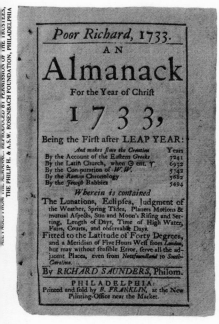

The title page of Franklin's first Poor Richard *almanac*

Almost every printer in Colonial America published an almanac—or wanted to publish one. They were widely read by farmers of the simpler sort, who sometimes took them seriously. Each almanac had a resident philomath who studied the stars, made his astronomical calculations and predictions, and split the profits with the printer. Franklin, with his usual shrewdness, noted that sensible people did not really believe in these predictions. Most people read almanacs for amusement, although they found in them such useful information as court dates and a calendar of other meeting dates. Franklin, therefore, decided to become his own philomath, inventing him as he did so many of his *Gazette* correspondents. His name was Richard Saunders and his candid introduction to the first edition explained why the work was titled *Poor Richard*.

Poor Richard, 1733

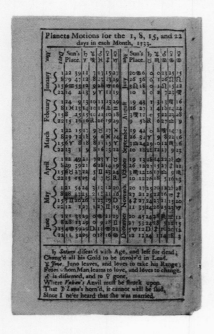

Courteous Reader,

I might in this place attempt to gain thy Favour, by declaring that I write Almanacks with no other View than that of the publick Good; but in this I should not be sincere; and Men are now a-days too wise to be deceiv'd by Pretences how specious soever. The plain Truth of the Matter is, I am excessive poor, and my Wife, good Woman, is, I tell her, excessive proud; she cannot bear, she says, to sit spinning in her Shift of Tow, while I do nothing but gaze at the Stars; and has threatned more than once to burn all my Books and Rattling-Traps (as she calls my Instruments) if I do not make some profitable Use of them for the good of my Family. The Printer has offer'd me some considerable share of the Profits, and I have thus begun to comply with my Dame's desire....

R. SAUNDERS

Poor Richard was soon the most successful almanac in America, selling more than ten thousand copies a year. The source of this success was not only the appeal of Poor Richard's ingenuous personality. His almanac's pages were crowded with amusing verses, proverbs, and aphorisms. Franklin took many of these from earlier almanacs and from collections of epigrams and sayings. But he constantly improved upon previous anthologists, by sharpening, simplifying, and balancing the epigrams that made "Poor Richard says" a household phrase throughout Colonial America. Here is a sampling of Franklin's best efforts, drawn from the twenty years during which he edited and wrote the *Almanack*.

Kings and Bears often worry their keepers.

He's a Fool that makes his Doctor his Heir.

Beware of meat twice boil'd, and an old foe reconcil'd.

The poor have little, beggars none, the rich too much, *enough* not one.

After 3 days men grow weary, of a wench, a guest, and weather rainy.

Men and Melons are hard to know.

Where there's Marriage without Love, there will be Love without Marriage.

Neither a Fortress nor a Maidenhead will hold out long after they begin to parly.

An Egg today is better than a Hen tomorrow.

He that waits upon Fortune, is never sure of a Dinner.

Marry your Son when you will, but your Daughter when you can.

Approve not of him who commends all you say.

Three may keep a Secret, if two of them are dead.

Opportunity is the great Bawd.

Here comes the Orator! with his Flood of Words, and his Drop of Reason.

An old young man, will be a young old man.

Sal laughs at every thing you say. Why? Because she has fine Teeth.

Fish and Visitors stink in 3 days.

He that lives upon Hope, dies farting.

Let thy maidservant be faithful, strong, and homely.

Admiration is the Daughter of Ignorance.

She that paints her Face, thinks of her Tail.

A countryman between 2 Lawyers, is like a fish between two cats.

There are no ugly Loves, nor handsome Prisons.

Write with the learned, pronounce with the vulgar.

Keep your eyes wide open before marriage, half shut afterwards.

Thou can'st not joke an Enemy into a Friend; but thou may'st a Friend into an Enemy.

He that falls in love with himself, will have no Rivals.

To bear other People's afflictions, every one has Courage enough, and to spare.

Learn of the skilful: He that teaches himself, hath a fool for his master.

Epitaph on a Scolding Wife by her Husband. Here my poor Bridget's Corps doth lie, she is at rest—and so am I.

A Plowman on his Legs is higher than a Gentleman on his knees.

If your head is wax, don't walk in the Sun.

You can bear your own Faults, and why not a Fault in your Wife.

The Golden Age never was the present Age.

Old Boys have their Playthings as well as young Ones; the Difference is only in the Price.

The Proud hate Pride—in others.

He that is of Opinion Money will do every Thing, may well be suspected of doing every Thing for Money.

Love your Neighbor; yet don't pull down your Hedge.

Love your enemies, for they tell you your faults.

While the business flourished, a personal tragedy struck the Franklin family. Deborah had given birth to a son, whom they named Francis Folger Franklin. At the age of four, the boy died of smallpox. Franklin was to feel the bitter sorrow of the boy's death for the rest of his life, for he had hesitated to have him inoculated. The sorrowing parents placed on little Frankie's gravestone the words, "The DELIGHT of all that knew him." Good newspaperman that he was, Franklin tried to make his loss benefit the public, in the following story.

Portrait engraving of Francis Folger Franklin, who died of smallpox

The Pennsylvania Gazette,
December 30, 1736

Understanding 'tis a current Report, that my Son Francis, who died lately of the Small Pox, had it by Inoculation; and being desired to satisfy the Publick in that Particular; inasmuch as some People are, by that Report (join'd with others of the like kind, and perhaps equally groundless) deter'd from having that Operation perform'd on their Children, I do hereby sincerely declare, that he was not inoculated, but receiv'd the Distemper in the common Way of Infection: And I suppose the Report could only arise from its being my known Opinion, that Inoculation was a safe and beneficial Practice; and from my having said among my Acquaintance, that I intended to have my Child inoculated, as soon as he should have recovered sufficient Strength from a Flux with which he had been long afflicted.

B. FRANKLIN

Franklin's respect and affection for his father and mother continued to be a factor in his life, although he was now a mature man of thirty-two. This respect, however, did not prevent him from making it clear to them that he was no longer being guided by their religious beliefs. This letter was occasioned by an unfortunate incident, in which Franklin was involved. Some pranksters pretended to initiate a simple-minded apprentice named Daniel Rees into the Masons with a garish ceremony, which included a devil dressed in a cow's hide with horns. A bowl of brandy, lighted to add an eerie glow to the scene, was accidentally spilled on the boy, and he died of his burns two days later. Franklin was accused of being part of the hoax in Andrew Bradford's *Mercury*. The story spread to other papers, and was reprinted in Boston, where his parents heard about it and reacted with great alarm.

Oldest American Masonic seal

Title page of Franklin's magazine, three days too late to be the first magazine published in America

[Philadelphia] April 13. 1738

Honour'd Father and Mother

I have your Favour of the 21st of March in which you both seem concern'd lest I have imbib'd some erroneous Opinions. Doubtless I have my Share, and when the natural Weakness and Imperfection of Human Understanding is considered, with the unavoidable Influences of Education, Custom, Books and Company, upon our Ways of thinking, I imagine a Man must have a good deal of Vanity who believes, and a good deal of Boldness who affirms, that all the Doctrines he holds, are true; and all he rejects, are false. And perhaps the same may be justly said of every Sect, Church and Society of men when they assume to themselves that Infallibility which they deny to the Popes and Councils. I think Opinions should be judg'd of by their Influences and Effects; and if a Man holds none that tend to make him less Virtuous or more vicious, it may be concluded he holds none that are dangerous; which I hope is the Case with me. I am sorry you should have any Uneasiness on my Account, and if it were a thing possible for one to alter his Opinions in order to please others, I know none whom I ought more willingly to oblige in that respect than your selves: But since it is no more in a Man's Power *to think* than *to look* like another, methinks all that should be expected from me is to keep my Mind open to Conviction, to hear patiently and examine attentively whatever is offered me for that end; and if after all I continue in the same Errors, I believe your usual Charity will induce you rather to pity and excuse than blame me. In the mean time your Care and Concern for me is what I am very thankful for. . . .

. . . I am Your dutiful Son

BF

Nothing sums up Franklin's relationship with his wife better than the song to Deborah that he wrote some time in 1742. According to Franklin's friend Dr. John Bard, the inspiration came from a discussion, possibly at the Junto, about the number of poems written in praise of mistresses, and the far fewer written in praise of wives. The next morning Bard received the following verses from Franklin with a note asking him to sing them at their next meeting. "Joggy" was a term for a homely woman.

[c. 1742]

Song

Of their Chloes and Phillisses Poets may prate
    I sing my plain Country Joan
Now twelve Years my Wife, still the Joy of my Life
    Blest Day that I made her my own,
        My dear Friends
    Blest Day that I made her my own.

2

Not a Word of her Face, her Shape, or her Eyes,
    Of Flames or of Darts shall you hear;
Tho' I Beauty admire 'tis Virtue I prize,
    That fades not in seventy Years,
        My dear Friends

3

In Health a Companion delightfull and dear,
    Still easy, engaging, and Free,
In Sickness no less than the faithfullest Nurse
    As tender as tender can be,
        My dear Friends

4

In Peace and good Order, my Household she keeps
    Right Careful to save what I gain
Yet chearfully spends, and smiles on the Friends
    I've the Pleasures to entertain
        My dear Friends

5

She defends my good Name ever where I'm to blame,
    Friend firmer was ne'er to Man giv'n,
Her compassionate Breast, feels for all the Distrest,
    Which draws down the Blessing from Heav'n,
        My dear Friends

6

Am I laden with Care, she takes off a large Share,
    That the Burthen ne'er makes [me] to reel,
Does good Fortune arrive, the Joy of my Wife,
    Quite doubles the Pleasures I feel,
        My dear Friends

7

In Raptures the giddy Rake talks of his Fair,
    Enjoyment shall make him Despise,
I speak my cool sence, that long Experience,
    And Enjoyment have chang'd in no wise,
        My dear Friends

*Members of the Junto borrowing
each other's books to read*

[Some Faults we have all, and so may my Joan,
But then they're exceedingly small;
And now I'm us'd to 'em, they're just like my own,
I scarcely can see 'em at all,
My dear Friends,
I scarcely can see them at all.]
8
Were the fairest young Princess, with Million in Purse
To be had in Exchange for my Joan,
She could not be a better Wife, mought be a Worse,
So I'd stick to my Joggy alone
My dear Friends
I'd cling to my lovely ould Joan.

Perhaps it was his Boston birth, and his residence in Philadelphia, that gave Franklin a continental view of America. In this letter to William Strahan, a London printer who became a trusted correspondent, he revealed that, from a business point of view, he already thought of the Colonies as a whole. He had set up printers in Charleston, South Carolina, and New York, as well as operating his own shop in Philadelphia. The young man that Strahan sent over as a result of this letter was David Hall, a Scot who eventually became Franklin's partner. Mr. Read, mentioned in the first line, was a cousin of Deborah Read's.

Philada. July 10. 1743
Mr. Read has communicated to me part of a Letter from you, recommending a young Man whom you would be glad to see in better Business than that of a Journeyman Printer. I have already three Printing-Houses in three different Colonies, and purpose to set up a fourth if I can meet with a proper Person to manage it, having all Materials ready for that purpose. If the young Man will venture over hither, that I may see and be acquainted with him, we can treat about the Affair, and I make no doubt but he will think my Proposals reasonable; If we should not agree, I promise him however a Twelvemonths Good Work, and to defray his Passage back if he enclines to return to England.

Hall arrived carrying a friendly reply from Strahan, to which Franklin promptly responded. The letter is important not only because it marked the beginning of one of his most important friendships, but also because of the way Franklin wrote to the Londoner as a humble colonial.

Philada. July 4. 1744
I receiv'd your Favour per Mr. Hall, who arriv'd here

*Portrait of William Strahan
by Sir Joshua Reynolds*

about two Weeks since, and from the short Acquaintance I have had with him, I am persuaded he will answer perfectly the Character you had given of him. I make no doubt but his Voyage, tho' it has been expensive, will prove advantageous to him: I have already made him some Proposals, which he has under Consideration, and as we are like to agree on them, we shall not, I believe, differ on the Article of his Passage Money. . . .

I have long wanted a Friend in London whose Judgment I could depend on, to send me from time to time such new Pamphlets as are worth Reading on any Subject (Religious Controversy excepted) for there is no depending on Titles and Advertisements. This Favour I take the Freedom to beg of you, and shall lodge Money in your Hands for that purpose.

We have seldom any News on our Side the Globe that can be entertaining to you on yours. All our Affairs are *petit*. They have a miniature Resemblance only, of the grand Things of Europe. Our Governments, Parliaments, Wars, Treaties, Expeditions, Factions, &c. tho' Matters of great and Serious Consequence to us, can seem but Trifles to you.

While he worked and prospered, Franklin never lost his interest in morality and religion, which he had inherited from Puritan Boston. He created his own set of religious exercises, some of which he recited daily. Even more interesting was his attempt to achieve moral perfection — and the conclusions he drew from the experiment. He told the story in his *Autobiography*.

Autobiography, 1771

It was about this time that I conceiv'd the bold and arduous Project of arriving at moral Perfection. I wish'd to live without committing any Fault at any time; I would conquer all that either Natural Inclination, Custom, or Company might lead me into. As I knew, or thought I knew, what was right and wrong, I did not see why I might not *always* do the one and avoid the other. But I soon found I had undertaken a Task of more Difficulty than I had imagined. While my *Attention was taken up* in guarding against one Fault, I was often surpriz'd by another. Habit took the Advantage of Inattention. Inclination was sometimes too strong for Reason. I concluded at length, that the mere speculative Conviction that it was our Interest to be compleatly virtuous, was not sufficient to prevent our Slipping, and that the contrary Habits must be broken and good ones acquired and established, before we can have any Dependence on a steady uniform Rectitude of Conduct. For this purpose I therefore contriv'd the following Method.

In the various Enumerations of the moral Virtues I had met with in my Reading, I found the Catalogue more or less numerous, as different Writers included more or fewer Ideas under the same Name. Temperance, for Example, was by some confin'd to Eating and Drinking, while by others it was extended to mean the moderating every other Pleasure, Appetite, Inclination or Passion, bodily or mental, even to our Avarice and Ambition. I propos'd to myself, for the sake of Clearness, to use rather more Names with fewer Ideas annex'd to each, than a few Names with more Ideas; and I included under Thirteen Names of Virtues all that at that time occurr'd to me as necessary or desirable, and annex'd to each a short Precept, which fully express'd the Extent I gave to its Meaning.

These names of Virtues with their Precepts were

1. TEMPERANCE.

Eat not to Dulness.

Drink not to Elevation.

2. SILENCE.

Speak not but what may benefit others or yourself. Avoid trifling Conversation.

3. ORDER.

Let all your Things have their Places. Let each Part of your Business have its Time.

4. RESOLUTION.

Resolve to perform what you ought. Perform without fail what you resolve.

5. FRUGALITY.

Make no Expence but to do good to others or yourself: i.e. Waste nothing.

6. INDUSTRY.

Lose no Time. Be always employ'd in something useful. Cut off all unnecessary Actions.

7. SINCERITY.

Use no hurtful Deceit.

Think innocently and justly; and, if you speak, speak accordingly.

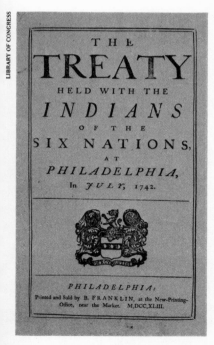

THE
TREATY
HELD WITH THE
INDIANS
OF THE
SIX NATIONS,
AT
PHILADELPHIA,
In JULY, 1742.

PHILADELPHIA:
Printed and Sold by B. FRANKLIN, at the New-Printing-Office, near the Market. M,DCC,XLIII.

Title page of one of Franklin's most elegant printing efforts

8. JUSTICE.

Wrong none, by doing Injuries or omitting the Benefits that are your Duty.

9. MODERATION.

Avoid Extreams. Forbear resenting Injuries so much as you think they deserve.

10. CLEANLINESS.

Tolerate no Uncleanness in Body, Cloaths or Habitation.

11. TRANQUILITY.

Be not disturbed at Trifles, or at Accidents common or unavoidable.

12. CHASTITY.

Rarely use Venery but for Health or Offspring; Never to Dulness, Weakness, or the Injury of your own or another's Peace or Reputation.

13. HUMILITY.

Imitate Jesus and Socrates.

My Intention being to acquire the *Habitude* of all these Virtues, I judg'd it would be well not to distract my Attention by attempting the whole at once, but to fix it on one of them at a time, and when I should be Master of that, then to proceed to another, and so on till I should have gone thro' the thirteen. And as the previous Acquisition of some might facilitate the Acquisition of certain others, I arrang'd them with that View as they stand above. *Temperance* first, as it tends to procure that Coolness and Clearness of Head, which is so necessary where constant Vigilance was to be kept up, and Guard maintained, against the unremitting Attraction of ancient Habits, and the Force of perpetual Temptations. This being acquir'd and establish'd, *Silence* would be more easy, and my Desire being to gain Knowledge at the same time that I improv'd in Virtue, and considering that in Conversation it was obtain'd rather by the use of the Ears than of the Tongue, and therefore wishing to break a Habit I was getting into of Prattling, Punning and Joking, which only made me acceptable to trifling Company, I gave *Silence* the second Place. This, and the next, *Order,* I expected would allow me more Time for attending to my Project and my Studies; RESOLUTION, once become habitual, would keep me firm in my Endeavours to obtain all the subsequent Virtues; *Frugality* and *Industry,* by freeing me from my remaining Debt, and producing Affluence and Independance, would

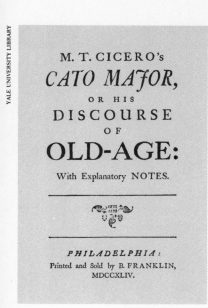

M. T. CICERO's

CATO MAJOR,

OR HIS

DISCOURSE

OF

OLD-AGE:

With Explanatory NOTES.

PHILADELPHIA:
Printed and Sold by B. FRANKLIN,
MDCCXLIV.

Title page of the Cato Major,
*considered by Franklin to be his
most distinguished printed book*

make more easy the Practice of *Sincerity* and *Justice,* &c. &c. Conceiving then that agreable to the Advice of Pythagoras in his Golden Verses daily Examination would be necessary, I contriv'd the following Method for conducting that Examination.

I made a little Book in which I allotted a Page for each of the Virtues. I rul'd each Page with red Ink, so as to have seven Columns, one for each Day of the Week, marking each Column with a Letter for the Day. I cross'd these Columns with thirteen red Lines, marking the Beginning of each Line with the first Letter of one of the Virtues, on which Line and in its proper Column I might mark by a little black Spot every Fault I found upon Examination to have been committed respecting that Virtue upon that Day.

I determined to give a Week's strict Attention to each of the Virtues successively. Thus in the first Week my great Guard was to avoid every the least Offence against Temperance, leaving the other Virtues to their ordinary Chance, only marking every Evening the Faults of the Day. Thus if in the first Week I could keep my first Line marked T clear of Spots, I suppos'd the Habit of that virtue so much strengthen'd and its opposite weaken'd, that I might venture extending my Attention to include the next, and for the following Week keep both Lines clear of Spots. Proceeding thus to the last, I could go thro' a Course compleat in Thirteen Weeks, and four Courses in a Year. And like him who having a Garden to weed, does not attempt to eradicate all the bad Herbs at once, which would exceed his Reach and his Strength, but works on one of the Beds at a time, and having accomplish'd the first proceeds to a Second; so I should have, (I hoped) the encouraging Pleasure of seeing on my Pages the Progress I made in Virtue, by clearing successively my Lines of their Spots, till in the End by a Number of Courses, I should be happy in viewing a clean Book after a thirteen Weeks daily Examination. . . .

I enter'd upon the Execution of this Plan for Self Examination, and continu'd it with occasional Intermissions for some time. I was surpriz'd to find myself so much fuller of Faults than I had imagined, but I had the Satisfaction of seeing them diminish. To avoid the Trouble of renewing now and then my little Book, which by scraping out the Marks on the Paper of old Faults to make room for new Ones in a new Course, became full of Holes: I transferr'd my Tables and Precepts to the Ivory Leaves of a Memorandum Book, on which the Lines were drawn with red Ink that made a durable Stain, and on those Lines I mark'd my Faults with a black Lead Pencil, which Marks I could easily wipe out with a wet Sponge. After a while I went thro' one Course only in a Year, and afterwards only one in several Years, till at length I omitted them entirely, being employ'd in Voyages and Business abroad with a Multiplicity of Affairs, that interfered, but I always carried my little Book with me.

Franklin's search for moral perfection did not prevent him from writing this very cheerful drinking song around this time.

[*c.* 1745]

The Antediluvians were all very sober
For they had no Wine, and they brew'd no October;
All wicked, bad Livers, on Mischief still thinking,
For there can't be good Living where there is not good
     Drinking.

                      Derry down

'Twas honest old Noah first planted the Vine,
And mended his Morals by drinking its Wine;
He justly the drinking of Water decry'd;
For he knew that all Mankind, by drinking it, dy'd.

                      Derry down

From this Piece of History plainly we find
That Water's good neither for Body or Mind;
That Virtue and Safety in Wine-bibbing's found
While all that drink Water deserve to be drown'd.

                      Derry down

So For Safety and Honesty put the Glass round.

As he grew older, Franklin did not lose his keen interest in sex. The following letter was for many years suppressed by various Franklin editors and librarians of his papers. Paul Leicester Ford, author of *The Many-Sided Franklin* (1899), for instance, thought it would "shock modern taste," and Albert Henry Smyth omitted it from his ten-volume edition, *The Writings of Benjamin Franklin* (1905-7), remarking that it would not be tolerated by "the public sentiment of the present age." Since 1926, when it was printed in a biography of Franklin by Phillips Russell, it has appeared in print frequently. No one knows to whom it was addressed. The editors of *The Papers of Benjamin Franklin* are inclined to believe that it is really an essay in the form of a letter; Franklin himself gave it the title "Old Mistresses Apologue."

June 25. 1745

My dear Friend,

I know of no Medicine fit to diminish the violent natural Inclinations you mention; and if I did, I think I should not communicate it to you. Marriage is the proper Remedy. It is the most natural State of Man, and therefore the State in which you are most likely to find solid Happiness. Your Reasons against entring into it at present, appear to me not well-founded. The circumstantial Advantages you have in View by postponing it, are not only uncertain, but they are small in comparison with that of the Thing itself, the being *married and settled.* It is the Man and Woman united that make the compleat human Being. Separate, she wants his Force of Body and Strength of Reason; he, her Softness, Sensibility and acute Discernment. Together they are more likely to succeed in the World. A single Man has not nearly the Value he would have in that State of Union. He is an incomplete Animal. He resembles the odd Half of a Pair of Scissars. If you get a prudent healthy Wife, your Industry in your Profession, with her good Oeconomy, will be a Fortune sufficient.

But if you will not take this Counsel, and persist in thinking a Commerce with the Sex inevitable, then I repeat my former Advice, that in all your Amours you should *prefer old Women to young ones.* You call this a Paradox, and demand my Reasons. They are these:

1. Because as they have more Knowledge of the World and their Minds are better stor'd with Observations, their Conversation is more improving and more lastingly agreable.

2. Because when Women cease to be handsome, they study to be good. To maintain their Influence over Men, they supply the Diminution of Beauty by an Augmentation of Utility. They learn to do a 1000 Services small and great, and are the most tender and useful of all Friends when you are sick. Thus they continue amiable. And hence there is hardly such a thing to be found as an old Woman who is not a good Woman.

3. Because there is no hazard of Children, which

irregularly produc'd may be attended with much Inconvenience.

4. Because thro' more Experience, they are more prudent and discreet in conducting an Intrigue to prevent Suspicion. The Commerce with them is therefore safer with regard to your Reputation. And with regard to theirs, if the Affair should happen to be known, considerate People might be rather inclin'd to excuse an old Woman who would kindly take care of a young Man, form his Manners by her good Counsels, and prevent his ruining his Health and Fortune among mercenary Prostitutes.

5. Because in every Animal that walks upright, the Deficiency of the Fluids that fill the Muscles appears first in the highest Part: The Face first grows lank and wrinkled; then the Neck, then the Breast and Arms; the lower Parts continuing to the last as plump as ever: So that covering all above with a Basket, and regarding only what is below the Girdle, it is impossible of two Women to know an old from a young one. And as in the dark all Cats are grey, the Pleasure of corporal Enjoyment with an old Woman is at least equal, and frequently superior, every Knack being by Practice capable of Improvement.

6. Because the Sin is less. The debauching a Virgin may be her Ruin, and make her for Life unhappy.

7. Because the Compunction is less. The having made a young Girl *miserable* may give you frequent bitter Reflections; none of which can attend the making an old Woman *happy*.

8[thly and Lastly] They are *so grateful!!* Thus much for my Paradox. But still I advise you to marry directly; being sincerely Your affectionate Friend.

Around the same time, Franklin produced another famous bit of sexual foolery. "The Speech of Miss Polly Baker" was not printed in *The Pennsylvania Gazette*. Its first known public appearance was in the London newspaper *The General Advertiser* on April 15, 1747. Within a week, five London papers reprinted it, and they were soon imitated by five monthly magazines. Before the end of the year, many American newspapers followed suit. It was widely regarded in England, France, and many parts of America as fact. The Abbé Raynal cited it in his book, *Histoire Philosophique et Politique*, as an example of the supposed severity of laws in New England.

The General Advertiser,
April 15, 1747

The SPEECH of Miss POLLY BAKER, before a Court of Judicature, at Connecticut near Boston in New-England; where she was prosecuted the Fifth Time, for having a Bastard Child: Which influenced the Court to dispense with her Punishment, and induced one of her Judges to marry her the next Day.

May it please the Honourable Bench to indulge me in a few Words: I am a poor unhappy Woman, who have no Money to fee Lawyers to plead for me, being hard put to it to get a tolerable Living. I shall not trouble your Honours with long Speeches; for I have not the Presumption to expect, that you may, by any Means, be prevailed on to deviate in your Sentence from the Law, in my Favour. All I humbly hope is, That your Honours would charitably move the Governor's Goodness on my Behalf, that my Fine may be remitted. This is the Fifth Time, Gentlemen, that I have been dragg'd before your Court on the same Account; twice I have paid heavy Fines, and twice have been brought to Publick Punishment, for want of Money to pay those Fines. This may have been agreeable to the Laws, and I don't dispute it; but since Laws are sometimes unreasonable in themselves, and therefore repealed, and others bear too hard on the Subject in particular Circumstances; and therefore there is left a Power somewhat to dispense with the Execution of them; I take the Liberty to say, That I think this Law, by which I am punished, is both unreasonable in itself, and particularly severe with regard to me, who have always lived an inoffensive Life in the Neighbourhood where I was born, and defy my Enemies (if I have any) to say I ever wrong'd Man, Woman, or Child. Abstracted from the Law, I cannot conceive (may it please your Honours) what the Nature of my Offence is. I have brought Five fine Children into the World, at the Risque of my Life; I have maintain'd them well by my own Industry, without burthening the Township, and would have done it better, if it had not been for the heavy Charges and Fines I have paid. Can it be a Crime (in the Nature of Things I mean) to add to the Number of the King's Subjects, in a new Country that really wants People? I own it, I should think it a Praise-worthy, rather than a punishable Action. I have debauched no

An eighteenth-century printing house as shown in Diderot's Encyclopedia

other Woman's Husband, nor enticed any Youth; these Things I never was charg'd with, nor has any one the least Cause of Complaint against me, unless, perhaps, the Minister, or Justice, because I have had Children without being married, by which they have missed a Wedding Fee. But, can ever this be a Fault of mine? I appeal to your Honours. You are pleased to allow I don't want Sense; but I must be stupified to the last Degree, not to prefer the Honourable State of Wedlock, to the Condition I have lived in. I always was, and still am willing to enter into it; and doubt not my behaving well in it, having all the Industry, Frugality, Fertility, and Skill in Oeconomy, appertaining to a good Wife's Character. I defy any Person to say, I ever refused an Offer of that Sort: On the contrary, I readily consented to the only Proposal of Marriage that ever was made me, which was when I was a Virgin; but too easily confiding in the Person's Sincerity that made it, I unhappily lost my own Honour, by trusting to his; for he got me with Child, and then forsook me: That very Person you all know; he is now become a Magistrate of this Country; and I had Hopes he would have appeared this Day on the Bench, and have endeavoured to moderate the Court in my Favour; then I should have scorn'd to have mention'd it; but I must now complain of it, as unjust and unequal, That my Betrayer and Undoer, the first Cause of all my Faults and Miscarriages (if they must be deemed such) should be advanc'd to Honour and Power in the Government, that punishes my Misfortunes with Stripes and Infamy. I should be told, 'tis like, That were there no Act of Assembly in the Case, the Precepts of Religion are violated by my Transgressions. If mine, then, is a religious Offence, leave it to religious Punishments. You have already excluded me from the Comforts of your Church-Communion. Is not that sufficient? You believe I have offended Heaven, and must suffer eternal Fire: Will not that be sufficient? What Need is there, then, of your additional Fines and Whipping? I own, I do not think as you do; for, if I thought what you call a Sin, was really such, I could not presumptuously commit it. But, how can it be believed, that Heaven is angry at my having Children, when to the little done by me towards it, God has been pleased to add his Divine Skill and admirable Workmanship in the Formation of their

The earliest known portrait of Franklin, attributed to Robert Feke, shows him as a prosperous business-man of around forty years of age.

Bodies, and crown'd it, by furnishing them with rational and immortal Souls. Forgive me, Gentlemen, if I talk a little extravagantly on these Matters; I am no Divine, but if you, Gentlemen, must be making Laws, do not turn natural and useful Actions into Crimes, by your Prohibitions. But take into your wise Consideration, the great and growing Number of Batchelors in the Country, many of whom from the mean Fear of the Expences of a Family, have never sincerely and honourably courted a Woman in their Lives; and by their Manner of Living, leave unproduced (which is little better than Murder) Hundreds of their Posterity to the Thousandth Generation. Is not this a greater Offence against the Publick Good, than mine? Compel them, then, by Law, either to Marriage, or to pay double the Fine of Fornication every Year. What must poor young Women do, whom Custom have forbid to solicit the Men, and who cannot force themselves upon Husbands, when the Laws take no Care to provide them any; and yet severely punish them if they do their Duty without them; the Duty of the first and great Command of Nature, and of Nature's God, *Encrease and Multiply*. A Duty, from the steady Performance of which, nothing has been able to deter me; but for its Sake, I have hazarded the Loss of the Public Esteem, and have frequently endured Publick Disgrace and Punishment; and therefore ought, in my humble Opinion, instead of a Whipping, to have a Statue erected to my Memory.

By the age of forty-two, Franklin was a distinctly successful man. His printing business was earning him well over two thousand pounds a year. Looking back on his experience, he wrote an essay that was to be reprinted numerous times in subsequent years. The raw young man who had arrived in Philadelphia with only a dollar and a few pennies in his pocket now spoke with the seasoned voice of success.

[July 21, 1748]

ADVICE TO A YOUNG TRADESMAN, WRITTEN BY AN OLD ONE.

To my Friend A.B.

As you have desired it of me, I write the following Hints, which have been of Service to me, and may, if observed, be so to you.

Remember that TIME is Money. He that can earn Ten Shillings a Day by his Labour, and goes abroad, or sits idle one half of that Day, tho' he spends but Sixpence

Verse, weather predictions, and aphorisms were intermingled in Poor Richard's *monthly pages, on which Franklin later made marginal notations of the actual weather.*

during his Diversion or Idleness, ought not to reckon That the only Expence; he has really spent or rather thrown away Five Shillings besides.

Remember that CREDIT is Money. If a Man lets his Money lie in my Hands after it is due, he gives me the Interest, or so much as I can make of it during that Time. This amounts to a considerable Sum where a Man has good and large Credit, and makes good Use of it.

Remember that Money is of a prolific generating Nature. Money can beget Money, and its Offspring can beget more, and so on. Five Shillings turn'd, is *Six*: Turn'd again, 'tis Seven and Three Pence; and so on 'til it becomes an Hundred Pound. The more there is of it, the more it produces every Turning, so that the Profits rise quicker and quicker. He that kills a breeding Sow, destroys all her Offspring to the thousandth Generation. He that murders a Crown, destroys all it might have produc'd, even Scores of Pounds.

Remember that Six Pounds a Year is but a Groat a Day. For this little Sum (which may be daily wasted either in Time or Expence unperceived) a Man of Credit may on his own Security have the constant Possession and Use of an Hundred Pounds. So much in Stock briskly turn'd by an industrious Man, produces great Advantage.

Remember this Saying, *That the good Paymaster is Lord of another Man's Purse*. He that is known to pay punctually and exactly to the Time he promises, may at any Time, and on any Occasion, raise all the Money his Friends can spare. This is sometimes of great Use: Therefore never keep borrow'd Money an Hour beyond the Time you promis'd, lest a Disappointment shuts up your Friends Purse forever.

The most trifling Actions that Affect a Man's Credit, are to be regarded. The Sound of your Hammer at Five in the Morning or Nine at Night, heard by a Creditor, makes him easy Six Months longer. But if he sees you at a Billiard Table, or hears your Voice in a Tavern, when you should be at Work, he sends for his Money the next Day. Finer Cloaths than he or his Wife wears, or greater Expence in any particular than he affords himself, shocks his Pride, and he duns you to humble you. Creditors are a kind of People, that have the sharpest Eyes and Ears, as well as the best Memories of any in the World.

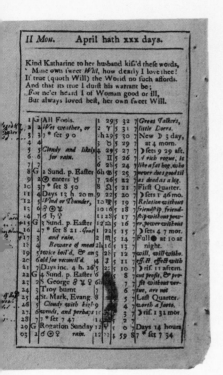

Good-natur'd Creditors (and such one would always chuse to deal with if one could) feel Pain when they are oblig'd to ask for Money. Spare 'em that Pain, and they will love you. When you receive a Sum of Money, divide it among 'em in Proportion to your Debts. Don't be asham'd of paying a small Sum because you owe a greater. Money, more or less, is always welcome; and your Creditor had rather be at the Trouble of receiving Ten Pounds voluntarily brought him, tho' at ten different Times or Payments, than be oblig'd to go ten Times to demand it before he can receive it in a Lump. It shews, besides, that you are mindful of what you owe; it makes you appear a careful as well as an honest Man; and that still encreases your Credit.

Beware of thinking all your own that you possess, and of living accordingly. 'Tis a Mistake that many People who have Credit fall into. To prevent this, keep an exact Account for some Time of both your Expences and your Incomes. If you take the Pains at first to mention Particulars, it will have this good Effect; you will discover how wonderfully small trifling Expences mount up to large Sums, and will discern what might have been, and may for the future be saved, without occasioning any great Inconvenience.

In short, the Way to Wealth, if you desire it, is as plain as the Way to Market. It depends chiefly on two Words, INDUSTRY and FRUGALITY; i.e. Waste neither Time nor Money, but make the best Use of both. He that gets all he can honestly, and saves all he gets (necessary Expences excepted) will certainly become RICH; If that Being who governs the World, to whom all should look for a Blessing on their honest Endeavours, doth not in his wise Providence otherwise determine.

A new serenity was becoming an evident part of Franklin's life. Perhaps the best proof of this was his introduction to *Poor Richard* for 1746. Here the distinction between Franklin and Richard Saunders all but disappeared, and he painted a word picture of his way of life as he entered middle age.

Poor Richard, 1746

Who is Poor Richard? People oft enquire,
Where lives? What is he?—never yet the nigher.
Somewhat to ease your Curiositie,
Take these slight Sketches of my Dame and me.

Thanks to kind Readers and a careful Wife,
With Plenty bless'd, I lead an easy Life;
My Business Writing; hers to drain the Mead,
Or crown the barren Hill with useful Shade;
In the smooth Glebe to see the Plowshare worn,
And fill the Granary with needful Corn.
Press nectarous Cyder from my loaded Trees,
Print the sweet Butter, turn the drying Cheese.
Some Books we read, tho' few there are that hit
The happy Point where Wisdom joins with Wit;
That set fair Virtue naked to our View,
And teach us what is *decent*, what is *true*.
The Friend sincere, and honest Man, with Joy
Treating or treated oft our Time employ.
Our Table neat, Meals temperate; and our Door
Op'ning spontaneous to the bashful Poor.
Free from the bitter Rage of Party Zeal,
All those we love who seek the publick Weal.
Nor blindly follow Superstition's Lore,
Which cheats deluded Mankind o'er and o'er.
Not over righteous, quite beyond the Rule,
Conscience perplext by every canting Tool.
Nor yet when Folly hides the dubious Line,
Where Good and Bad their blended Colours join;
Rush indiscreetly down the dangerous Steep,
And plunge uncertain in the darksome Deep.
Cautious, if right; if wrong resolv'd to part
The Inmate Snake that folds about the Heart.
Observe the *Mean*, the *Motive* and the *End*;
Mending our selves, or striving still to mend.
Our Souls sincere, our Purpose fair and free,
Without Vain Glory or Hypocrisy:
Thankful if well; if ill, we kiss the Rod;
Resign with Hope, and put our Trust in GOD.

Chapter 4

America's Newton

In a letter to his mother in April, 1750, Franklin remarked that when he died he would rather have it said "he lived usefully, than he died rich." No sooner had he achieved financial security, than his spacious mind began seeking new frontiers to challenge. First, and most intriguing, was science. In the summer of 1747, Franklin offered David Hall, who was by then working as his foreman, an opportunity to become a partner in his printing business. Hall was to run the print shop, publish the newspaper and almanac, and pay Franklin 50 per cent of the profits. At the end of eighteen years, this arrangement would cease, and Hall would become the full owner of the business. Franklin, meanwhile, was free to devote all his time to the science that was to make him famous: electricity. The following letter was written to a man who was to play a very important role in Franklin's life—Peter Collinson, a London Quaker merchant with a strong interest in natural science.

Philadelphia, March 28, 1747

Your kind present of an electric tube, with directions for using it, has put several of us on making electrical experiments, in which we have observed some particular phaenomena that we look upon to be new. I shall, therefore communicate them to you in my next, though possibly they may not be new to you, as among the numbers daily employed in those experiments on your side of the water, 'tis probable some one or other has hit on the same observations. For my own part, I never was before engaged in any study that so totally engrossed my attention and my time as this has lately done; for what with making experiments when I can be alone, and repeating them to my Friends and Acquaintance, who, from the novelty of the thing, come continually in crouds to see them, I have, during some months past, had little leisure for any thing else.

Electricity was at this period more of a curiosity than a science. It had attracted the attention of numerous learned men in Europe, but no one knew what it was or how it worked. In another letter to Collinson, Franklin moved toward one of his most significant discoveries, the importance of pointed bodies in attracting and repelling electric current. From this discovery Franklin progressed to an even more significant insight, the creation of the terms *negative* and *positive* to describe the two kinds of electricity that caused bodies to repel and attract each other. "Watson's Sequel," which Franklin mentions several times, was a book by the noted English electrical scientist William Watson: *A Sequel to the Experiments and Observations Tending to illustrate the Nature and Properties of Electricity.*

Philada. May 25. 1747

In my last I informed you that In pursuing our Electrical Enquiries, we had observ'd some particular Phaenomena, which we lookt upon to be new, and of which I promised to give you some Account; tho' I apprehended they might possibly not be new to you, as so many Hands are daily employed in Electrical Experiments on your Side the Water, some or other of which would probably hit on the same Observations.

The first is the wonderful Effect of Points both in *drawing* off and *throwing* off the Electrical Fire. For Example,

Place an Iron shot of three or four Inches Diameter on the Mouth of a clean dry Glass Bottle. By a fine silken Thread from the Ceiling, right over the Mouth of the Bottle, suspend a small Cork Ball, about the Bigness of a Marble: the Thread of such a Length, as that the Cork Ball may rest against the Side of the Shot. Electrify the Shot, and the Ball will be repelled to the Distance of 4 or 5 Inches, more or less according to the Quantity of Electricity. When in this State, if you present to the Shot the Point of a long, slender, sharp Bodkin at 6 or 8 Inches Distance, the Repellency is instantly destroy'd, and the Cork flies to it. A blunt Body must be brought within an Inch, and draw a Spark to produce the same Effect. To prove that the Electrical Fire is drawn off by the Point: if you take the Blade of the Bodkin out of the wooden Handle, and fix it in a Stick of Sealing Wax, and then present it at the Distance aforesaid no such Effect follows; but slide one Finger along the Wax till you touch the Blade, and the Ball flies to the Shot immediately. If you present the Point in the Dark, you will see, sometimes at a Foot Distance and more, a Light gather upon it like that of a Fire-Fly or Glow-Worm; the less sharp the Point, the nearer you must bring it to observe this Light: and at whatever Distance you see the Light, you may draw off the Electrical Fire, and destroy the Repellency. If a Cork Ball, so suspended, be repelled by the Tube, and a Point be presented quick to it, tho' at a considerable Distance, tis surprizing to see how suddenly it flies back to the Tube. Points of Wood do as well as those of Metal, provided the Wood is not dry.

To shew that Points will *throw* off, as well as *draw* off the Electrical Fire: Lay a long sharp Needle upon the Shot, and you can not electrise the Shot, so as to make it repel the Cork Ball. Fix a Needle to the End of a suspended Gun Barrel, so as to point beyond it like a little Bayonet, and while it remains there, the Gun Barrel can not be electrised (by the Tube applied to the other End) so as to give a Spark; the Fire is continually running out silently at the Point. In the Dark you may see it make the same Appearance as it does in the Case before mentioned.

The Repellency between the Cork Ball and Shot is likewise destroy'd; 1. By sifting find Sand on it; this does it gradually: 2. By breathing on it: 3. By making a Smoke about it from burning Wood: 4. By Candle Light, even tho' the Candle is at a Foot Distance: These do it suddenly. The Light of a bright Coal from a Wood Fire, and the Light of a red-hot Iron do it likewise; but not at so great a Distance. Smoke from dry Rosin dropt into a little hot Letter Founders Ladle under the Shot does not destroy the Repellency; but is attracted by both the Shot and the Cork-Ball, forming proportionable Atmospheres round them, making them look beautifully; somewhat like some of the Figures in Burnets or Whiston's Theory of the Earth.

N.B. This Experiment should be made [in a closet] where the Air is very still.

The Light of the Sun thrown strongly on both Shot and Cork by a Looking Glass for a long Time together does not impair the Repellency in the least. This Difference between Fire Light and Sun Light is another Thing that seems new and extraordinary to us.

We had for some Time been of Opinion, that the Electrical Fire was not created by Friction, but collected, being an Element diffused among, and attracted by other Matter, particularly by Water and Metals. We had even discovered and demonstrated its Afflux to the Electrical Sphere, as well as its Efflux, by Means of little light Wind-Mill Wheels made of stiff Paper Vanes, fixt obliquely, and turning freely

Peter Collinson of London

*Engraving of Franklin's crude
electrical generator, c. 1747*

on fine Wire Axes. Also by little Wheels of the same Matter, but formed like Water Wheels. Of the Disposition and Application of which Wheels, and the various Phaenomena resulting, I could, if I had Time, and it were necessary, fill you a Sheet.

The Impossibility of Electrising one's self (tho' standing on Wax) by Rubbing the Tube and drawing the Fire from it: and the Manner of doing it by passing the Tube near a Person, or Thing standing on the Floor &c. had also occurred to us some Months before Mr. Watsons ingenious *Sequel* came to hand; and these were some of the new Things I intended to have communicated to you: But now I need only mention some Particulars not hinted in that Piece, with our Reasonings thereon; tho' perhaps the latter might well enough be spared.

1. A Person standing on Wax and rubbing the Tube; and another Person on Wax drawing the Fire, they will both of them (provided they do not stand so as to touch one another) appear to be electrised to a Person standing on the Floor; that is, he will perceive a Spark on approaching each of them.

2. But if the Persons standing on Wax touch one another during the exciting of the Tube, neither of them will appear to be electrised.

3. If they touch one another after exciting the Tube, and drawing the Fire as aforesaid, there will be a stronger Spark between them than was between either of them and the Person on the Floor.

4. After such strong Spark, neither of them discovers any Electricity.

These Appearances we attempt to account for thus. We suppose as aforesaid, That Electrical Fire is a common Element, of which every one of the three Persons abovementioned has his equal Share before any Operation is begun with the Tube. *A* who stands on Wax, and rubs the Tube, collects the Electrical Fire from himself into the Glass; and his Communication with the common Stock being cut off by the Wax, his Body is not again immediately supply'd. *B*, who stands upon Wax likewise, passing his Knuckle along near the Tube, receives the Fire which was collected by the Glass from *A*; and his Communication with the common Stock being likewise cutt off, he retains the additional Quantity received. To *C*, standing on the Floor, both appear to be electrised; for he having only the middle Quantity of Electrical Fire receives a Spark on approaching *B*, who has an over-quantity, but gives one to *A*, who has an under-quantity. If *A* and *B* touch each other, the Spark between them is stronger, because the Difference between them is greater. After such Touch, there is no Spark between either of them and *C*; because the Electrical Fire in all is reduced to the original Equality. If they touch while Electrising, the Equality is never destroyed, the Fire only circulating. Hence have arisen some new Terms among us. We say *B* (and other Bodies alike circumstanced) are electrised *positively*; *A negatively*: Or rather *B* is electrised *plus* and *A minus*. And we daily in our Experiments electrise bodies *plus* or *minus* as we think proper. *These Terms* we may use till your Philosophers give us better.

Franklin's progress into the mystery of electricity was neither simple nor easy. He spent four years working on the new science. In this letter to Peter Collinson, he confessed to—and yet simultaneously exulted in—his difficulties.

Philada. Augt. 14. 1747

I have lately written two long Letters to you on the Subject of Electricity, one by the Governor's Vessel, the other per Mesnard. On some further Experiments since, I have observ'd a Phenomenon or two that I cannot at present account for on the Principles laid down in those Letters, and am therefore become a little diffident of my Hypothesis, and asham'd that I have express'd myself in so positive a manner. In going on with these Experiments, how many pretty Systems do we build, which we soon find ourselves oblig'd to destroy! If there is no other Use discover'd of Electricity, this, however, is something considerable, that it may *help to make a vain Man humble*. I must now request that you would not expose those Letters; or if you communicate them to any Friends, you would at least conceal my Name.

As he did with almost everything, Franklin injected an element of fun into his electrical investigations. This experiment, described in another letter to Peter Collinson, also has some interest for its symbolic, prophetic role in Franklin's life.

Philada. Apl. 29. 1749

The Magical Picture is made thus. Having a large Mezzotinto with a Frame and Glass (Suppose of the King, God preserve him) Take out the Print, and cut a Pannel out of it, near two Inches all around distant from the Frame; if the Cut is thro' the Picture, tis not the Worse. With thin Paste or Gum Water, fix the Border, that is cut off, on the inside of the Glass, pressing it smoothe and close; then fill up the Vacancy by Gilding the Glass well with Leaf Gold or Brass; gild likewise the inner Edge of the Back of the Frame all round except the Top Part, and form a Communication between that Gilding and the Gilding behind the Glass: then put in the Board, and that side is finished. Turn up the Glass, and gild the foreside exactly over the Back Gilding; and when this is dry, cover it by pasting on the Pannel of the Picture that had been cut out, observing to bring the corresponding Parts of the Border and Picture together; by which the Picture will appear of a Piece as at first, only Part is behind the Glass and Part before. Hold the Picture horizontally by the Top, and place a little moveable gilt Crown on the Kings Head. If now the Picture be moderately electrified, and another Person take hold of the Frame with one Hand, so that his Fingers touch it's inside Gilding, and with the other Hand endeavour to take off the Crown, he will receive a terrible Blow and fail in the Attempt. If the Picture were highly charg'd, the Consequence might perhaps be as fatal as that of High Treason: For when the Spark is taken thro' a Quire of Paper laid on the Picture, by Means of a Wire Communication, it makes a fair Hole thro' every Sheet; that is thro' 48 Leaves (tho' a Quire of Paper is thought good Armour against the Push of a Sword, or even against a Pistol Bullet) and the Crack is exceeding loud. The Operator, who, to prevent its falling, holds the Picture by the upper End, where the inside of the Frame is not gilt, feels Nothing of the Shock, and may touch the Crown without Danger, which he pretends is a Test of his Loyalty. If a Ring of Persons take a Shock among them the Experiment is called the *Conspiracy....*

[Franklin ended the letter with a charming picture of Philadelphia's "Electricians" relaxing in the country.]

Chagrin'd a little that We have hitherto been able to discover Nothing in this Way of Use to Mankind, and the hot Weather coming on, when Electrical Experiments are not so agreable; 'tis proposed to put an End to them for this Season somewhat humorously in a Party of Pleasure on the Banks of Schuyl-Kill, (where Spirits are at the same

An engraving of Franklin after the Mason Chamberlin portrait shows him looking at bells that rang when electricity passed through them; outside the window a storm swirls around his lightning rod.

Time to be fired by a Spark sent from Side to Side thro'
the River). A Turky is to be killed for our Dinners by the
Electrical Shock; and roasted by the electrical Jack, before
a Fire kindled by the Electrified Bottle; when the Healths
of all the famous Electricians in England, France and
Germany, are to be drank in Electrified Bumpers, under
the Discharge of Guns from the Electrical Battery.

Even as he wrote these words, Franklin was moving to-
ward his most important practical discovery—the one that would make him
world-famous. He described his progress in a letter he wrote a few years
later to John Lining of Charleston, South Carolina.

Philadelphia, March 18, 1755
Your question, how I came first to think of proposing the
experiment of drawing down the lightning, in order to
ascertain its sameness with the electric fluid, I cannot
answer better than by giving you an extract from the
minutes I used to keep of the experiments I made, with
memorandums of such as I purposed to make, the reasons
for making them, and the observations that arose upon
them, from which minutes my letters were afterwards
drawn. By this extract you will see that the thought was
not so much "an out-of-the-way one," but that it might
have occurred to any electrician.
"Nov. 1, 1749. Electrical fluid agrees with lightning in
these particulars: 1. Giving light. 2. Colour of the light.
3. Crooked direction. 4. Swift motion. 5. Being conducted by metals. 6. Crack or noise in exploding. 7. Subsisting in water or ice. 8. Rending bodies it passes
through. 9. Destroying animals. 10. Melting metals.
11. Firing inflammable substances. 12. Sulphureous
smell. The electric fluid is attracted by points. We do not
know whether this property is in lightning. But since they
agree in all the particulars wherein we can already compare them, is it not probable they agree likewise in this?
Let the experiment be made."

By July 29, 1750, Franklin had worked out the details
for an experiment to prove that lightning and electricity were the same. Here
is a description of the event from a paper entitled "Opinions and Conjectures
concerning the Properties and Effects of the Electrical Matter, arising from
Experiments and Observations made in Philadelphia, 1749." A copy of the
paper was forwarded with a letter to his London correspondent Peter Collinson in mid-1750.

Philada. July 29 1750

21. To determine the Question, Whether the Clouds that contain Lightning are electrified or not, I would propose an Experiment to be try'd where it may be done conveniently.

On the Top of some high Tower or Steeple, place a Kind of Sentry Box big enough to contain a Man and an electrical Stand. From the Middle of the Stand let an Iron Rod rise, and pass bending out of the Door, and then upright 20 or 30 feet, pointed very sharp at the End. If the Electrical Stand be kept clean and dry, a Man standing on it when such Clouds are passing low, might be electrified, and afford Sparks, the Rod drawing Fire to him from the Cloud. If any Danger to the Man should be apprehended (tho' I think there would be none) let him stand on the Floor of his Box, and now and then bring near to the Rod, the Loop of a Wire, that has one End fastened to the Leads; he holding it by a Wax-Handle. So the Sparks, if the Rod is electrified, will Strike from the Rod to the Wire and not affect him.

In Europe this proposal was quickly dubbed the Philadelphia Experiment. Europeans learned about it from Franklin's collected letters, which Peter Collinson arranged to have published in 1751 as *Experiments and Observations on Electricity, Made in Philadelphia in America, by Mr. Benjamin Franklin.* Franklin himself did not attempt the experiment, because there was no structure high enough in Philadelphia to give it a chance to succeed. English scientists, who had no lack of church steeples to work from, were strangely uninterested in attempting it — an early example of the mother country's instinctive hauteur toward Americans. When *Experiments and Observations* was translated into French, in 1752, two French electricians, Delor and Dalibard, each successfully performed the sentry box experiment in the spring of that year. Word of their success crossed the Channel, and the English confirmed the triumph of Franklin's hypothesis several times during the summer of 1752. Meanwhile, in Philadelphia, Franklin was trying out an idea of his own. In June of 1752, before he heard about the success of the French and English experiments, he sent his conductor high enough to draw electricity from the clouds by flying it on a kite during a thunder shower. On October 19, 1752, Franklin reported the success of this experiment in a rather cryptic fashion, in *The Pennsylvania Gazette.*

Philadelphia, October 19 [1752]

As frequent Mention is made in the News Papers from Europe, of the Success of the Philadelphia Experiment for drawing the Electric Fire from Clouds by Means of

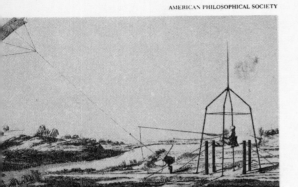

An improvement of Franklin's electrical kite experiment is tested by a French scientist.

EXPERIMENTS

AND

OBSERVATIONS

ON

ELECTRICITY,

MADE AT

Philadelphia in *America,*

BY

Mr. BENJAMIN FRANKLIN,

AND

Communicated in several Letters to Mr. P. COLLINSON,
of *London,* F. R. S.

LONDON:
Printed and fold by E. Cave, at *St. John's Gate.* 1751
(Price 2s. 6d.)

SUPPLEMENTAL

Experiments and Obfervations

ON

ELECTIRCITY,

PART II.

MADE AT

Philadelphia in *America,*

BY

BENJAMIN FRANKLIN, *Efq;*

AND

Communicated in feveral Letters to P. COLLINSON, *Efq;*
of *London,* F. R. S.

LONDON·
Printed and fold by E. Cave, at *St. John's Gate.* 1753
(Price 6d.)

Title pages of the first and supplemental editions of Franklin's experiments reveal an embarrassing spelling error in the key word.

pointed Rods of Iron erected on high Buildings, &c. it may be agreeable to the Curious to be inform'd, that the same Experiment has succeeded in Philadelphia, tho' made in a different and more easy Manner, which any one may try, as follows.

Make a small Cross of two light Strips of Cedar, the Arms so long as to reach the four Corners of a large thin Silk Handkerchief when extended; tie the Corners of the Handkerchief to the Extremities of the Cross, so you have the Body of a Kite; which being properly accommodated with a Tail, Loop and String, will rise in the Air, like those made of Paper; but this being of Silk is fitter to bear the Wet and Wind of a Thunder Gust without tearing. To the Top of the upright Stick of the Cross is to be fixed a very sharp pointed Wire, rising a Foot or more above the Wood. To the End of the Twine, next the Hand, is to be tied a silk Ribbon, and where the Twine and the silk join, a Key may be fastened. This Kite is to be raised when a Thunder Gust appears to be coming on, and the Person who holds the String must stand within a Door, or Window, or under some Cover, so that the Silk Ribbon may not be wet; and Care must be taken that the Twine does not touch the Frame of the Door or Window. As soon as any of the Thunder Clouds come over the Kite, the pointed Wire will draw the Electric Fire from them, and the Kite, with all the Twine, will be electrified, and the loose Filaments of the Twine will stand out every Way, and be attracted by an approaching Finger. And when the Rain has wet the Kite and Twine, so that it can conduct the Electric Fire freely, you will find it stream out plentifully from the Key on the Approach of your Knuckle. At this Key the Phial may be charg'd; and from Electric Fire thus obtain'd, Spirits may be kindled, and all the other Electric Experiments be perform'd, which are usually done by the Help of a rubbed Glass Globe or Tube; and thereby the *Sameness* of the Electric Matter with that of Lightning compleatly demonstrated.

In *Poor Richard* for 1753, Franklin published the final phase of his discovery—the practical application known as the lightning rod.

Poor Richard, 1753

It has pleased God in his Goodness to Mankind, at length to discover to them the Means of securing their Habitations and other Buildings from Mischief by Thunder and Lightning. The Method is this: Provide a small Iron Rod (it may be made of the Rod-iron used by the Nailers) but of such a Length, that one End being three or four Feet in the moist Ground, the other may be six or eight Feet above the highest Part of the Building. To the upper End of the Rod fasten about a Foot of Brass Wire, the Size of a common Knitting-needle, sharpened to a fine Point; the Rod may be secured to the House by a few small Staples. If the House or Barn be long, there may be a Rod and Point at each End, and a middling Wire along the Ridge from one to the other. A House thus furnished will not be damaged by Lightning, it being attracted by the Points, and passing thro the Metal into the Ground without hurting any Thing. Vessels also, having a sharp pointed Rod fix'd on the Top of their Masts, with a Wire from the Foot of the Rod reaching down, round one of the Shrouds, to the Water, will not be hurt by Lightning.

As Franklin noted in his experiment on the magical picture, electricity was a powerful substance. He described how nearly fatal to him personally was one electrical experiment, in this letter that he wrote to his brother John Franklin.

Phila. Decr. 25. 1750

I have lately made an Experiment in Electricity that I desire never to repeat. Two nights ago being about to kill a Turkey by the Shock from two large Glass Jarrs containing as much electrical fire as forty common Phials, I inadvertently took the whole thro' my own Arms and Body, by receiving the fire from the united Top Wires with one hand, while the other held a Chain connected with the outsides of both Jars. The Company present (whose talking to me, and to one another I suppose occasioned my Inattention to what I was about) Say that the flash was very great and the crack as loud as a Pistol; yet my Senses being instantly gone, I neither Saw the one nor heard the other; nor did I feel the Stroke on my hand, tho' I afterwards found it raised a round swelling where the fire enter'd as big as half a Pistol Bullet by which you may judge of the Quickness of the Electrical Fire, which by this Instance Seems to be greater than that of Sound, Light and animal Sensation. What I can remember of the matter, is, that I was about to try whether the Bottles or Jars were fully charged, by the Strength and Length of the stream issuing to my hands as I commonly used to do, and which I might safely

Exp. II.

One of the lightning rod illustrations from Franklin's book on electricity

Testing Franklin's experiment proved fatal to a Russian scientist.

eno' have done if I had not held the chain in the other hand; I then felt what I know not how well to describe; an universal Blow thro'out my whole Body from head to foot which seem'd within as well as without; after which the first thing I took notice of was a violent quick Shaking of my body which gradually remitting, my sense as gradually return'd, and then I tho't the Bottles must be discharged but Could not conceive how, till att last I Perceived the Chain in my hand, and Recollected what I had been About to do: that part of my hand and fingers which held the Chain was left white as tho' the Blood had been Driven Out, and Remained so 8 or 10 Minutes After, feeling like Dead flesh, and I had a Numbness in my Arms and the back of my Neck, which Continued till the Next Morning but wore off. Nothing Remains now of this Shock but a Soreness in my breast Bone, which feels As if it had been Brused. I Did not fall, but Suppose I should have been Knocked Down if I had Received the Stroke in my head: the whole was Over in less than a minute.

You may Communicate this to Mr. Bowdoin As A Caution to him, but do not make it more Publick, for I am Ashamed to have been Guilty of so Notorious A Blunder; A Match for that of the Irishman, Sister Told me of, who to Divert his Wife pour'd the Bottle of Gun Powder on the live Coal; or of that Other, who being About to Steal Powder, made a Hole in the Cask with a Hott Iron.

Electricity was by no means the only science that absorbed Franklin's mind. He was also intensely interested in meteorology, and in this letter to his friend Jared Eliot, pastor of the Congregational Church in Killingworth, Connecticut, he explained an important discovery—the origin of northeast storms.

Philada. Feb. 13. 1749, 50 [1750]
You desire to know my Thoughts about the N.E. Storms beginning to Leeward. Some Years since there was an Eclipse of the Moon at 9 in the Evening, which I intended to observe, but before 8 a Storm blew up at NE., and continued violent all Night and all next Day, the Sky thick clouded, dark and rainy, so that neither Moon nor Stars could be seen. The Storm did a great deal of Damage all along the Coast, for we had Accounts of it in the News Papers from Boston, Newport, New York, Maryland and Virginia. But what surpriz'd me, was to find in the Boston Newspapers an Account of an Observation of that

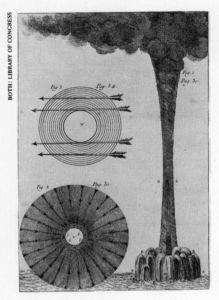

*Diagram of a waterspout used to
illustrate Franklin's theory on the
causes of this phenomenon of the sea*

Eclipse made there: For I thought, as the Storm came from the NE. it must have begun sooner at Boston than with us, and consequently have prevented such Observation. I wrote to my Brother about it, and he inform'd me, that the Eclipse was over there, an hour before the Storm began. Since which I have made Enquiries from time to time of Travellers, and of my Correspondents N Eastward and S. Westward, and observ'd the Accounts in the News-papers from N England, N York, Maryland, Virginia and South Carolina, and I find it to be a constant Fact, that N East Storms begin to Leeward; and are often more violent there than farther to Windward. Thus the last October Storm, which with you was on the 8th. began on the 7th in Virginia and N Carolina, and was most violent there. As to the Reason of this, I can only give you my Conjectures. Suppose a great Tract of Country, Land and Sea, to wit Florida and the Bay of Mexico, to have clear Weather for several Days, and to be heated by the Sun and its Air thereby exceedingly rarefied; Suppose the Country North Eastward, as Pennsilvania, New England, Nova Scotia, Newfoundland, &c. to be at the same time cover'd with Clouds, and its Air chill'd and condens'd. The rarefied Air being lighter must rise, and the Dense Air next to it will press into its Place; that will be follow'd by the next denser Air, that by the next, and so on. Thus when I have a Fire in my Chimney, there is a Current of Air constantly flowing from the Door to the Chimney; but the beginning of the Motion was at the Chimney, where the air being rarefied by the Fire, rising, its Place was supply'd by the cooler Air that was next to it, and the Place of that by the next, and so on to the Door. So the Water in a long Sluice or Mill Race, being stop'd by a Gate, is at Rest like the Air in a Calm; but as soon as you open the Gate at one End to let it out, the Water next the Gate begins first to move, that which is next to it follows; and so tho' the Water proceeds forward to the Gate, the Motion which began there runs backwards, if one may so speak, to the upper End of the Race, where the Water is last in Motion. We have on this Continent a long Ridge of Mountains running from N east to S west; and the Coast runs the same Course. These may, perhaps, contribute towards the Direction [of the winds or at least influence] them in some Degree, [missing]. If these Conjectures do not [satisfy you, I wish] to have yours on the Subject.

Almost as important as electricity in winning Franklin fame as a scientist in his own time was his essay on population. Franklin wrote it in 1751 — at a time when the British Iron Act of 1750, prohibiting the expansion of the iron industry in America, threatened the growth of the Colonies. Although he circulated the essay privately among his English and American friends, he did not consent to its publication until 1754. Thereafter, it was reprinted frequently and had a strong influence on other students of population, such as Thomas Malthus, and on economists, such as Adam Smith, who owned two copies of the essay. On English politicians, however, it seems to have had an opposite effect from the one Franklin intended. Instead of inspiring them to give the Colonies more freedom, the knowledge that America would soon match England in numbers and wealth made many politicians favor additional repressive measures. Franklin's prediction that the population of America would double every twenty years was amazingly accurate. It held true for a hundred years after he made it. It probably would have continued to hold true had not the massive influx of immigrants in the last half of the nineteenth century added a new, accelerating element to the nation's growth.

1751

OBSERVATIONS concerning the Increase of Mankind, Peopling of Countries, &c.

1.   Tables of the Proportion of Marriages to Births, of Deaths to Births, of Marriages to the Numbers of Inhabitants, &c. form'd on Observations made upon the Bills of Mortality, Christnings, &c. of populous Cities, will not suit Countries; nor will Tables form'd on Observations made on full settled old Countries, as Europe, suit new Countries, as America.

2.   For People increase in Proportion to the Number of Marriages, and that is greater in Proportion to the Ease and Convenience of supporting a Family. When Families can be easily supported, more Persons marry, and earlier in Life.

3.   In Cities, where all Trades, Occupations and Offices are full, many delay marrying, till they can see how to bear the Charges of a Family; which Charges are greater in Cities, as Luxury is more common: many live single during Life, and continue Servants to Families, Journeymen to Trades, &c. hence Cities do not by natural Generation supply themselves with Inhabitants; the Deaths are more than the Births.

4.   In Countries full settled, the Case must be nearly the same; all Lands being occupied and improved to the Heighth: those who cannot get Land, must Labour for

When Franklin found that glasses "proper for Reading" were not best "for greater Distances," he was not long in making the first bifocals.

97

SCIENTIST, INVENTOR, AND GADGETEER

Franklin's scientific and inventive genius ran the gamut from his extraordinary discoveries in the field of electricity to a mathematical stunt of numbering squares so that the sums of every row, horizontal, perpendicular, or diagonal, should be equal (bottom). A British admirer said of him: "He could make an experiment with less apparatus . . . than any other philosopher we ever saw." The plate of diagrams at right is from Franklin's own copy of his *Experiments and Observations on Electricity* and the explanation of Fig. VI is in his own handwriting. Also by his own hand is the drawing of the "Boat for Pleasure on the Delaware River" (below, left), which illustrates how one would fix the sail in a horizontal position during a tempest. Other maritime inventions included a sea anchor to alleviate the problems illustrated by the two little ships below, which are in danger of having their anchor chains snapped in a storm; and on his various transatlantic crossings he determined the course of the Gulf Stream (bottom, far right). In 1753, he offered readers of *Poor Richard* a diagram charting the coming transit of Mercury across the face of the sun (bottom, left). But the invention that made his name a household word was the ingenious Franklin stove (bottom, near right), which vastly improved the heating of cold Colonial rooms.

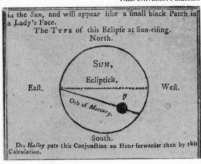

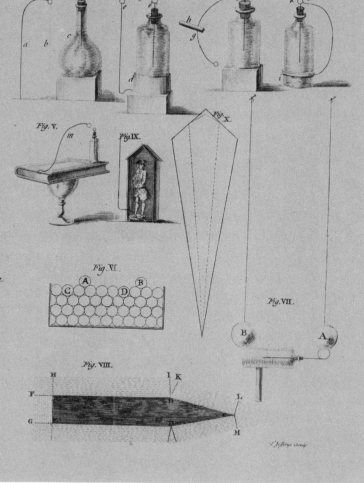

Fig. VI. Profile of a Piece of Water. C & D are amongst the Particles of the Surface. A & B above the Surface. Small Shot would represent it better than this Figure.

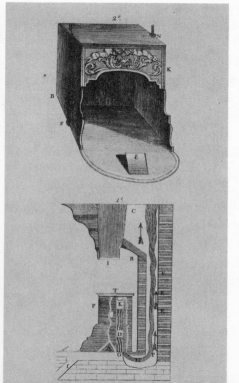

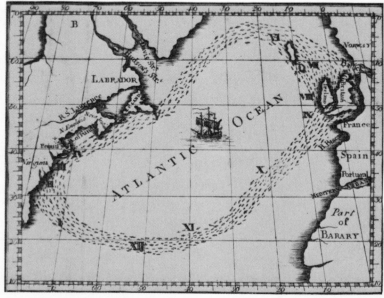

others that have it; when Labourers are plenty, their Wages will be low; by low Wages a Family is supported with Difficulty; this Difficulty deters many from Marriage, who therefore long continue Servants and single. Only as the Cities take Supplies of People from the Country, and thereby make a little more Room in the Country; Marriage is a little more incourag'd there, and the Births exceed the Deaths.

5.   Europe is generally full settled with Husbandmen, Manufacturers, &c. and therefore cannot now much increase in People: America is chiefly occupied by Indians, who subsist mostly by Hunting. But as the Hunter, of all Men, requires the greatest Quantity of Land from whence to draw his Subsistence, (the Husbandman subsisting on much less, the Gardner on still less, and the Manufacturer requiring least of all), The Europeans found America as fully settled as it well could be by Hunters; yet these having large Tracks, were easily prevail'd on to part with Portions of Territory to the new Comers, who did not much interfere with the Natives in Hunting, and furnish'd them with many Things they wanted.

6. Land being thus plenty in America, and so cheap as that a labouring Man, that understands Husbandry, can in a short Time save Money enough to purchase a Piece of new Land sufficient for a Plantation, whereon he may subsist a Family; such are not afraid to marry; for if they even look far enough forward to consider how their Children when grown up are to be provided for, they see that more Land is to be had at Rates equally easy, all Circumstances considered.

7.   Hence Marriages in America are more general, and more generally early, than in Europe. And if it is reckoned there, that there is but one Marriage per Annum among 100 Persons, perhaps we may here reckon two; and if in Europe they have but 4 Births to a Marriage (many of their Marriages being late) we may here reckon 8, of which if one half grow up, and our Marriages are made, reckoning one with another at 20 Years of Age, our People must at least be doubled every 20 years.

8.   But notwithstanding this Increase, so vast is the Territory of North-America, that it will require many Ages to settle it fully; and till it is fully settled, Labour will never be cheap here, where no Man continues long a Labourer for others, but gets a Plantation of his own, no Man continues

Thomas Malthus (above) and Adam Smith (below) were both influenced by Franklin's population study.

long a Journeyman to a Trade, but goes among those new Settlers, and sets up for himself, &c. Hence Labour is no cheaper now, in Pennsylvania, than it was 30 Years ago, tho' so many Thousand labouring People have been imported.

9.   The Danger therefore of these Colonies interfering with their Mother Country in Trades that depend on Labour, Manufactures, &c. is too remote to require the Attention of Great-Britain.

10.   But in Proportion to the Increase of the Colonies, a vast Demand is growing for British Manufactures, a glorious Market wholly in the Power of Britain, in which Foreigners cannot interfere, which will increase in a short Time even beyond her Power of supplying, tho' her whole Trade should be to her Colonies: Therefore Britain should not much restrain Manufactures in her Colonies. A wise and good Mother will not do it. To distress, is to weaken, and weakening the Children, weakens the whole Family.

11.   Besides if the Manufactures of Britain (by Reason of the American Demands) should rise too high in Price, Foreigners who can sell cheaper will drive her Merchants out of Foreign Markets; Foreign Manufactures will thereby be encouraged and increased, and consequently foreign Nations, perhaps her Rivals in Power, grow more populous and more powerful; while her own Colonies, kept too low, are unable to assist her, or add to her Strength.

12.   'Tis an ill-grounded Opinion that by the Labour of Slaves, America may possibly vie in Cheapness of Manufactures with Britain. The Labour of Slaves can never be so cheap here as the Labour of working Men is in Britain. Any one may compute it. Interest of Money is in the Colonies from 6 to 10 per Cent. Slaves one with another cost £30 Sterling per Head. Reckon then the Interest of the first Purchase of a Slave, the Insurance or Risque on his Life, his Cloathing and Diet, Expences in his Sickness and Loss of Time, Loss by his Neglect of Business (Neglect is natural to the Man who is not to be benefited by his own Care or Diligence), Expence of a Driver to keep him at Work, and his Pilfering from Time to Time, almost every Slave being *by Nature* a Thief, and compare the whole Amount with the Wages of a Manufacturer of Iron or Wool in England, you will see that Labour is much cheaper there than it ever can

be by Negroes here. Why then will Americans purchase Slaves? Because Slaves may be kept as long as a Man pleases, or has Occasion for their Labour; while hired Men are continually leaving their Master (often in the midst of his Business,) and setting up for themselves.

13. As the Increase of People depends on the Encouragement of Marriages, the following Things must diminish a Nation, viz. 1. The being conquered; for the Conquerors will engross as many Offices, and exact as much Tribute or Profit on the Labour of the conquered, as will maintain them in their new Establishment, and this diminishing the Subsistence of the Natives discourages their Marriages, and so gradually diminishes them, while the Foreigners increase. 2. Loss of Territory. Thus the Britons being driven into Wales, and crowded together in a barren Country insufficient to support such great Numbers, diminished 'till the People bore a Proportion to the Produce, while the Saxons increas'd on their abandoned Lands; 'till the Island became full of English. And were the English now driven into Wales by some foreign Nation, there would in a few Years be no more Englishmen in Britain, than there are now People in Wales. 3. Loss of Trade. Manufactures exported, draw Subsistence from Foreign Countries for Numbers; who are thereby enabled to marry and raise Families. If the Nation be deprived of any Branch of Trade, and no new Employment is found for the People occupy'd in that Branch, it will also be soon deprived of so many People. 4. Loss of Food. Suppose a Nation has a Fishery, which not only employs great Numbers, but makes the Food and Subsistence of the People cheaper; If another Nation becomes Master of the Seas, and prevents the Fishery, the People will diminish in Proportion as the Loss of Employ, and Dearness of Provision, makes it more difficult to subsist a Family. 5. Bad Government and insecure Property. People not only leave such a Country, and settling Abroad incorporate with other Nations, lose their native Language, and become Foreigners; but the Industry of those that remain being discourag'd, the Quantity of Subsistence in the Country is lessen'd, and the Support of a Family becomes more difficult. So heavy Taxes tend to diminish a People. 6. The Introduction of Slaves. The Negroes brought into the English Sugar Islands, have greatly

(42)

OBSERVATIONS

CONCERNING THE

INCREASE of MANKIND,

Peopling of Countries, &c.

1. TABLES of the Proportion of Marriages to Births, of Deaths to Births, of Marriages to the Numbers of Inhabitants, &c. formed on Observations made upon the Bills of Mortality, Christenings, &c. of populous Cities, will not suit Countries; nor will Tables formed on Observations made on full settled old Countries, as *Europe*, suit new Countries, as *America*.

2. For People increase in Proportion to the Number of the Marriages, and that is greater in Proportion to the Ease and Convenience of supporting a Family. When Families can be easily supported, more Persons marry, and earlier in Life.

3. In

A page from a 1755 London reprint of Franklin's essay on population diminish'd the Whites there; the Poor are by this Means depriv'd of Employment, while a few Families acquire vast Estates; which they spend on Foreign Luxuries, and educating their Children in the Habit of those Luxuries; the same Income is needed for the Support of one that might have maintain'd 100. The Whites who have Slaves, not labouring, are enfeebled, and therefore not so generally prolific; the Slaves being work'd too hard, and ill fed, their Constitutions are broken, and the Deaths among them are more than the Births; so that a continual Supply is needed from Africa. The Northern Colonies having few Slaves increase in Whites. Slaves also pejorate the Families that use them; the white Children become proud, disgusted with Labour, and being educated in Idleness, are rendered unfit to get a Living by Industry.

14. Hence the Prince that acquires new Territory, if he finds it vacant, or removes the Natives to give his own People Room; the Legislator that makes effectual Laws for promoting of Trade, increasing Employment, improving Land by more or better Tillage; providing more Food by Fisheries; securing Property, &c. and the Man that invents new Trades, Arts or Manufactures, or new Improvements in Husbandry, may be properly called *Fathers* of their Nation, as they are the Cause of the Generation of Multitudes, by the Encouragement they afford to Marriage.

15. As to Privileges granted to the married, (such as the *Jus trium Liberorum* among the Romans), they may hasten the filling of a Country that has been thinned by War or Pestilence, or that has otherwise vacant Territory; but cannot increase a People beyond the Means provided for their Subsistence.

16. Foreign Luxuries and needless Manufactures imported and used in a Nation, do, by the same Reasoning, increase the People of the Nation that furnishes them, and diminish the People of the Nation that uses them. Laws therefore that prevent such Importations, and on the contrary promote the Exportation of Manufactures to be consumed in Foreign Countries, may be called (with Respect to the People that make them) *generative Laws*, as by increasing Subsistence they encourage Marriage. Such Laws likewise strengthen a Country, doubly, by increasing its own People and

diminishing its Neighbours. . . .

18.   Home Luxury in the Great, increases the Nation's Manufacturers employ'd by it, who are many, and only tends to diminish the Families that indulge in it, who are few. The greater the common fashionable Expence of any Rank of People, the more cautious they are of Marriage. Therefore Luxury should never be suffer'd to become common.

19.   The great Increase of Offspring in particular Families, is not always owing to greater Fecundity of Nature, but sometimes to Examples of Industry in the Heads, and industrious Education; by which the Children are enabled to provide better for themselves, and their marrying early, is encouraged from the Prospect of good Subsistence.

20.   If there be a Sect therefore, in our Nation, that regard Frugality and Industry as religious Duties, and educate their Children therein, more than others commonly do; such Sect must consequently increase more by natural Generation, than any other Sect in Britain.

21.   The Importation of Foreigners into a Country that has as many Inhabitants as the present Employments and Provisions for Subsistence will bear; will be in the End no Increase of People; unless the New Comers have more Industry and Frugality than the Natives, and then they will provide more Subsistence, and increase in the Country; but they will gradually eat the Natives out. Nor is it necessary to bring in Foreigners to fill up any occasional Vacancy in a Country; for such Vacancy . . . will soon be filled by natural Generation. . . .

22.   There is in short, no Bound to the prolific Nature of Plants or Animals, but what is made by their crowding and interfering with each others Means of Subsistence. Was the Face of the Earth vacant of other Plants, it might be gradually sowed and overspread with one Kind only; as, for Instance, with Fennel; and were it empty of other Inhabitants, it might in a few Ages be replenish'd from one Nation only; as, for Instance, with Englishmen. Thus there are suppos'd to be now upwards of One Million English Souls in North-America, (tho' 'tis thought scarce 80,000 have been brought over Sea) and yet perhaps there is not one the fewer in Britain, but rather many more, on Account of the Employment the Colonies afford to Manufacturers at Home. This Million doubling,

suppose but once in 25 Years, will in another Century be more than the People of England, and the greatest Number of Englishmen will be on this Side the Water. What an Accession of Power to the British Empire by Sea as well as Land! What Increase of Trade and Navigation! What Numbers of Ships and Seamen! We have been here but little more than 100 Years, and yet the Force of our Privateers in the late War, united, was greater, both in Men and Guns, than that of the whole British Navy in Queen Elizabeth's Time....

23.   In fine, A Nation well regulated is like a Polypus; take away a Limb, its Place is soon supply'd; cut it in two, and each deficient Part shall speedily grow out of the Part remaining. Thus if you have Room and Subsistence enough, as you may by dividing, make ten Polypes out of one, you may of one make ten Nations, equally populous and powerful; or rather, increase a Nation ten fold in Numbers and Strength.

And since Detachments of English from Britain sent to America, will have their Places at Home so soon supply'd and increase so largely here; why should the Palatine Boors be suffered to swarm into our Settlements, and by herding together establish their Language and Manners to the Exclusion of ours? Why should Pennsylvania, founded by the English, become a Colony of *Aliens,* who will shortly be so numerous as to Germanize us instead of our Anglifying them, and will never adopt our Language or Customs, any more than they can acquire our Complexion.

24.   Which leads me to add one Remark: That the Number of purely white People in the World is proportionably very small. All Africa is black or tawny. Asia chiefly tawny. America (exclusive of the new Comers) wholly so. And in Europe, the Spaniards, Italians, French, Russians and Swedes, are generally of what we call a swarthy Complexion; as are the Germans also, the Saxons only excepted, who with the English, make the principal Body of White People on the Face of the Earth. I could wish their Numbers were increased. And while we are, as I may call it, *Scouring* our Planet, by clearing America of Woods, and so making this Side of our Globe reflect a brighter Light to the Eyes of Inhabitants in Mars or Venus, why should we in the Sight of Superior Beings, darken its People? why increase the Sons of Africa, by Planting them

Fanciful German version of the fresh air bath, an innovation Franklin suggested, and practiced, in 1768

105

in America, where we have so fair an Opportunity, by excluding all Blacks and Tawneys, of increasing the lovely White and Red? But perhaps I am partial to the Complexion of my Country, for such Kind of Partiality is natural to Mankind.

Perhaps the most admirable thing about Franklin the scientist was his modesty. In a letter to his friend Jared Eliot he cheerfully dismissed, in typical Franklin style, the praise that had come his way as a result of his electrical discoveries.

> Philada. April 12. 1753
>
> The Tatler tells us of a Girl who was observ'd to grow suddenly proud, and none could guess the Reason, till it came to be known that she had got on a pair of new Silk Garters. Lest you should be puzzel'd to guess the Cause when you observe any thing of the kind in me, I think I will not hide my new Garters under my Petticoats, but take the Freedom to show them to you, in a Paragraph of our Friend Collinson's last Letter viz.—But I ought to mortify, and not indulge, this Vanity; I will not transcribe the Paragraph.—Yet I cannot forbear. "If any of thy Friends (says Peter) should take Notice that thy Head is held a little higher up than formerly, let them know; when the Grand Monarch of France strictly commands the Abbé Mazeas to write a Letter in the politest Terms to the Royal Society, to return the Kings Thanks and Compliments in an express Manner to Mr. Franklin of Pennsilvania, for the useful Discoveries in Electricity, and Application of the pointed Rods to prevent the terrible Effects of Thunderstorms. I say, after all this, is not some Allowance to be made if the Crest is a little elevated. There are four Letters containing very curious Experiments on thy Doctrine of Points and its Verification, which will be printed in the New Transactions. I think now I have stuck a Feather on thy Cap, I may be allowed to conclude in wishing thee long to wear it. Thine, P. Collinson." On reconsidering this Paragraph, I fear I have not so much Reason to be proud as the Girl had; for a Feather in the Cap is not so useful a Thing, or so serviceable to the Wearer, as a Pair of good Silk Garters.

Because of his reputation, soon grown to worldwide proportions, Franklin was sought out by other scientists for advice, information, and opinions. On a trip west in 1766, Franklin's friend George Croghan picked up some interesting fossils at a place in Kentucky appropriately called Big Bone Lick. Back in Philadelphia, Croghan split his collection in two and sent part to Lord Shelburne, the Secretary of State, and part to Franklin, also then in England. The shipment to Franklin included:

"Four great tusks, of different sizes.

One broken in halves, near six feet long.

One much decayed, the center looks like chalk, or lime.

A part was cut off from one of these teeth, that has all of the appearances of fine white ivory.

A joint of the vertebrae.

Three of the large pronged teeth; one has four rows of fangs."

Franklin acknowledged receipt of the interesting gift in a letter to Croghan and a few months later passed the fossils on to Abbé Jean Chappe d'Auteroche, a distinguished French astronomer, for another opinion. Following are the letters to Croghan and the Abbé Chappe.

London, Aug. 5, 1767.

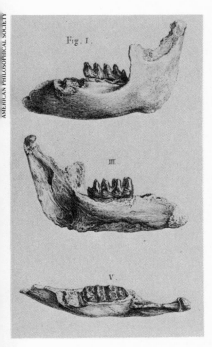

Engravings of mastodon bones from Big Bone Lick, Kentucky

I return you many thanks for the box of elephants' tusks and grinders. They are extremely curious on many accounts; no living elephants having been seen in any part of America by any of the Europeans settled there, or remembered in any tradition of the Indians. It is also puzzling to conceive what should have brought so many of them to die on the same spot; and that no such remains should be found in any other part of the continent, except in that very distant country Peru, from whence some grinders of the same kind formerly brought, are now in the museum of the Royal Society. The tusks agree with those of the African and Asiatic elephant, in being nearly of the same form and texture; and some of them, notwithstanding the length of time they must have lain, being still good ivory. But the grinders differ, being full of knobs, like the grinders of a carnivorous animal; when those of the elephant, who eats only vegetables, are almost smooth. But then we know of no other animal with tusks like an elephant to whom such grinders might belong. It is remarkable, that elephants now inhabit naturally only hot countries where there is no winter, and yet these remains are found in a winter country; and it is no uncommon thing to find elephants' tusks in Siberia, in great quantities, when their rivers overflow, and wash away the earth, though Siberia is still more a wintery country than that on the Ohio; which looks as if the earth had anciently been in another position, and the climates differently placed from what they are at present.

London, Jan. 31. 1768

I sent you sometime since, directed to the Care of M. Molini, a Bookseller near the Quây des Augustins a Tooth that I mention'd to you when I had the Pleasure of meeting with you at the Marquis de Courtanvaux's. It was found near the River Ohio in America, about 200 Leagues below Fort du Quesne, at what is called the Great Licking Place, where the Earth has a Saltish Taste that is agreable to the Bufaloes and Deer, who come there at certain Seasons in great Numbers to lick the same. At this [pla]ce have been found the Skeletons of near 30 [large?] Animals suppos'd to be Elephants, several Tusks like those of Elephants, being found with those Grinder Teeth. Four of these Grinders were sent me by the Gentleman who brought them from the Ohio to New York, together with 4 Tusks, one of which is 6 Feet long and in the thickest Part near 6 Inches Diameter, and also one of the Vertebrae. My Lord Shelbourn receiv'd at the same time 3 or four others with a Jaw Bone and one or two Grinders remaining in it. Some of Our Naturalists here, however, contend, that these are not the Grinders of Elephants but of some carnivorous Animal unknown, because such Knobs or Prominances on the Face of the Tooth are not to be found on those of Elephants, and only, as they say, on those of carnivorous Animals. But it appears to me that Animals capable of carrying such large and heavy Tusks, must themselves be large Creatures, too bulky to have the Activity necessary for pursuing and taking Prey; and therefore I am enclin'd to think those Knobs are only a small Variety, Animals of the same kind and Name often differing more materially, and that those Knobs might be as useful to grind the small Branches of Trees, as to chaw Flesh. However I should be glad to have your Opinion, and to know from you whether any of the kind have been found in Siberia.

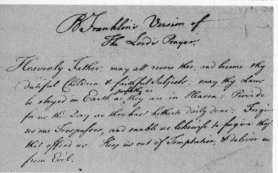

Although Franklin was not deeply religious, his interest in linguistics may have drawn him to this revision of the Lord's Prayer.

Franklin the scientist is best remembered for his experiments with electricity, but his active mind continued to find other subjects for research and speculation. Indeed, his broad range of interests and his truly deep thinking on some subjects entitle him to be called "America's Newton." Although his American orientation usually inclined Franklin to look for practical applications of science, his mind continued to range widely over the whole field of knowledge, speculating on such things as the nature of matter and—in this letter to Barbeu-Dubourg—on raising the dead.

[London, April–May, 1773]

Your observations on the causes of death, and the experiments which you propose for recalling to life those who appear to be killed by lightning, demonstrate equally your sagacity and your humanity. It appears that the doctrines of life and death in general are yet but little understood.

A toad buried in sand will live, it is said, till the sand becomes petrified; and then, being enclosed in the stone, it may still live for we know not how many ages. The facts which are cited in support of this opinion are too numerous, and too circumstantial, not to deserve a certain degree of credit. As we are accustomed to see all the animals with which we are acquainted eat and drink, it appears to us difficult to conceive how a toad can be supported in such a dungeon; but if we reflect that the necessity of nourishment which animals experience in their ordinary state proceeds from the continual waste of their substance by perspiration, it will appear less incredible that some animals in a torpid state, perspiring less because they use no exercise, should have less need of aliment; and that others, which are covered with scales or shells, which stop perspiration, such as land and sea turtles, serpents, and some species of fish, should be able to subsist a considerable time without any nourishment whatever. A plant, with its flowers, fades and dies immediately, if exposed to the air without having its root immersed in a humid soil, from which it may draw a sufficient quantity of moisture to supply that which exhales from its substance and is carried off continually by the air. Perhaps, however, if it were buried in quicksilver, it might preserve for a considerable space of time its vegetable life, its smell, and colour. If this be the case, it might prove a commodious method of transporting from distant countries those delicate plants, which are unable to sustain the inclemency of the weather at sea, and which require particular care and attention. I have seen an instance of common flies preserved in a manner somewhat similar. They had been drowned in Madeira wine, apparently about the time when it was bottled in Virginia, to be sent hither [to London]. At the opening of one of the bottles, at the house of a friend where I then was, three drowned flies fell into the first glass that was filled. Having heard it remarked that drowned flies were capable

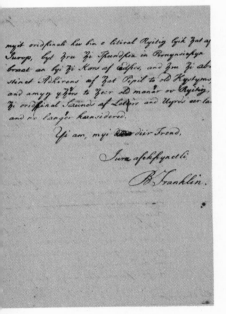

Around 1768 Franklin became interested in phonetic spelling; this letter to Polly [Poli] Stevenson is the first known use of his new alphabet.

of being revived by the rays of the sun, I proposed making the experiment upon these; they were therefore exposed to the sun upon a sieve, which had been employed to strain them out of the wine. In less than three hours, two of them began by degrees to recover life. They commenced by some convulsive motions of the thighs, and at length they raised themselves upon their legs, wiped their eyes with their fore feet, beat and brushed their wings with their hind feet, and soon after began to fly, finding themselves in Old England, without knowing how they came thither. The third continued lifeless till sunset, when, losing all hopes of him, he was thrown away.

I wish it were possible, from this instance, to invent a method of embalming drowned persons, in such a manner that they may be recalled to life at any period, however distant; for having a very ardent desire to see and observe the state of America a hundred years hence, I should prefer to any ordinary death, the being immersed in a cask of Madeira wine, with a few friends, till that time, to be then recalled to life by the solar warmth of my dear country! But since in all probability we live in an age too early and too near the infancy of science, to hope to see such an art brought in our time to its perfection, I must for the present content myself with the treat, which you are so kind as to promise me, of the resurrection of a fowl or a turkey cock.

In a letter of October, 1750, to Cadwallader Colden, a fellow American scientist, who was also a prominent politician in New York, Franklin had cautioned against the scientist's natural inclination to abandon "Publick Business" completely. "But let not your Love of Philosophical Amusements have more than its due Weight with you. Had Newton been Pilot but of a single common Ship, the finest of his Discoveries would scarce have excus'd, or atton'd for his abandoning the Helm one Hour in Time of Danger; how much less if she had carried the Fate of the Commonwealth." This conviction soon forced Franklin to desert science for the far more uncertain world of politics.

A Picture Portfolio

Ben Franklin's Philadelphia

MAN OF THE CITY

Benjamin Franklin was decidedly an urban product. Raised in Boston, he matured and prospered in Philadelphia and later delighted in both London and Paris. The city for him was a stimulant and a challenge to which he responded with all his native ingenuity. In Philadelphia he never lived far from the heart of things, from the day in 1723 when he landed at the Market Street wharf, located to the left of the tallest spire—Christ Church—in the print opposite. The many places in which he lived and worked were all on this same busy street, then called High, close by the market houses (below). No picture of any of his homes is known to exist, but at his death in 1790, his grandson, using a standard newspaper cut of the day, advertised: "To be Let—the Mansion House of the late Dr. Franklin."

A REASONABLE MARRIAGE

Franklin took Deborah Read to wife in Philadelphia in 1730, perhaps as much to help him avoid "Intrigues with low Women" as for any other reason. She was no match for her brilliant husband, but he
fondly wrote in his *Autobiography:* "...she prov'd a good and faithful Helpmate, assisted me much

by attending the Shop, we throve together, and have ever mutually endeavour'd to make each other happy." For the long years he would be separated from her on his missions abroad, he had Benjamin Wilson paint their portraits to be hung together in their Philadelphia home.

SUBSCRIPTION LIBRARY

Franklin's contributions to Philadelphia were legion. In 1727, he started a congenial club called the Junto, which met once a week in a tavern to discuss the topics of the day. Its need for books led Franklin to set up a subscription library, and thus the Library Company of Philadelphia came into being. Among Franklin's contributions to the infant company was a copy of *Logic* bearing his signature (right), possibly the earliest example of his handwriting. When the library later moved into the handsome new building below, in 1790, the year Franklin died, he was honored by a statue in the niche above the door.

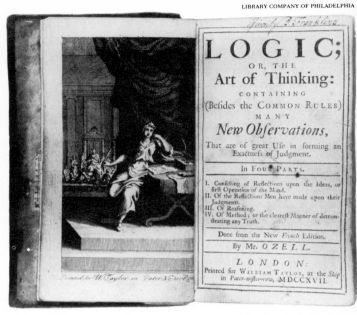

PHILOSOPHERS' HAVEN

Another remarkable institution that owed its existence to Franklin was the American Philosophical Society, whose building adjoining the State House is seen behind the trees above. Modeled on the Royal Society of London, it attracted a select group of scientifically minded men, with Franklin as their energetic organizing secretary. As its president from 1769 until his death, Franklin signed membership certificates like the one at left, admitting John Ewing, provost of the University of Pennsylvania to the society.

117

BOTH: INSURANCE COMPANY OF NORTH AMERICA

HISTORICAL SOCIETY OF PENNSYLVANIA

118

URBAN IMPROVEMENTS

Colonial cities were prone to devastating fires and to violence in their dimly lit streets. Franklin responded to such problems in characteristic fashion by proposing a regular paid corps of watchmen, instead of volunteers, and by suggesting that both their watchboxes (far left) and all street lamps be equipped with four panes of glass instead of the old globes to facilitate replacing and keeping them clean. To reduce the wild confusion at the scene of fires, Franklin recommended forming volunteer fire companies trained both in putting out fires and in rescue work, as in the eighteenth-century engraving below. He is shown at left, below, in the white chief's hat of his own Union Fire Company, the first in Philadelphia. Although this painting was done a century after the fact, the fire mark of the four clasped hands at left dates from 1752, the year Franklin founded the first successful fire insurance company in the Colonies. These emblems were nailed to the face of insured buildings and warned firefighters to be careful in their work.

PLAIN TRUTH:

OR,

SERIOUS CONSIDERATIONS

On the PRESENT STATE of the

CITY of PHILADELPHIA,

AND

PROVINCE of PENNSYLVANIA.

By a TRADESMAN of *Philadelphia.*

Capta urbe, nihil fit reliqui victis. Sed, per Deos immortales, vos ego appello, qui semper domos, villas, signa, tabulas vestras, tantæ æstimationis fecistis ; si ista, cujuscumque modi sint, quæ amplexamini, retinere, si voluptatibus vestris otium præbere vultis; expergiscimini aliquando, & expositè rempublicam. Non agitur nunc de sociorum injuriis ; LIBERTAS & ANIMA nostra in dubio est. Dux hostium cum exercitu supra caput est. Vos cunctamini etiam nunc, & dubitatis quid faciatis ? Scilicet, res ipsa aspera est, sed vos non timetis eam. Imo vero maxumè ; sed inertiâ & mollitiâ animi, alius alium expectantes, cunctamini ; videlicet, Diis immortalibus confisi, qui hanc rempublicam in maxumis periculis servavere. NON VOTIS, NEQUE SUPPLICIIS MULIEBRERUS, AUXILIA DEORUM PARANTUR : vigilando, agendo, bene consulendo, prospere omnia cedunt. Ubi socordiæ tete atque ignaviæ tradideris, nequicquam Deos implores ; irati, infestique sunt. M. POR. CAT. in SALUST.

Printed in the YEAR MDCCXLVII.

120

AN OUNCE OF PREVENTION

In 1747, with England at war against France and Spain, Franklin tried to prod the Pennsylvania Assembly into providing for its defense by writing the pamphlet *Plain Truth* (below, left) urging a "voluntary Association of the People." Its frontispiece was a woodcut (far left), thought to be the first attempt printed in America to symbolize a political situation; it shows a farmer praying for help to Hercules, who is telling him to help himself. When the Assembly failed to act, Franklin held a lottery and with its proceeds saw that a fort was erected on the Delaware River to protect Philadelphia and where "among the rest I regularly took my turn of duty...as a common soldier." Nine years later, he was appointed special commissioner in charge of the Pennsylvania frontier. Traveling to the Moravian outposts of Bethlehem (left) and Gnadenhütten, where the Indians had been dangerously hostile, he built several forts and organized the local militias. On his return, although he was now a man of fifty and going to fat, Franklin had achieved sufficient military stature to be elected colonel of the city's militia regiment, supported by regular British troops, seen below in their Philadelphia barracks.

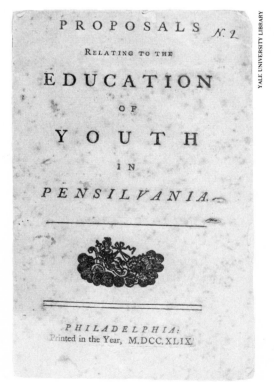

KNOWLEDGE FOR THE YOUNG

Spurred on by an anonymous pamphlet (below, left), actually written and printed by Franklin, the "principal inhabitants" of Philadelphia dug into their pocketbooks for the funds necessary to establish an academy, later to become the University of Pennsylvania. Opened in 1751, in the old Whitefield tabernacle on Fourth Street (seen at left in a contemporary sketch by Pierre Eugène Du Simitière), its first provost was an Anglican clergyman, William Smith (below), with Franklin as president of the board of trustees. The two men did not remain friends, and Franklin was to write in 1763: "I made that Man my Enemy by doing him too much Kindness. Tis the honestest Way of acquiring an Enemy. And since 'tis convenient to have at least one Enemy, who by his Readiness to revile one on all Occasions may make one careful of one's Conduct, I shall keep him an Enemy for that purpose . . . ."

"RELIEF OF THE SICK AND MISERABLE"

"There is no such thing as carrying through a public-spirited project without you are concerned in it," wrote Franklin's intimate friend Dr. Thomas Bond in regard to the foundation of a privately managed hospital for Philadelphians. Thanks to Franklin's energy and propaganda skills—he used the builder's intended plan (above) and an account of the creation (right) to get the necessary aid from the Colonial assembly—the building "for the Relief of the Sick and Miserable" was opened in 1756. The original manuscript of Franklin's inscription for the hospital's cornerstone is at upper right—dated in a year during which George II was "happily reigning" and Philadelphia was "flourishing."

the Elevation of the intended Plan.
...unded, for the Relief of the Sick and Miserable

In the Year of Christ,
1755;
George the second happily reigning;
(For he sought the Happiness of his People)
Philadelphia flourishing,
(For its Inhabitants were publick-spirited)
This Building,
By the Bounty of the Government,
And of many private Persons,
Was piously founded,
For the Relief of the Sick and Miserable.
May the God of Mercies
Bless the Undertaking!

James Pemberton

SOME

ACCOUNT

OF THE

Pennsylvania Hospital;

From its first RISE, to the Beginning
of the *Fifth Month*, called *May*, 1754.

PHILADELPHIA:
Printed by B. FRANKLIN, and D. HALL, MDCCLIV.

MONEY AND THE MAIL

Franklin's first attempt to sway public opinion with a book explained the need for a paper currency (below, far right). It was so successful that he ended up with the job of printing the money, for which he cleverly designed a leaf pattern to discourage counterfeiting (below, right). He was appointed Postmaster of Philadelphia in 1737 and immediately set about streamlining the system and keeping records (below, left), running the Post Office from his own shop in Market Street. From 1753 until his dismissal in 1774 he was Deputy Postmaster General of America. In 1775, when the Post Office was located in the London Coffee House (right), the Continental Congress—recognizing that it was now necessary to supersede the royal authority—nominated Franklin, just home from London, first Postmaster General of the budding nation. He promptly issued a circular using the rude woodcut of a post rider (below), and used as his official frank "B. *Free*, Franklin" (bottom) in place of "*Free*, B. Franklin," in a humorous display of patriotism.

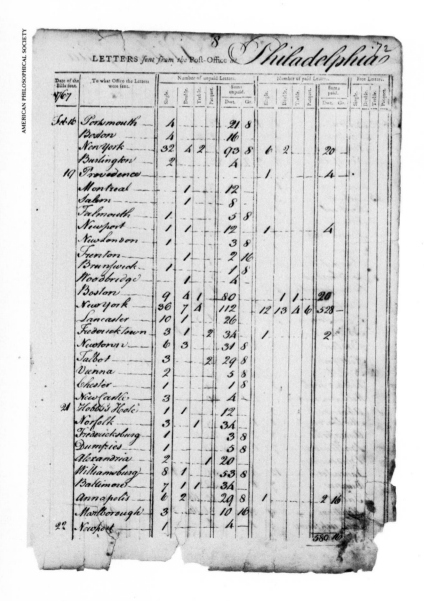

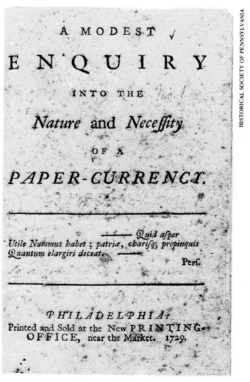

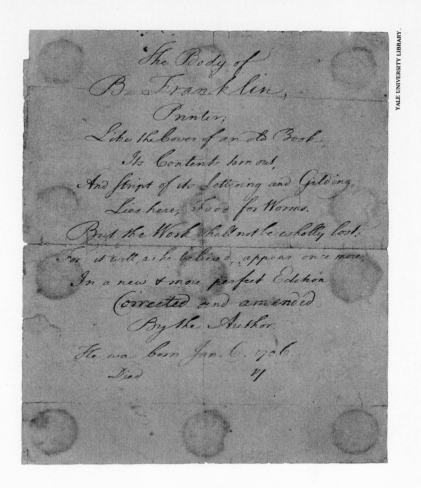

The Body of
B. Franklin,
Printer;
Like the Cover of an old Book,
Its Contents torn out,
And stript of its Lettering and Gilding,
Lies here, Food for Worms.
But the Work shall not be wholly lost.
For it will, as he believed, appear once more,
In a new & more perfect Edition
Corrected and amended
By the Author.
He was born Jan. 6. 1706.
Died

PHILADELPHIA'S PATRIARCH

Unquestionably Philadelphia's most prominent citizen, Franklin was sent to London in 1757 to represent the people of Pennsylvania as their Colonial agent. When he returned nearly twenty years later, after war had broken out between England and her Colonies, he was promptly elected to the Second Continental Congress. Serving ably on numerous committees, he was often observed by his colleague John Adams as being "fast asleep in his chair," and indeed he appears to be dozing in the painting at left depicting Congress voting for independence on July 2, 1776. Dispatched abroad again that same year to negotiate a treaty of alliance with France, he did not return to his beloved Philadelphia until 1785. Given a hero's welcome, he was elected President of the Supreme Executive Council of Pennsylvania and, at the age of eighty-one, he became a delegate to the Constitutional Convention. Three years later death claimed him, but he had farsightedly provided his own famous epitaph (above), written sixty-two years earlier. The whole world mourned him, and it has been perfectly said that "no other town burying its great man ever buried more of itself than Philadelphia with Franklin."

Chapter 5

Pennsylvania Politician

Even when Franklin's researches into electricity were at their most intense, he did not abandon his strong interest and rising influence in Pennsylvania politics. In 1747, he was chiefly responsible for creating the Colony's first militia, to defend Pennsylvania against possible French and Spanish attacks during the War of the Austrian Succession, known in America as King George's War. Previously he had played a leading role in the creation of Philadelphia's first fire department and had persuaded his fellow citizens to hire watchmen to guard the streets at night—the first tentative step toward a police department. Next he helped found the Academy of Philadelphia, from which the University of Pennsylvania eventually grew. In 1751, the Pennsylvania Hospital was chartered, again under Franklin's leadership. On August 13, 1751, his fellow citizens acknowledged his talent for political and social leadership by electing him to the Pennsylvania Assembly. Although some of the letters and essays he wrote in connection with these local activities are lively and vivid, they no longer hold as much interest for modern readers as does Franklin's response to the larger political problems of the American Colonies as a whole. One of the liveliest expressions of his interest in politics was the letter he wrote on May 9, 1751, to *The Pennsylvania Gazette* under the pseudonym Americanus. Recent editions of the *Gazette* had carried numerous stories about the murders, robberies, and other criminal acts committed by convict servants in Virginia, Maryland, and Pennsylvania.

May 9, 1751

To the Printers of the Gazette.

By a Passage in one of your late Papers, I understand that the Government at home will not suffer our mistaken Assemblies to make any Law for preventing or discouraging the Importation of Convicts from Great Britain, for this kind Reason, "*That such Laws are against the Publick Utility, as they tend to prevent the* IMPROVE-MENT *and* WELL PEOPLING of the Colonies."

Such a tender *parental* Concern in our *Mother Country* for the *Welfare* of her Children, calls aloud for the highest *Returns* of Gratitude and Duty. This every one must be sensible of: But 'tis said, that in our present Circumstances it is absolutely impossible for us to make *such* as are adequate to the Favour. I own it; but nevertheless let us do our Endeavour. 'Tis something to show a grateful Disposition.

In some of the uninhabited Parts of these Provinces, there are Numbers of these venomous Reptiles we call RATTLE-SNAKES; Felons-convict from the Beginning of the World: These, whenever we meet with them, we put to Death, by Virtue of an old Law, *Thou shalt bruise his Head.* But as this is a sanguinary Law, and may seem too cruel; and as however mischievous those Creatures are with us, they may possibly change their Natures, if they were to change the Climate; I would humbly propose, that this general Sentence of *Death* be changed for *Transportation.*

In the Spring of the Year, when they first creep out of their Holes, they are feeble, heavy, slow, and easily taken; and if a small Bounty were allow'd *per* Head, some Thousands might be collected annually, and *transported* to Britain. There I would propose to have them carefully distributed in St. James's Park, in the Spring-Gardens and other Places of Pleasure about London; in the Gardens of all the Nobility and Gentry throughout the Nation; but particularly in the Gardens of the *Prime Ministers,* the *Lords of Trade* and *Members of Parliament*; for to them we are *most particularly* obliged.

There is no human Scheme so perfect, but some Inconveniencies may be objected to it: Yet when the Conveniencies far exceed, the Scheme is judg'd rational, and fit to be executed. Thus Inconveniencies have been objected to that *good* and *wise* Act of Parliament, by virtue of which all the Newgates and Dungeons in Britain are emptied into the Colonies. It has been said, that these Thieves and Villains introduc'd among us, spoil the Morals of Youth in the Neighbourhoods that entertain them, and perpetrate many horrid Crimes: But let not *private Interests* obstruct *publick Utility.* Our *Mother* knows what is best for us. What is a little *Housebreaking,*

This rare broadside proclaimed a general fast that Franklin proposed to the Council in 1747 and which "they Embraced"; it was one of Franklin's efforts to unite the people of Philadelphia in self-defense.

One of the Colonial flags of the Pennsylvania "Associators" was designed by Franklin in 1747.

Shoplifting, or *Highway Robbing*; what is a *Son* now and then *corrupted* and *hang'd*, a Daughter *debauch'd* and *pox'd*, a Wife *stabb'd*, a Husband's *Throat cut*, or a Child's *Brains beat out* with an Axe, compar'd with this "IMPROVEMENT and WELL PEOPLING of the Colonies!"

Thus it may perhaps be objected to my Scheme, that the *Rattle-Snake* is a mischievous Creature, and that his changing his Nature with the Clime is a mere Supposition, not yet confirm'd by sufficient Facts. What then? Is not Example more prevalent than Precept? And may not the honest rough British Gentry, by a Familiarity with these Reptiles, learn to *creep*, and to *insinuate*, and to *slaver*, and to *wriggle* into Place (and perhaps to *poison* such as stand in their Way) Qualities of no small Advantage to Courtiers! In comparison of which "*Improvement and Publick Utility*," what is a *Child* now and then kill'd by their venomous Bite,—or even a favourite *Lap-Dog*? . . .

AMERICANUS

Although Franklin said in his *Autobiography* that he never sought an office, or resigned one, the fact is that he could not resist the opportunity to become Deputy Postmaster General of America. He got into the postal business almost in self-defense. Newspaper publishers in all the Colonies sought the appointment because it enabled them to send their papers free while barring their local competition. Franklin had become Postmaster of Philadelphia in 1737. The ensuing years gave him the chance to study the American postal system, which was very poorly run. In the following letter to Peter Collinson, Franklin, after a few lines about the flourishing state of the library and the academy, got down to the business of asking Collinson's help. The appointment came two years later, in 1753, and he held office for two decades, until his dismissal in 1774 for pro-Colonial activities considered disloyal to the Crown.

Philada. May 21. 1751

The Occasion of my writing this, viâ Ireland, is, That I have just receiv'd Advice that the Deputy-Postmaster General of America (Mr. Elliot Benger residing in Virginia) who has for some time been in a declining Way, is tho't to be near his End. My Friends advise me to apply for that Post, and Mr. Allen (our Chief Justice) has wrote the enclos'd to his Correspondent Mr. Simpson in my favour, requesting his Interest and Application in the Affair, and impowering him to advance a considerable Sum if it should be necessary. I have not heretofore made much Scruple of giving you Trouble when the Publick Good was to be promoted by it; but 'tis with great Reluctance that I think of asking you to interest yourself in my private Concerns, as I know you have little Time to spare. The Place is in the Disposal of the Postmasters General of Britain, with some of whom or their Friends you may possibly have Acquaintance. Mr. Allen has desir'd Mr. Simpson to confer with you on the Affair, and if you can, without much Inconvenience to your self, advise and assist in endeavouring to secure the Success of this Application, you will, whatever may be the Event, add greatly to the Obligations you have already confer'd on me; and if it succeeds, I hope that as my *Power* of doing Good increases, my *Inclination* will always at least keep pace with it.

I am quite a Stranger to the Manner of Managing these Applications, so can offer no particular Instructions. I enclose a Copy of the Commission of a former Dep. Postmaster General, which may be of some Use: The Articles of Agreement refer'd to in the Commission I have never seen, but suppose they have always been nearly the same whoever is appointed, and have been usually sent over to America to be executed by the new Officer; for I know neither of the three last Officers went to England for the Commission. The Place has been commonly reputed worth about £150 a Year, but would be otherways very suitable to me, particularly as it would enable me to execute a Scheme long since form'd, of which I send you enclos'd a Copy, and which I hope would soon produce something agreable to you and to all Lovers of Useful Knowledge, for I have now a large Acquaintance among ingenious Men in America. I need not tell you, that Philadelphia being the Center of the Continent Colonies, and having constant Communication with the West India Islands, is by much a fitter Place for the Situation of a General Post Office than Virginia, and that it would be some Reputation to our Province, to have it establish'd here. ...I have heard £200 was given for this Office by Mr. Benger, and the same by his Predecessor; I know not whose Perquisite it was: But lest that should not be Sufficient, and there may be some contingent Fees and Charges, Mr. Allen has ordered £300. However, the less it costs the better, as 'tis an Office for Life only, which is a very uncertain Tenure.

Post rider of Franklin's day

Meanwhile, the pulse of world politics began to quicken, and its beat was felt in Pennsylvania. France and England were girding for the climactic conflict that would decide which would rule North America. In the winter of 1754 an obscure Virginia militia officer named George Washington had carried a message from the Governor of Virginia, warning the French to cease their penetration of the Ohio country. The French returned the warning with insults, and then, in an aggressive move that clearly endangered both Pennsylvania and Virginia, swept down the Ohio and routed the Virginians who were building a fort at the forks of the Ohio River, on the site of present-day Pittsburgh. Franklin instantly recognized the essence of the French threat to the thirteen English Colonies. The French were united and had a plan. In this news story from *The Pennsylvania Gazette* (which he sent to Richard Partridge, Pennsylvania's agent in London, suggesting that he have it inserted in "some of your most publick Papers"), Franklin summed up the threat and presented his solution— backed up with America's first political cartoon.

The Pennsylvania Gazette,
May 9, 1754

Friday last an Express arrived here from Major Washington, with Advice, that Mr. Ward, Ensign of Capt. Trent's Company, was compelled to surrender his small Fort in the Forks of Monongahela to the French, on the 17th past.... We hear farther, that some few of the English Traders on the Ohio escaped, but 'tis supposed the greatest Part are taken, with all their Goods, and Skins, to the Amount of near £20,000. The Indian Chiefs, however, have dispatch'd Messages to Pennsylvania, and Virginia, desiring that the English would not be discouraged, but send out their Warriors to join them, and drive the French out of the Country before they fortify; otherwise the Trade will be lost, and, to their great Grief, an eternal Separation made between the Indians and their Brethren the English, 'Tis farther said, that besides the French that came down from Venango, another Body of near 400, is coming up the Ohio; and that 600 French Indians, of the Chippaways and Ottaways, are coming down Siota River, from the Lake, to join them; and many more French are expected from Canada; the Design being to establish themselves, settle their Indians, and build Forts just on the Back of our Settlements in all our Colonies; from which Forts, as they did from Crown-Point, they may send out their Parties to kill and scalp the Inhabitants, and ruin the Frontier Counties. Accordingly we hear, that the Back Settlers in Virginia,

America's first political cartoon,
probably designed by Franklin

are so terrify'd by the Murdering and Scalping of the Family last Winter, and the Taking of this Fort, that they begin already to abandon their Plantations, and remove to Places of more Safety.—The Confidence of the French in this Undertaking seems well-grounded on the present disunited State of the British Colonies, and the extreme Difficulty of bringing so many different Governments and Assemblies to agree in any speedy and effectual Measures for our common Defence and Security; while our Enemies have the very great Advantage of being under one Direction, with one Council, and one Purse. Hence, and from the great Distance of Britain, they presume that they may with Impunity violate the most solemn Treaties subsisting between the two Crowns, kill, seize and imprison our Traders, and confiscate their Effects at Pleasure (as they have done for several Years past) murder and scalp our Farmers, with their Wives and Children, and take an easy Possession of such Parts of the British Territory as they find most convenient for them; which if they are permitted to do, must end in the Destruction of the British Interest, Trade and Plantations in America.

A few weeks later, in a letter to Peter Collinson, Franklin added new depth to his vision of Colonial unity. Collinson had written from London, the preceding March, to express his concern over the "Comotion" in the Virginia and New York legislatures—and to state that it was difficult for anyone to determine who was right unless he could hear both sides.

Philada: 28th May. 1754

I am heartily concern'd with you, at the Dissensions so unseasonably kindling in the Colony Assemblies, when unanimity is became more than ever necessary to Frustrate the Designs of the French. May I presume to whisper my Sentiments in a private Letter? Britain and her Colonies should be considered as one Whole, and not as different States with separate Interests.

Instructions from the Crown to the Colonies, should have in View the Common Weal of that Whole, to which partial Interests ought to give way: And they should never Aim at extending the Prerogative beyond its due Bounds, nor abridging the just Liberties of the people: In short, they should be plainly just and reasonable, and rather savour of Fatherly Tenderness and Affection, than of Masterly harshness and Severity. Such Instructions might safely be made publick; but if they are of a different kind, they must be kept secret. Then the Representatives of the People, knowing nothing of the Instructions, frame Laws which cannot pass. Governors not daring to produce the Instructions invent other Reasons for refusing the Bill. False Reasons seldom appear good, their Weakness is discover'd and expos'd. The Governor persists and is despised. The people lose their Respect for him, grow Angry and rude. And if at length the Instruction appears, perhaps to justify the Governor's conduct, they say, why was it not produc'd before? for then all this Time spent in Framing the Bill, and disputing the point, might have been saved, the heavy charge of long Sessions prevented and Harmony preserved.—But enough of this.

The British, aware that some degree of Colonial unity was a military necessity, ordered the royal governors to convene an intercolonial congress at Albany to discuss a coordinated policy toward the Indians, who were showing signs of going over en masse to the French. Franklin was chosen by his fellow Pennsylvanians as one of the delegates, or commissioners, as they were called, to this conference. In New York, Franklin met an old friend, James Alexander, a prominent merchant and New Jersey landowner. The conversation turned to the problems of uniting the Colonies, and Franklin remarked that he thought he had a plan that might be workable. Alexander eagerly asked for something in writing, and Franklin sent him the following rough outline of what eventually became known to historians as the Albany Plan of Union.

N York June 8. 1754

Short hints towards a scheme for uniting the Northern Colonies

A Governour General

To be appointed by the King.

To be a Military man

To have a Salary from the Crown

To have a negation on all acts of the Grand Council, and carry into execution what ever is agreed on by him and that Council.

Grand Council

One member to be chosen by the Assembly of each of the smaller Colonies and two or more by each of the larger, in proportion to the Sums they pay Yearly into the General Treasury.

Members Pay

—Shillings sterling per Diem deuring their sitting and mileage for Travelling Expences.

Place and Time of meeting

To meet — times in every Year, at the Capital of each Colony in Course, unless particular circumstances and emergencies require more frequent meetings and Alteration in the Course, of places. The Governour General to Judge of those circumstances &c. and call by his Writts.

General Treasury

Its Fund, an Excise on Strong Liquors pretty equally drank in the Colonies or Duty on Liquor imported, or — shillings on each Licence of Publick House or Excise on Superfluities as Tea &c. &c. all which would pay in some proportion to the present wealth of each Colony, and encrease as that wealth encreases, and prevent disputes about the Inequality of Quotas.

To be Collected in each Colony, and Lodged in their Treasury to be ready for the payment of Orders issuing from the Governour General and Grand Council jointly.

DUTY AND POWER

of the Governour General and Grand Council

To order all Indian Treaties.

make all Indian purchases not within proprietary Grants

make and support new settlements by building Forts, raising and paying Soldiers to Garison the Forts, defend the frontiers and annoy the Ennemy.

equip Grand Vessels to scour the Coasts from Privateers in time of war, and protect the Trade

and every thing that shall be found necessary for the defence and support of the Colonies in General, and encreasing and extending their settlements &c.

For the Expence they may draw on the fund in the Treasury of any Colony.

Manner of forming this Union

The scheme being first well considered corrected and improved by the Commissioners at Albany, to be sent home, and an Act of Parliament obtain'd for establishing it.

Franklin's Plan of Union was accepted with only minor changes by the Albany Congress, but it was either rejected or ignored by every Colony, including Franklin's Pennsylvania, which caused him, he admitted in his *Autobiography* "no small mortification." In a letter of

December 29, 1754, to Peter Collinson, he was candid about his disillusionment with his fellow Americans. "Every Body cries, a Union is absolutely necessary; but when they come to the Manner and Form of the Union, their weak Noddles are presently distracted. So if ever there be an Union, it must be form'd at home by the Ministry and Parliament." Meanwhile, Governor William Shirley of Massachusetts, one of the most far-seeing and competent Crown officials in America, discussed the plan with Franklin when he visited Boston. Shirley offered an alternative plan. Franklin's plan had called for a kind of American parliament or grand council, composed of representatives from the assemblies of each Colony. Shirley's alternative was a much smaller council composed of the governors of all the Colonies, plus one or two members of their respective councils. Such an arrangement would have effectively excluded the people from choosing any representatives to the council, since all the governors except those of Rhode Island and Connecticut were appointed by the Crown, as were their councilors. Franklin and Shirley discussed the two plans in an exchange of letters. Franklin all but predicted the American Revolution as he explained to the Royal Governor why Americans would resent being taxed by a governing body in which they had no representatives.

Boston. December 4. 1754

Sir,

I mention'd it Yesterday to your Excellency as my Opinion, that Excluding the People of the Colonies from all Share in the Choice of the Grand Council would probably give extreme Dissatisfaction, as well as the Taxing them by Act of Parliament where they have no Representative. In Matters of General Concern to the People, and especially where Burthens are to be laid upon them, it is of Use to consider as well what they will *be apt* to think and say, as what they *ought* to think: I shall, therefore, as your Excellency requires it of me, briefly mention what of either Kind occurs at present, on this Occasion.

First, they will say, and perhaps with Justice, that the Body of the People in the Colonies are as loyal, and as firmly attach'd to the present Constitution and reigning Family, as any Subjects in the King's Dominions; that there is no Reason to doubt the Readiness and Willingness of their Representatives to grant, from Time to Time, such Supplies, for the Defence of the Country, as shall be judg'd necessary, so far as their Abilities will allow: That the People in the Colonies, who are to feel the immediate Mischiefs of Invasion and Conquest by an Enemy, in the Loss of their Estates, Lives and Liberties,

Governor William Shirley

are likely to be better Judges of the Quantity of Forces necessary to be raised and maintain'd, Forts to be built and supported, and of their own Abilities to bear the Expence, than the Parliament of England at so great a Distance. That Governors often come to the Colonies meerly to make Fortunes, with which they intend to return to Britain, are not always Men of the Best Abilities and Integrity, have no Estates here, nor any natural Connections with us, that should make them heartily concern'd for our Welfare; and might possibly be sometimes fond of raising and keeping up more Forces than necessary, from the Profits accruing to themselves, and to make Provision for their Friends and Dependents. That the Councellors in most of the Colonies, being appointed by the Crown, on the Recommendation of Governors, are often of small Estates, frequently dependant on the Governors for Offices, and therefore too much under Influence. That there is therefore great Reason to be jealous of a Power in such Governors and Councils, to raise such Sums as they shall judge necessary, by Draft on the Lords of the Treasury, to be afterwards laid on the Colonies by Act of Parliament, and paid by the People here; since they might abuse it, by projecting useless Expeditions, harrassing the People, and taking them from their Labour to execute such Projects, and meerly to create Offices and Employments, gratify their Dependants and divide Profits. That the Parliament of England is at a great Distance, subject to be misinform'd by such Governors and Councils, whose united Interests might probably secure them against the Effect of any Complaints from hence. That it is suppos'd an undoubted Right of Englishmen not to be taxed but by their own Consent given thro' their Representatives. That the Colonies have no Representatives in Parliament. That to propose taxing them by Parliament, and refusing them the Liberty of chusing a Representative Council, to meet in the Colonies, and consider and judge of the Necessity of any General Tax and the Quantum, shews a Suspicion of their Loyalty to the Crown, or Regard for their Country, or of their Common Sense and Understanding, which they have not deserv'd. That compelling the Colonies to pay Money without their Consent would be rather like raising Contributions in an Enemy's Country, than taxing of Englishmen for their own publick Benefit. That it would be treating them as a conquer'd People, and not as true British Subjects. That a Tax laid by the Representatives of the Colonies might easily be lessened as the Occasions should lessen, but being once laid by Parliament, under the Influence of the Representations made by Governors, would probably be kept up and continued, for the Benefit of Governors, to the grievous Burthen and Discouragement of the Colonies, and preventing their Growth and Increase. That a Power in Governors to march the Inhabitants from one End of the British and French Colonies to the other, being a Country of at least 1500 Miles square, without the Approbation or Consent of their Representatives first obtain'd to such Expeditions, might be grievous and ruinous to the People, and would put them on a Footing with the Subjects of France in Canada, that now groan under such Oppression from their Governor, who for two Years past has harrass'd them with long and destructive Marches to the Ohio. That if the Colonies in a Body may be well governed by Governors and Councils appointed by the Crown, without Representatives, particular Colonies may as well or better by so governed; a Tax may be laid on them all by Act of Parliament, for Support of Government, and their Assemblies be dismiss'd as a useless Part of their Constitution. That the Powers propos'd, by the Albany Plan of Union to be vested in a Grand Council representative of the People, even with Regard to Military Matters, are not so great as those the Colonies of Rhode-Island and Connecticut are intrusted with, and have never abused; for by this Plan the President-General is appointed by the Crown, and controlls all by his Negative; but in those Governments the People chuse the Governor, and yet allow him no Negative. That the British Colonies, bordering on the French, are properly Frontiers of the British Empire; and that the Frontiers of an Empire are properly defended at the joint Expence of the Body of People in such Empire. . . . if the Frontiers in America must bear the Expence of their own Defence, it seems hard to allow them no Share in Voting the Money, judging of the Necessity and Sum, or advising the Measures. That besides the Taxes necessary for the Defence of the Frontiers, the Colonies pay yearly great Sums to the Mother Country unnotic'd: For Taxes, paid in Britain by the Land holder or Artificer, must enter into and increase the Price of the Produce of Land, and of Manufactures made of it; and great Part of this is paid by Consumers in the Colonies, who thereby pay a considerable Part of the British Taxes. We are restrain'd in our Trade with Foreign Nations, and where we could be supplied with any Manufactures cheaper from them, but must buy the same dearer from Britain, the Difference of Price is a clear Tax to Britain. We are oblig'd to carry great Part of our Produce directly to Britain, and where the Duties there laid upon it lessens its Price to the Planter, or it sells for less than it would in Foreign Markets, the Difference is a Tax paid to Britain. Some Manufactures we could make, but are forbid, and must take them of British Merchants; the whole Price of these is a Tax paid to Britain. By our greatly increasing the *Consumption* and *Demand* of British Manufactures, their Price is considerably rais'd of late Years; the Advance is clear Profit to Britain, and enables its People better to pay great Taxes; and much of it being paid by us is clear Tax to Britain. In short, as we are not suffer'd to regulate our Trade, and restrain the Importation and Consumption of British Superfluities, (as Britain can the Consumption of Foreign Superfluities) our whole Wealth centers finally among the Merchants and Inhabitants of Britain, and if we make them richer, and enable them better to pay their Taxes, it is nearly the same as being taxed ourselves, and equally beneficial to the Crown. These Kind of Secondary Taxes, however, we do not complain of, tho' we have no Share in the Laying or Disposing of them; but to pay immediate heavy Taxes, in the Laying Appropriation or Disposition of which, we have no Part, and which perhaps we may know to be as unnecessary as grievous, must seem hard Measure to Englishmen, who cannot conceive, that by hazarding their Lives and Fortunes in subduing and settling new Countries, extending the Dominion and encreasing the Commerce of their Mother Nation, they have forfeited the native Rights of Britons, which they think ought rather to have been given them, as due to such Merit, if they had been before in a State of Slavery.

These, and such Kind of Things as these, I apprehend will be thought and said by the People, if the propos'd Alteration of the Albany Plan should take Place. Then, the Administration of the Board of Governors and Council so appointed, not having any Representative Body of the People to approve and unite in its Measures, and conciliate the Minds of the People to them, will probably become suspected and odious. Animosities and dangerous Feuds will arise between the Governors and Governed, and every Thing go into confusion.

During this visit to Boston, Franklin, aged forty-nine, had a kind of May-December romance with twenty-four-year-old Catherine Ray. She had come to Boston to visit her sister, who had married into the Boston branch of the Franklin family. She traveled with Franklin to Westerly, Rhode Island, where they visited her sister Anna, wife of Samuel Ward. Then "Katy" was hastily summoned back to Block Island to the bedside of her critically ill father. Franklin continued his journey to Philadelphia, where he wrote her the first of many letters they were to exchange.

Philada. March 4. 1755

It gives me great Pleasure to hear that you got home safe and well that Day. I thought too much was hazarded, when I saw you put off to Sea in that very little Skiff, toss'd by every Wave. But the Call was strong and just, a sick Parent. I stood on the Shore, and look'd after you, till I could no longer distinguish you, even with my Glass; then returned to your Sister's, praying for your safe Passage. Towards Evening all agreed that you must certainly be arriv'd before that time, the Weather having been so favourable; which made me more easy and chearful, for I had been truly concern'd for you.

I left New England slowly, and with great Reluctance: Short Days Journeys, and loitering Visits on the Road, for three or four Weeks, manifested my Unwillingness to quit a Country in which I drew my first Breath, spent my earliest and most pleasant Days, and had now received so many fresh Marks of the People's Goodness and Benevolence, in the kind and affectionate Treatment I had every where met with. I almost forgot I had a Home; till I was more than half-way towards it; till I had, one by one, parted with all my New England Friends, and was got into the western Borders of Connecticut, among meer Strangers: then, like an old Man, who, having buried all he lov'd in this World, begins to think of Heaven, I begun to think of and wish for Home; and as I drew nearer, I found the Attraction stronger and stronger, my Diligence and Speed increas'd with my Impatience, I drove on violently, and made such long Stretches that a very few Days brought me to my

Sketch by Charles Willson Peale of Franklin and one of his lady friends

own House, and to the Arms of my good old Wife and Children, where I remain, Thanks to God, at present well and happy.

Persons subject to the Hyp, complain of the North East Wind as increasing their Malady. But since you promis'd to send me Kisses in that Wind, and I find you as good as your Word, 'tis to me the gayest Wind that blows, and gives me the best Spirits. I write this during a N. East Storm of Snow, the greatest we have had this Winter: Your Favours come mixd with the Snowy Fleeces which are pure as your Virgin Innocence, white as your lovely Bosom,—and as cold:—But let it warm towards some worthy young Man, and may Heaven bless you both with every kind of Happiness.

The war that Franklin had foreseen in his *Gazette* story on Major Washington's dispatch now began in earnest. The British sent Major General Edward Braddock with two regiments of regular troops to drive the French from the fort they had seized from the Virginians. In this passage from the section of his *Autobiography* composed late in his life, Franklin told how he became involved in the expedition.

Autobiography, 1788

The British Government not chusing to permit the Union of the Colonies, as propos'd at Albany, and to trust that Union with their Defence, lest they should thereby grow too military, and feel their own Strength, Suspicions and Jealousies at this time being entertain'd of them; sent over General Braddock with two Regiments of Regular English Troops for that purpose. He landed at Alexandria in Virginia, and thence march'd to Frederic Town in Maryland, where he halted for Carriages. Our Assembly apprehending, from some Information, that he had conceived violent Prejudices against them, as averse to the Service, wish'd me to wait upon him, not as from them, but as Postmaster General, under the guise of proposing to settle with him the Mode of conducting with most Celerity and Certainty the Dispatches between him and the Governors of the several Provinces, with whom he must necessarily have continual Correspondence, and of which they propos'd to pay the Expence. My Son accompanied me on this Journey. We found the General at Frederic Town, waiting impatiently for the Return of those he had sent thro' the back Parts of Maryland and Virginia to collect Waggons. I staid with him several

Days, Din'd with him daily, and had full Opportunity of removing all his Prejudices, by the Information of what the Assembly had before his Arrival actually done and were still willing to do to facilitate his Operations.

When I was about to depart, the Returns of Waggons to be obtain'd were brought in, by which it appear'd that they amounted only to twenty-five, and not all of those were in serviceable Condition. The General and all the Officers were surpriz'd, declar'd the Expedition was then at an End, being impossible, and exclaim'd against the Ministers for ignorantly landing them in a Country destitute of the Means of conveying their Stores, Baggage, &c. not less than 150 Waggons being necessary. I happen'd to say, I thought it was pity they had not been landed rather in Pennsylvania, as in that Country almost every Farmer had his Waggon. The General eagerly laid hold of my Words, and said, "Then you, Sir, who are a Man of Interest there, can probably procure them for us; and I beg you will undertake it." I ask'd what Terms were to be offer'd the Owners of the Waggons; and I was desir'd to put on Paper the Terms that appear'd to me necessary. This I did, and they were agreed to, and a Commission and Instructions accordingly prepar'd immediately.

Battery proposed by Franklin for the defense of Philadelphia

In two weeks, Braddock had 150 wagons and 259 pack horses in his camp. But this help from Franklin only facilitated his advance to the forest ambush that destroyed him and his army. Franklin wrote that he sensed trouble well before the disaster occurred.

Autobiography, 1788

This General was I think a brave Man, and might probably have made a Figure as a good Officer in some European War. But he had too much self-confidence, too high an Opinion of the Validity of Regular Troops, and too mean a One of both Americans and Indians. George Croghan, our Indian Interpreter, join'd him on his March with 100 of those People, who might have been of great Use to his Army as Guides, Scouts, &c. if he had treated them kindly; but he slighted and neglected them, and they gradually left him.

In Conversation with him one day, he was giving me some Account of his intended Progress. "After taking Fort Du Quesne, says he, I am to proceed to Niagara; and having taken that, to Frontenac, if the Season will allow time; and I suppose it will; for Duquesne can hardly

Engraving of the "Defeat and Death of General Braddock" from Russel's History of England

detain me above three or four Days; and then I see nothing that can obstruct my March to Niagara." Having before revolv'd in my Mind the long Line his Army must make in their March, by a very narrow Road to be cut for them thro' the Woods and Bushes; and also what I had read of a former Defeat of 1500 French who invaded the Iroquois Country, I had conceived some Doubts and some Fears for the Event of the Campaign. But I ventur'd only to say, To be sure, Sir, if you arrive well before Duquesne, with these fine Troops so well provided with Artillery, that Place, not yet compleatly fortified, and as we hear with no very strong Garrison, can probably make but a short Resistance. The only Danger I apprehend of Obstruction to your March, is from the Ambuscades of Indians, who by constant Practice are dextrous in laying and executing them. And the slender Line near four Miles long, which your Army must make, may expose it to be attack'd by Surprize in its Flanks, and to be cut like a Thread into several Pieces, which from their Distance cannot come up in time to support each other. He smil'd at my Ignorance, and reply'd, "These Savages may indeed be a formidable Enemy to your raw American Militia; but upon the King's regular and disciplin'd Troops, Sir, it is impossible they should make any Impression." I was conscious of an Impropriety in my Disputing with a military Man in Matters of his Profession, and said no more.

In Pennsylvania, meanwhile, Franklin found himself caught in the middle of a continuing quarrel between the Proprietors (the sons of Pennsylvania's founder, William Penn) and the people. The core of the argument was the Proprietors' insistence that their lands be exempted from any tax levied to raise funds for the defense of the province. The Proprietors and their supporters in Pennsylvania attempted to defend their position by attacking the Quakers, who composed the bulk of the majority party, arguing that the refusal of the Quakers to bear arms in defense of the country was a far more serious dereliction. In this letter to Peter Collinson, Franklin summed up the situation. The "Brief State" that he mentioned was a pamphlet, A *Brief State of the Province of Pennsylvania,* attacking Franklin and the Quaker Party. It had in fact been written by William Smith, the Anglican clergyman whom Franklin had hired to head the Academy of Philadelphia. Franklin had not yet perceived Smith's devious character.

Philada. Augt. 27. 1755.

We are all in Flames, as you will see by the Papers. I

145

have wrote to our Agent, Mr. Partridge, a short, but I believe a clear Account of our late Bill for giving £50,000 refus'd by the Governor because the Proprietary Estate was thereby to be taxed with others. He will show it to you if you desire it, as I have not now time to repeat it. These Obstructions of the General Interest from particular Disputes in the Colonies, show more and more the Necessity of the projected UNION, which I hope will be compleated soon; for depend on it, no American War will ever be well carried on without it.

I wrote to you, via New York, a full Account of our shameful Defeat on the Ohio. The General presum'd too much, and was too secure. This the Event proves; but it was my Opinion from the time I saw him and convers'd with him....

I do not find that our Assembly have any Inclination to answer the Brief State. They think it below them. Perhaps they slight it too much. The design was to get Quakers out of the Assembly, on this Principle, or at least on this Pretence, *That they could not or would not do the Duty of Assembly-men in defending the Country.* Great Pains was taken to this Purpose at our last Election, when I was absent in New England, but in vain. If the End was, simply, to get the Country defended by Grants of Money, the Quakers have now shown that they can give and dispose of Money for that purpose as freely as any People. If this does not give Satisfaction, the Pique against them must seem to be personal and private, and not founded on Views for the publick Good. I know the Quakers now think it their Duty, when chosen, to consider themselves as Representatives of the *Whole People,* and not of their own Sect only; they consider the public Money as raised from and belonging to the *whole Publick,* and not to their Sect only; and therefore, tho' they can neither bear Arms themselves, nor compel others to do it, yet very lately, when our Frontier Inhabitants, who are chiefly Presbyterians or Churchmen, thought themselves in Danger, and the Poor among them were unable to provide Arms, and petitioned the House, a Sum was voted for that purpose, and put into the Hands of a Committee to procure and supply them. I have accordingly purchas'd and sent up a considerable Quantity; with the Governor's Approbation, as to the Disposition; for as he is Captain General we think it our Duty not to

Scene in a Quaker meeting house

arm the People without his Consent, tho' we are other-wise at Variance with him. . . . A Number of Falshoods are now privately propagated to blast my Character, of which I shall take no Notice 'till they grow bold enough to show their Faces in publick. Those who caress'd me a few Months since, are now endeavouring to defame me every where by every base Art. . . . if I did not love the Country and the People, [I] would remove immediately into a more quiet Government, Connecticut, where I am also happy enough to have many Friends.

Franklin's correspondence with young Catherine Ray gave him an opportunity to escape from Pennsylvania politics.

Philada. Sept. 11. 1755

Begone, Business, for an Hour, at least, and let me chat a little with my Katy. . . .

You ask in your last, How I do, and what I am doing, and whether every body loves me yet, and why I make 'em do so? In [the first place, I am so well?] Thanks to God, that I do not remember I was ever better. I still relish all the Pleasures of Life that a temperate Man can in reason desire, and thro' Favour I have them all in my Power. This happy Situation shall continue as long as God pleases, who knows what is best for his Creatures, and I hope will enable me to bear with Patience and duti-ful Submission any Change he may think fit to make that is less agreable. As to the second Question, I must con-fess, (but don't you be jealous) that many more People love me now than ever did before: For since I saw you, I have been enabled to do some general Services to the Country, and to the Army, for which both have thank'd and prais'd me; and say they love me; they *say so,* as you us'd to do; and if I were to ask any Favours of them, would, perhaps, as readily refuse me: So that I find little real Advantage in being belov'd, but it pleases my Humour.

Now it is near four Months since I have been favour'd with a single Line from you; but I will not be angry with you, because 'tis my fault. I ran in debt to you three or four Letters, and as I did not pay, you would not trust me any more, and you had some Reason: But believe me, I am honest, and tho' I should never make equal Returns, you shall see I'll keep fair Accounts. Equal Returns I can never make, tho' I should write to you by every Post: For

Quakers going to meeting

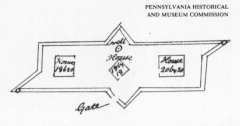

*Top, Franklin's own sketch of Fort
Allen; center, building the stockade
of the fort; below, back from the
frontier, he parades in triumph with
the men of his regiment.*

the Pleasure I receive from one of yours, is more than you
can have from two of mine....

I long to hear whether you have continu'd ever since in
that Monastery; or have broke into the World again, doing
pretty Mischief; how the Lady Wards do, and how many of
them are married, or about it; what is become of Mr. B.
and Mr. L. and what the State of your Heart is at this
Instant? but that, perhaps I ought not to know; and therefore I will not conjure, as you sometimes say I do....

I commend your prudent Resolutions in the Article of
granting Favours to Lovers: But if I were courting you, I
could not heartily approve such Conduct. I should even be
malicious enough to say you were too *knowing*....

You have spun a long Thread, 5022 Yards! It will reach
almost from Block Island hither. I wish I had hold of one
End of it, to pull you to me: But you would break it
rather than come. The Cords of Love and Friendship are
longer and stronger, and in Times past have drawn me
farther; even back from England to Philadelphia. I guess
that some of the same kind will one day draw you out
of that Island.

I was extreamly pleas'd with the Turff you sent me.
The Irish People who have seen it, say, 'tis the right Sort;
but I cannot learn that we have anything like it here. The
Cheeses, particularly one of them, were excellent: All
our Friends have tasted it, and all agree that it exceeds
any English Cheese they ever tasted. Mrs. Franklin was
very proud, that a young Lady should have so much
Regard for her old Husband, as to send him such a Present.
We talk of you every Time it comes to Table; She is sure
you are a sensible Girl, and a notable Housewife; and
talks of bequeathing me to you as a Legacy; But I ought
to wish you a better, and hope she will live these 100
Years; for we are grown old together, and if she has any
faults, I am so us'd to 'em that I don't perceive 'em....
Indeed I begin to think she has none, as I think of you.
And since she is willing I should love you as much as
you are willing to be lov'd by me; let us join in wishing
the old Lady a long Life and a happy.

Pennsylvania soon summoned Franklin back to duty —
duty that included his assumption of the role of general. With Braddock's
army defeated, and its survivors having retreated all the way to New Jersey,
the Pennsylvania frontier was left almost totally exposed to marauding

French and Indians. The town of Gnadenhütten in the Lehigh Gap was burned and its inhabitants massacred. Early in January, 1756, Franklin led some three hundred volunteers out of Philadelphia to restore order in the western counties. His son William accompanied him and handled the military details of the expedition. The mission was successful. The two Franklins organized local militia in frontier towns and then marched to Gnadenhütten, where they built a fort. In that desolate place, Franklin wrote the following cheerful letter to his wife Deborah. He addressed her in the sentimental phrase they both used when they wrote to each other: "My dear child."

Gnadenhathen, January 25, 1756.

My Dear Child,

This day week we arrived here, I wrote to you the same day, and once since. We all continue well, thanks be to God. We have been hindered with bad weather, yet our fort is in a good defensible condition, and we have every day, more convenient living. Two more are to be built, one on each side of this, at about fifteen miles distance. I hope both will be done in a week or ten days, and then I purpose to bend my course homewards.

We have enjoyed your roast beef, and this day began on the roast veal; all agree that they are both the best that ever were of the kind. Your citizens, that have their dinners hot and hot, know nothing of good eating; we find it in much greater perfection when the kitchen is four score miles from the dining room. . . .

As to our lodging, 'tis on deal feather beds, in warm blankets, and much more comfortable than when we lodged at our inn, the first night after we left home, for the woman being about to put very damp sheets on the bed we desired her to air them first; half an hour afterwards, she told us the bed was ready, and the sheets *well aired.* I got into bed, but jumped out immediately, finding them as cold as death, and partly frozen. She had *aired* them indeed, but it was out upon the *hedge.* I was forced to wrap myself up in my great coat and woollen trowsers, every thing else about the bed was shockingly dirty. . . .

B FRANKLIN

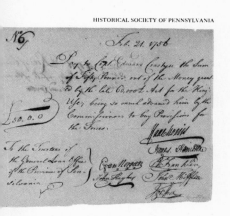

HISTORICAL SOCIETY OF PENNSYLVANIA

Order to pay Captain Edward Croston for troop provisions, written in Franklin's hand and signed by all seven of the provincial commissioners

Returning to Philadelphia, Franklin found sad news. His favorite brother, John, had died of the bladder ailment that had distressed him for many years. Writing to John's stepdaughter, Elizabeth Hubbart, Franklin composed a letter about life and death that quickly achieved fame. At first it was copied by hand to solace others similarly bereaved, and later it was frequently printed.

Philadelphia, February 22, 1756

I condole with you, we have lost a most dear and valuable relation, but it is the will of God and Nature that these mortal bodies be laid aside, when the soul is to enter into real life; 'tis rather an embrio state, a preparation for living; a man is not completely born until he be dead: Why then should we grieve that a new child is born among the immortals? A new member added to their happy society? We are spirits. That bodies should be lent us, while they can afford us pleasure, assist us in acquiring knowledge, or doing good to our fellow creatures, is a kind and benevolent act of God—when they become unfit for these purposes and afford us pain instead of pleasure—instead of an aid, become an incumbrance and answer none of the intentions for which they were given, it is equally kind and benevolent that a way is provided by which we may get rid of them. Death is that way. We ourselves prudently choose a partial death. In some cases a mangled painful limb, which cannot be restored, we willingly cut off. He who plucks out a tooth, parts with it freely since the pain goes with it, and he that quits the whole body, parts at once with all pains and possibilities of pains and diseases it was liable to, or capable of making him suffer.

Our friend and we are invited abroad on a party of pleasure—that is to last for ever. His chair was first ready and he is gone before us. We could not all conveniently start together, and why should you and I be grieved at this, since we are soon to follow, and we know where to find him.

Later that year, Franklin wrote another letter, which did not achieve fame but foreshadowed one of the most important preoccupations of his later years—founding a colony on the Ohio River. It was written to George Whitefield, famous as a preacher both in America and England.

New York, July 2. 1756

You mention your frequent Wish that you were a Chaplain to an American Army. I sometimes wish, that you and I were jointly employ'd by the Crown to settle a Colony on the Ohio. I imagine we could do it effectually, and without putting the Nation to much Expence. But I fear we shall never be call'd upon for such a Service. What a glorious Thing it would be, to settle in that fine Country a large Strong Body of Religious and Industrious

John Franklin's bookplate

People! What a Security to the other Colonies; and Advantage to Britain, by Increasing her People, Territory, Strength and Commerce. Might it not greatly facilitate the Introduction of pure Religion among the Heathen, if we could, by such a Colony, show them a better Sample of Christians than they commonly see in our Indian Traders, the most vicious and abandoned Wretches of our Nation? Life, like a dramatic Piece, should not only be conducted with Regularity, but methinks it should finish handsomely. Being now in the last Act, I begin to cast about for something fit to end with. Or if mine be more properly compar'd to an Epigram, as some of its few Lines are but barely tolerable, I am very desirous of concluding with a bright Point. In such an Enterprize I could spend the Remainder of Life with Pleasure; and I firmly believe God would bless us with Success, if we undertook it with a sincere Regard to his Honour, the Service of our gracious King, and (which is the same thing) the Publick Good.

Reverend George Whitefield

Relations between the Pennsylvania Assembly and the proprietary government worsened steadily. The Proprietors stubbornly insisted that their lands should be exempted from taxation, and the Quaker Assembly in return refused to vote any money for the defense of the Colony or contribute any of its much-needed resources to the war with France. Finally, Franklin and the other members of the Assembly decided that the only answer to the impasse was direct negotiations with the Proprietors in England. In this letter to his London friend and fellow printer William Strahan, Franklin predicted his early arrival in the British capital and the beginning of another phase in his career. The son Billy he mentioned was Strahan's boy, who the two friends hoped would marry Franklin's daughter Sarah, then thirteen. "Smouting" is printer's slang for part-time work.

[Philadelphia,] Jan. 31. 1757

It gives me great Pleasure to hear so good an Account of our Son Billy. In Return, let me tell you, that our Daughter Sally is indeed a very good Girl, affectionate, dutiful and industrious, has one of the best Hearts, and tho' not a Wit, is for one of her Years, by no means deficient in Understanding. She already takes off part of her Mother's Family Cares. This must give you and Mrs. Strahan Pleasure: So that Account is partly ballanced.

Our Assembly talk of sending me to England speedily. Then look out sharp, and if a fat old Fellow should come to your Printing House and request a little Smouting,

depend upon it, 'tis Your affectionate Friend and humble
Servant

B FRANKLIN

On the point of leaving for England, Franklin did not
forget his Boston relatives. His older half sister, Elizabeth Douse, was living
in a house he owned in Boston. Another sister, Jane Mecom, and some additional members of the family thought that it would be more economical to
sell the house and furniture, and move the old woman in with them. In this
wise letter to his sister Jane, Franklin demurred.

New York, April 19. 1757

I wrote a few Lines to you yesterday, but omitted to answer
yours relating to Sister Douse: As *having their own Way*, is
one of the greatest Comforts of Life, to old People, I
think their Friends should endeavour to accommodate
them in that, as well as in any thing else. When they have
long liv'd in a House, it becomes natural to them, they are
almost as closely connected with it as the Tortoise with
his Shell, they die if you tear them out of it. Old Folks
and old Trees, if you remove them, tis ten to one that
you kill them. So let our good old Sister be no more
importun'd on that head. We are growing old fast ourselves, and shall expect the same kind of Indulgencies. If
we give them, we shall have a Right to receive them in
our Turn.

And as to her few fine Things, I think she is in the
right not to sell them, and for the Reason she gives, that
they will fetch but little. When that little is spent, they
would be of no farther use to her; but perhaps the Expectation of Possessing them at her Death, may make that
Person tender and careful of her, and helpful to her, to
the amount of ten times their Value. If so, they are put to
the best Use they possibly can be.

I hope you visit Sister as often as your Affairs will permit, and afford her what Assistance and Comfort you
can, in her present Situation. *Old Age, Infirmities,* and
Poverty, join'd, are Afflictions enough; the *Neglect and
Slight* of Friends and near Relations, should never be
added. People in her Circumstances are apt to suspect
this sometimes without Cause; *Appearances* should
therefore be attended to, in our Conduct towards them,
as well as *Realities....*

We expect to sail in about a Week, so that I can hardly
hear from you again on this Side the Water.

On the voyage to England, Franklin prepared the text for *Poor Richard* of 1758. With plenty of time on his hands, he went through all his previous volumes, and wrote an introductory essay, *The Way to Wealth,* which was to become one of his most famous compositions—with a very unfortunate effect on his reputation. Poor Richard's advice on how to get rich achieved wide fame in Franklin's lifetime and was reprinted repeatedly in the hundred years after his death. It made Franklin's name synonymous with saving, and even with penny-pinching—an ironic fate for a man who abandoned what he called "the pursuit of wealth to no purpose" at the age of forty–two. Franklin did pinch his pennies as a young man, starting out in business with heavy debts. But, as his letters have already demonstrated, once he achieved financial security, he was generous and open-handed. The essay, in which Franklin created another of his memorable characters, wise old Father Abraham, was really more of an intellectual exercise. The tone is highly ironic and at times is even close to parody. Franklin was actually laughing just a little at himself and Poor Richard and the whole notion of persuading men to save money—while simultaneously working into the text a maximum number of quotations from his previous almanacs. Appropriately, it was the last Franklin himself wrote.

Poor Richard, 1758

...a great Number of People were collected at a Vendue [auction] of Merchant Goods. The Hour of Sale not being come, they were conversing on the Badness of the Times, and one of the Company call'd to a plain clean old Man, with white Locks, *Pray, Father Abraham, what think you of the Times? Won't these heavy Taxes quite ruin the Country? How shall we be ever able to pay them? What would you advise us to?*—Father Abraham stood up, and reply'd, If you'd have my Advice, I'll give it you in short, for a *Word to the Wise is enough,* and *many Words won't fill a Bushel,* as *Poor Richard says.* They join'd in desiring him to speak his Mind, and gathering round him, he proceeded as follows;

"Friends, says he, and Neighbours, the Taxes are indeed very heavy, and if those laid on by the Government were the only Ones we had to pay, we might more easily discharge them; but we have many others, and much more grievous to some of us. We are taxed twice as much by our *Idleness,* three times as much by our *Pride,* and four times as much by our *Folly,* and from these Taxes the Commissioners cannot ease or deliver us by allowing an Abatement. However let us hearken to good Advice, and something may be done for us; *God helps them that help themselves,* as Poor Richard says, in his Almanack

FATHER
Abraham's
SPEECH
To a great Number of People, at a *Vendue* of Merchant-Goods ;

Introduced to the PUBLICK by

Poor Richard,

A famous PENNSYLVANIA Conjurer, and Almanack-Maker,

In Anfwer to the following QUESTIONS.

Pray, Father Abraham, *what think you of the Times ? Won't thefe heavy Taxes quite ruin the Country ? How fhall we be ever able to pay them ? What would you advife us to ?*

To which are added,
SEVEN *curious* PIECES *of* WRITING.

BOSTON, NEW-ENGLAND,
Printed and Sold by Benjamin Mecom, *at* The NEW PRINTING-OFFICE, *Oppofite to the Old-Brick Meeting, near the Court-Houfe.*

NOTE, Very good Allowance to thofe who take them by the Hundred or Dozen, to fell again.

The title page of Father Abraham's Speech, *first published in 1758*

Father Abraham's Speech *became best known by its later title,* The Way to Wealth, *published in many editions, such as this 1807 British version.*

of 1733.

It would be thought a hard Government that should tax its People one tenth Part of their *Time,* to be employed in its Service. But *Idleness* taxes many of us much more, if we reckon all that is spent in absolute *Sloth,* or doing of nothing, with that which is spent in idle Employments or Amusements, that amount to nothing. *Sloth,* by bringing on Diseases, absolutely shortens Life. *Sloth, like Rust, consumes faster than Labour wears, while the used Key is always bright,* as Poor Richard says. But *dost thou love Life, then do not squander Time, for that's the Stuff Life is made of,* as Poor Richard says. How much more than is necessary do we spend in Sleep! forgetting that *The sleeping Fox catches no Poultry,* and that *there will be sleeping enough in the Grave,* as Poor Richard says. If Time be of all Things the most precious, *wasting Time* must be, as Poor Richard says, *the greatest Prodigality,* since, as he elsewhere tells us, *Lost Time is never found again;* and what we call *Time-enough, always proves little enough:* Let us then be up and be doing, and doing to the Purpose; so by Diligence shall we do more with less Perplexity. *Sloth makes all Things difficult, but Industry all easy,* as Poor Richard says; and *He that riseth late, must trot all Day, and shall scarce overtake his Business at Night.* While *Laziness travels so slowly, that Poverty soon overtakes him,* as we read in Poor Richard, who adds, *Drive thy Business, let not that drive thee;* and *Early to Bed, and early to rise, makes a Man healthy, wealthy and wise.*

So what signifies *wishing* and *hoping* for better Times. We may make these Times better if we bestir ourselves. *Industry need not wish,* as Poor Richard says, and *He that lives upon Hope will die fasting. There are no Gains, without Pains;* then *Help Hands, for I have no Lands,* or if I have, they are smartly taxed. And, as Poor Richard likewise observes, *He that Hath a Trade hath an Estate,* and *He that hath a Calling hath an Office of Profit and Honour;* but then the *Trade* must be worked at, and the *Calling* well followed, or neither the *Estate,* nor the *Office,* will enable us to pay our Taxes. If we are industrious we shall never starve; for, as Poor Richard says, *At the working Man's House Hunger looks in, but dares not enter.* Nor will the Bailiff nor the Constable enter, for *Industry pays Debts, while Despair encreaseth them,* says Poor Richard. What though you have found no Treasure, nor has any rich Relation left you a Legacy, *Diligence is the Mother of Good luck*, as Poor Richard says, and *God gives all Things to Industry*. Then *plough deep, while Sluggards sleep, and you shall have Corn to sell and to keep*, says Poor Dick. Work while it is called To-day, for you know not how much you may be hindered To-morrow, which makes Poor Richard say, *One To-day is worth two To-morrows*; and farther, *Have you somewhat to do To-morrow, do it To-day*. If you were a Servant, would you not be ashamed that a good Master should catch you idle? Are you then your own Master, *be ashamed to catch yourself idle*, as Poor Dick says. When there is so much to be done for yourself, your Family, your Country, and your gracious King, be up by Peep of Day; *Let not the Sun look down and say, Inglorious here he lies*. Handle your Tools without Mittens; remember that *the Cat in Gloves catches no Mice*, as Poor Richard says. 'Tis true there is much to be done, and perhaps you are weak handed, but stick to it steadily, and you will see great Effects, for *constant Dropping wears away Stones*, and by *Diligence and Patience the Mouse ate in two the Cable*; and *Little Strokes fell great Oaks*, as Poor Richard says in his Almanack, the Year I cannot just now remember.

Illustrations from the 1807 British edition with Poor Richard *sayings: "The cat in gloves catches no mice"; "There will be sleeping enough in the grave"; and "Never leave that till tomorrow, which you can do today."*

Methinks I hear some of you say, *Must a Man afford himself no Leisure?* I will tell thee, my Friend, what Poor Richard says, *Employ thy Time well if thou meanest to gain Leisure*; and, *since thou art not sure of a Minute, throw not away an Hour*. Leisure, is Time for doing something useful; this Leisure the diligent Man will obtain, but the lazy Man never; so that, as Poor Richard says, a *Life of Leisure and a Life of Laziness are two Things*. Do you imagine that Sloth will afford you more Comfort than Labour? No, for as Poor Richard says, *Trouble springs from Idleness, and grievous Toil from needless Ease. Many without Labour, would live by their* WITS *only, but they break for want of Stock*. Whereas Industry gives Comfort, and Plenty, and Respect: *Fly Pleasures, and they'll follow you. . . .*

But with our Industry, we must likewise be *steady, settled* and *careful*, and oversee our own Affairs *with our own Eyes*, and not trust too much to others; for, as Poor Richard says . . .

He that by the Plough would thrive,
Himself must either hold or drive.

And again, *The Eye of a Master will do more Work than both his Hands;* and again, *Want of Care does us more Damage than Want of Knowledge;* and again, *Not to oversee Workmen, is to leave them your Purse open.* . . . And farther, *If you would have a faithful Servant, and one that you like, serve yourself.* . . .

So much for Industry, my Friends, and Attention to one's own Business; but to these we must add *Frugality,* if we would make our *Industry* more certainly successful. A Man may, if he knows not how to save as he gets, *keep his Nose all his Life to the Grindstone,* and die not worth a *Groat* at last. *A fat Kitchen makes a lean Will.* . . . and, *If you would be wealthy,* says he, in another Almanack, *think of Saving as well as of Getting: The Indies have not made Spain rich, because her* Outgoes *are greater than her* Incomes. Away then with your expensive Follies, and you will not have so much Cause to complain of hard Times, heavy Taxes, and chargeable Families; for, as Poor Dick says,

Women and Wine, Game and Deceit,
Make the Wealth small, and the Wants great.

And farther, *What maintains one Vice, would bring up two Children.* You may think perhaps, That a *little* Tea, or a *little* Punch now and then, Diet a *little* more costly, Clothes a *little* finer, and a *little* Entertainment now and then, can be no *great* Matter; but remember what Poor Richard says . . . *Beware of* little *Expences; a small Leak will sink a great Ship;* and again, *Who Dainties love, shall Beggars prove.* . . .

Here you are all got together at this Vendue of *Fineries* and *Knicknacks.* You call them *Goods,* but if you do not take Care, they will prove *Evils* to some of you. You expect they will be sold *cheap,* and perhaps they may for less than they cost; but if you have no Occasion for them, they must be *dear* to you. Remember what Poor Richard says, *Buy what thou hast no Need of, and ere long thou shalt sell thy Necessaries.* And again, *At a great Pennyworth pause a while:* He means, that perhaps the Cheapness is *apparent* only, and not *real;* or the Bargain, by straitning thee in thy Business, may do thee more Harm than Good. . . . Many a one, for the Sake of Finery on the Back, have gone with a hungry Belly, and

Eight panels from an 1859 engraving, "Poor Richard Illustrated," with "Lessons for the Young and Old on Industry, Temperance, Frugality &c by Benjamin Franklin"

half starved their Families; *Silks and Satins, Scarlet and Velvets,* as Poor Richard says, *put out the Kitchen Fire.* These are not the *Necessaries* of Life; they can scarcely be called the *Conveniencies,* and yet only because they look pretty, how many *want* to *have* them. The *artificial* Wants of Mankind thus become more numerous than the *natural;* and, as Poor Dick says, *For one* poor *Person, there are an hundred* indigent. By these, and other Extravagancies, the Genteel are reduced to Poverty, and forced to borrow of those whom they formerly despised, but who through *Industry* and *Frugality* have maintained their Standing; in which Case it appears plainly, that a *Ploughman on his Legs is higher than a Gentleman on his Knees,* as Poor Richard says. Perhaps they have had a small Estate left them, which they knew not the Getting of; they think *'tis Day, and will never be Night;* that a little to be spent out of *so much,* is not worth minding; *(a Child and a Fool,* as Poor Richard says, *imagine Twenty Shillings and Twenty Years can never be spent)* but, *always taking out of the Meal-tub, and never putting in, soon comes to the Bottom;* then, as Poor Dick says, *When the Well's dry, they know the Worth of Water.* But this they might have known before, if they had taken his Advice; *If you would know the Value of Money, go and try to borrow some;* for, *he that goes a borrowing goes a sorrowing....*

    Fond Pride of Dress, *is sure a very Curse;*
    E'er Fancy *you consult, consult your Purse.*

...When you have bought one fine Thing you must buy ten more, that your Appearance may be all of a Piece; but Poor Dick says, *'Tis easier to* suppress *the first Desire, than to* satisfy *all that follow it....*

But what Madness must it be to *run in Debt* for these Superfluities! We are offered, by the Terms of this Vendue, *Six Months Credit;* and that perhaps has induced some of us to attend it, because we cannot spare the ready Money, and hope now to be fine without it. But, ah, think what you do when you run in Debt; *You give to another Power over your Liberty.* If you cannot pay at the Time, you will be ashamed to see your Creditor; you will be in Fear when you speak to him; you will make poor pitiful sneaking Excuses, and by Degrees come to lose your Veracity, and sink into base downright lying; for, as Poor Richard says, *The second Vice is*

Lying, the first is running in Debt. And again, to the same Purpose, *Lying rides upon Debt's Back....*

And now to conclude, *Experience keeps a dear School, but Fools will learn in no other, and scarce in that;* for it is true, *we may give Advice, but we cannot give Conduct,* as Poor Richard says: However, remember this, *They that won't be counselled, can't be helped,* as Poor Richard says....

Thus the old Gentleman ended his Harangue. The People heard it, and approved the Doctrine, and immediately practised the contrary, just as if it had been a common Sermon; for the Vendue opened, and they began to buy extravagantly, notwithstanding all his Cautions, and their own Fear of Taxes.

War was still raging between France and England when Franklin sailed from America. In this vivid passage from his *Autobiography,* Franklin told how close his ship came to disaster, because of the captain's fear of capture by the French.

Autobiography, 1788

We were several times chas'd on our Passage, but outsail'd every thing, and in thirty Days had Soundings. We had a good Observation, and the Captain judg'd himself so near our Port, (Falmouth) that if we made a good Run in the Night we might be off the Mouth of that Harbour in the Morning, and by running in the Night might escape the Notice of the Enemy's Privateers, who often cruis'd near the Entrance of the Channel. Accordingly all the Sail was set that we could possibly make, and the Wind being very fresh and fair, we went right before it, and made great Way. The Captain after his Observation, shap'd his Course as he thought so as to pass wide of the Scilly Isles; but it seems there is sometimes a strong Indraught setting up St. George's Channel which deceives Seamen.... This Indraught was probably the Cause of what happen'd to us. We had a Watchman plac'd in the Bow to whom they often call'd, *Look well out before, there;* and he as often answer'd, *Aye, aye!* But perhaps had his Eyes shut, and was half asleep at the time: they sometimes answering as is said mechanically: For he did not see a Light just before us which had been hid by the Studding Sails from the Man at Helm and from the rest of the Watch; but by an accidental Yaw of the Ship was discover'd, and occasion'd a great Alarm, we being very near it, the light appearing to me as big as a Cart Wheel. It was Midnight, and Our Captain fast asleep. But Capt. Kennedy jumping upon Deck, and seeing the Danger, ordered the Ship to wear round, all Sails standing, An Operation dangerous to the Masts, but it carried us clear, and we escap'd Shipwreck, for we were running right upon the Rocks on which the Lighthouse was erected. This Deliverance impress'd me strongly with the Utility of Lighthouses and made me resolve to encourage the building more of them in America, if I should live to return there.

In the Morning it was found by the Soundings, &c. that we were near our Port, but a thick Fog hid the Land from our Sight. About 9 a Clock the Fog began to rise, and seem'd to be lifted up from the Water like the Curtain at the Play-house, discovering underneath the Town of Falmouth, the Vessels in its Harbour, and the Fields that surrounded it. A most pleasing Spectacle to those who had been so long without any other Prospects, than the uniform View of a vacant Ocean!

William Franklin, now twenty-six years old, accompanied his father as his secretary. He also planned to study law in England and be admitted to the bar. For some years he had been reading in the law office of Joseph Galloway, Franklin's loyal lieutenant in the Pennsylvania Assembly. Father and son paused to sightsee a little on the three-hundred-mile trip from Falmouth, viewing Stonehenge, the prehistoric ruin on Salisbury Plain, and the Roman antiquities collected by Lord Pembroke in his house and gardens at Wilton. They arrived in London on July 26, 1757, and took rooms at the Bear Inn on the Southwark end of old London Bridge. The next day they visited Peter Collinson, and from his offices Franklin dashed off this note to Deborah reporting their safe arrival.

London, July 27. 1757

My dear Child

We arrived here well last Night, only a little fatigued with the last Day's Journey, being 70 Miles. I write only this Line, not knowing of any Opportunity to send it; but Mr. Collinson will enquire for one, as he is going out. If he finds one, I shall write more largely. I have just seen Mr. Strahan, who is well with his Family. Billy is with me here at Mr. Collinson's, and presents his Duty to you, and Love to his Sister. My Love to all. I am, my dear Child, Your loving Husband

B FRANKLIN

159

Chapter 6

To England with Love

A few days after Franklin arrived in London, and met the friends whom
he had known only by correspondence, William Strahan and Peter
Collinson, he declared himself ready to tackle the Penns. Collinson and
another Quaker friend of Pennsylvania, Dr. John Fothergill, a prominent
London physician, advised Franklin against complaining to Crown officials.
They recommended negotiating directly with the Proprietors to work out
a compromise, and Dr. Fothergill arranged an interview between Franklin
and the Penns. Thomas Penn, as principal Proprietor, was the spokesman.
Here, from the *Autobiography*, is Franklin's version of the meeting.

Autobiography, 1789–90

After some Days, Dr. Fothergill having spoken to the
Proprietaries, they agreed to a Meeting with me at Mr. T.
Penn's House in Spring Garden. The Conversation at first
consisted of mutual Declarations of Disposition to reasonable Accommodation; but I suppose each Party had its
own ideas of what should be meant by *reasonable*. We
then went into Consideration of our several Points of
Complaint which I enumerated. The Proprietaries justify'd
their Conduct as well as they could, and I the Assembly's.
We now appeared very wide, and so far from each other
in our Opinions, as to discourage all Hope of Agreement.
However, it was concluded that I should give them the
Heads of our Complaints in Writing, and they promis'd
then to consider them. I did so soon after; but they put
the Paper into the Hands of the Solicitor Ferdinando John
Paris, who manag'd for them all their Law Business in
their great Suit with the neighbouring Proprietary of
Maryland, Lord Baltimore, which had subsisted 70 Years,
and wrote for them all their Papers and Messages in their

Dispute with the Assembly. He was a proud angry Man; and as I had occasionally in the Answers of the Assembly treated his Papers with some Severity, they being really weak in point of Argument, and haughty in Expression, he had conceiv'd a mortal Enmity to me, which discovering itself whenever we met, I declin'd the Proprietary's Proposal that he and I should discuss the Heads of Complaint between our two selves, and refus'd treating with any one but them.

In the midst of this discouraging business, Franklin contracted one of the few serious illnesses of his life. He took to his bed, and not until November 22, 1757, did he have the strength to write Deborah and tell her of his ordeal. "Cupping" refers to bloodletting, a standard medical treatment of the day. The "bark" is quinine, frequently prescribed to fight fever. That Franklin survived this heroic approach to medicine is a tribute to his tough constitution.

Trade card of an English "cupper"

London, Nov. 22. 1757

The 2d of September I wrote to you that I had had a violent cold and something of a fever, but that it was almost gone. However, it was not long before I had another severe cold, which continued longer than the first, attended by great pain in my head, the top of which was very hot, and when the pain went off, very sore and tender. These fits of pain continued sometimes longer than at others; seldom less than 12 hours, and once 36 hours. I was now and then a little delirious: they cupped me on the back of the head which seemed to ease me for the present; I took a great deal of bark, both in substance and infusion, and too soon thinking myself well, I ventured out twice, to do a little business and forward the service I am engaged in, and both times got fresh cold and fell down again; my good Doctor grew very angry with me, for acting so contrary to his Cautions and Directions, and oblig'd me to promise more Observance for the future. He attended me very carefully and affectionately; and the good Lady of the House nursed me kindly; Billy was also of great Service to me, in going from place to place, where I could not go myself, and Peter was very diligent and attentive. I took so much bark in various ways that I began to abhor it; I durst not take a vomit, for fear of my head; but at last I was seized one morning with a vomiting and purging, the latter of which continued the greater part of the day, and I believe was a kind of crisis to the distemper, carrying it clear off; for ever since I feel quite lightsome, and am every day gathering strength; so I hope my seasoning is over, and that I shall enjoy better health during the rest of my stay in England....

I make no doubt but Reports will be spread by my Enemies to my Disadvantage, but let none of them trouble you. If I find I can do my Country no Good, I will take care, at least, not to do it any Harm. I will neither seek nor accept of any thing for my self; and though I may perhaps not be able to obtain for the People what they wish and expect, no Interest shall induce me to betray the Trust they have repos'd in me....

Had I been well, I intended to have gone round among the Shops, and bought some pretty things for you and my dear good Sally, (whose little hands you say eased your headache) to send by this ship, but I must now defer it to the next, having only got a crimson satin cloak for you, the newest fashion, and the black-silk for Sally; but Billy sends her a scarlet feather, muff, and tippet, and a box of fashionable linen for her dress;...

The agreable Conversation I meet with among Men of Learning, and the Notice taken of me by Persons of Distinction, are the principal Things that sooth me for the present under this painful Absence from my Family and Friends; yet those would not detain me here another Week, if I had not other Inducements, Duty to my Country and Hopes of being able to do it Service.

Trade card of the kind of London fabric shop frequented by Franklin

On January 14, 1758, Franklin told Deborah that he was growing "daily stronger and better," but was not yet his old self: "much writing still disorders me." He added that he "would be glad if I could tell you when I expected to be at home, but that is still in the dark." His report of a recent conference with the Penns, sent the same day to Isaac Norris, Speaker of the Pennsylvania Assembly, made it sound very much as though the argument was going to continue for a long time. The letter survives only in an extract that Norris made from it. But the third person opening quickly shifts to the first person, and undoubtedly contains most of Franklin's real language—language that outraged the Penns, when they heard about the letter through their informants in Pennsylvania.

[London] Dated Janry: 14. 1758.
Extract from Mr. Franklin's Letter.

Benjamin Franklin insisted in a Conference with the Proprietaries, that if, when Commissioners were named

Thomas Penn, "the principal Proprietor" of Pennsylvania, and his brother Richard (below)

in a Bill, the Governor might not strike out or change them at his Pleasure, as none but his own Creatures might be admitted, and the Assembly might as well trust him with the whole, and this it was an undoubted Right of the House of Commons to name Commissioners in Bills in all Cases where they thought it necessary and proper, and to have such Commissioners so named stand without Alteration and Amendment and therefore our Assembly claimed the said Privileges; To which He answered that in such Cases, that before the House of Commons inserted the Names of Commissioners in Bills, the List was privately settled with the Ministry by the Committees; but tho' it might be a Privilege of the House of Commons, it did not follow that it was the Privilege of a Pennsylvania Assembly. That We were only a kind of Corporation acting by a Charter from the Crown and could have no Privileges or Rights but what was granted by that Charter, in which no such Privilege as We now claim was any where mentioned. *But says I* Your Father's Charter expressly says that the Assembly of Pennsylvania shall have all the Power and Privileges of an Assembly according to the Rights of the Freeborn Subjects of England, and as is usual in any of the British Plantations in America. *Yes says he* but, if my Father granted Privileges he was not by the Royal Charter impowered to grant, Nothing can be claim'd by such Grant. *I said,* If then your Father had no Right to grant the Privileges He pretended to grant, and published all over Europe as granted those who came to settle in the Province upon the Faith of that Grant and in Expectation of enjoying the Privileges contained in it, were deceived, cheated and betrayed. *He answered* they should have themselves looked to that. That the Royal Charter was no Secret; they who came into the Province on my Father's Offer of Privileges, if, they were deceiv'd, it was their own Fault; and that He said with a Kind of triumphing laughing Insolence, such as a low Jockey might do when a Purchaser complained that He had cheated him in a Horse. I was astonished to see him thus meanly give up his Father's Character and conceived that Moment a more cordial and thorough Contempt for him than I ever before felt for any Man living—A Contempt that I cannot express in Words, but I believe my Countenance expressed it strongly. And that his Brother was looking at me, must have observed it; however finding myself grow warm I made no other Answer to this than that the poor People were no Lawyers themselves and confiding in his Father did not think it necessary to consult any.

Franklin's interest in his English ancestors inspired him to take a journey into Northamptonshire to find out more about the history of his family. In this long letter to Deborah, he told much of what he summarized in his *Autobiography* about the English Franklins. But this has the charm of added detail and fresh news. He began his journey after being feted at Cambridge's commencement in July.

Cambridge University looked like this when Franklin and his son attended commencement ceremonies there early in July of 1758.

London, September 6, 1758. After the commencement, we went from Cambridge, through Huntingdonshire into Northamptonshire, and at Wellingborough; on inquiry we found still living Mary Fisher, whose maiden name was Franklin, daughter and only child of Thomas Franklin, my father's eldest brother: she is five years older than sister Douse, and remembers her going away with my father and his then wife, and two other children to New England, about the year, 1685. We have had no correspondence with her since my uncle Benjamin's death, now near 30 years. I knew she had lived at Wellingborough, and had married there to one Mr. Richard Fisher, a grazier and tanner, about fifty years ago, but did not expect to see either of them alive, so inquired for their posterity; I was directed to their house and we found them both alive, but weak with age, very glad however to see us; she seems to have been a very smart, sensible woman. They are wealthy, have left off business, and live comfortably. They have had only one child, a daughter, who died, when about thirty years of age, unmarried; she gave me several of my uncle Benjamin's letters to her, and acquainted me where the other remains of the family lived, of which I have, since my return to London, found out a daughter of my father's only sister, very old, and was never married. She is a good clever woman, but poor, though vastly contented with her situation and very cheerful. The others are in different parts of the country: I intend to visit them, but they were too much out of our tour in that journey. From Wellingborough we went to Ecton, about three or four miles, being the village where my father was born, and where his father, grandfather, and great-grandfather had lived, and how many of the family before we know not. We went first to see the old house and grounds; they came to Mr.

In Ecton Franklin visited the small house where his father was born and the church where his ancestors had worshiped and were buried.

Fisher with his wife, and after letting them for some years finding his rent something ill paid, he sold them. The land is now added to another farm, and a school kept in the house: it is a decayed old stone building, but still known by the name of Franklin House. Thence we went to visit the rector of the parish, who lives close by the church, a very antient building. He entertained us very kindly, and showed us the old church register, in which were the births, marriages, and burials of our ancestors for 200 years, as early as his book began. His wife a good-natured chatty old lady, (grandaughter of the famous archdeacon Palmer, who formerly had that parish, and lived there,) remembered a great deal about the family; carried us out into the church-yard, and showed us several of their grave stones, which were so covered with moss that we could not read the letters till she ordered a hard brush and basin of water, with which Peter scoured them clean, and then Billy copied them. She entertained and diverted us highly with stories of Thomas Franklin, Mrs. Fisher's father, who was a conveyancer, something of a lawyer, clerk of the county courts, and clerk to the archdeacon, in his visitations; a very leading man in all county affairs, and much employed in public business. He set on foot a subscription for erecting chimes in their steeple, and completed it, and we heard them play. He found out an easy method of saving their village meadows from being drowned, as they used to be sometimes by the river, which method is still in being; but when first proposed, nobody could conceive how it could be; but however they said if Franklin says he knows how to do it, it will be done. His advice and opinion was sought for on all occasions, by all sorts of people, and he was looked upon, she said, by some, as something of a conjurer.

In the autumn of 1759, Franklin, with his son, journeyed to Scotland, where he received a degree of Doctor of Laws from the University of St. Andrews. He made many friends in the course of this journey, including the philosopher David Hume and the jurist and man of letters Henry Home, Lord Kames. His lordship was famous as a practical joker, but he met his match in Franklin. Visiting the Kames estate in Berwick, Franklin startled the jurist by declaring, one evening, that the Old Testament recommended toleration. Presbyterian educated, Kames knew his Bible well, and he emphatically disagreed. Franklin called for a Bible, and proceeded to recite the following passage, which he introduced as a chapter from Genesis.

Lord Kames

Milne Square in Edinburgh, where Franklin lodged in 1759

CHAP. XXVII

1. And it came to pass after these Things, that Abraham sat in the Door of his Tent, about the going down of the Sun.

2. And behold a Man, bowed with Age, came from the Way of the Wilderness, leaning on a Staff.

3. And Abraham arose and met him, and said unto him, Turn in, I pray thee, and wash thy Feet, and tarry all Night, and thou shalt arise early on the Morrow, and go on thy Way.

4. And the Man said, Nay, for I will abide under this Tree.

5. But Abraham pressed him greatly; so he turned, and they went into the Tent; and Abraham baked unleavened Bread, and they did eat.

6. And when Abraham saw that the Man blessed not God, he said unto him, Wherefore dost thou not worship the most high God, Creator of Heaven and Earth?

7. And the Man answered and said, I do not worship the God thou speakest of; neither do I call upon his Name; for I have made to myself a God, which abideth alway in mine House, and provideth me with all Things.

8. And Abraham's Zeal was kindled against the Man; and he arose, and fell upon him, and drove him forth with Blows into the Wilderness.

9. And at Midnight God called unto Abraham, saying, Abraham, where is the Stranger?

10. And Abraham answered and said, Lord, he would not worship thee, neither would he call upon thy Name; therefore have I driven him out from before my Face into the Wilderness.

11. And God said, Have I born with him these hundred ninety and eight Years, and nourished him, and cloathed him, notwithstanding his Rebellion against me, and couldst not thou, that art thyself a Sinner, bear with him one Night?

12. And Abraham said, Let not the Anger of my Lord wax hot against his Servant. Lo, I have sinned; forgive me, I pray Thee:

13. And Abraham arose and went forth into the Wilderness, and sought diligently for the Man, and found him, and returned with him to his Tent; and when he had entreated him kindly, he sent him away on the Morrow with Gifts.

14.   And God spake again unto Abraham, saying, For this thy Sin shall thy Seed be afflicted four Hundred Years in a strange Land:

15.   But for thy Repentance will I deliver them; and they shall come forth with Power, and with Gladness of Heart, and with much Substance.

This "Parable against Persecution," as it has come to be known, was, of course, another Franklin hoax—a skillful imitation of the King James version of the Bible. Franklin wrote several similar imitations in the course of his life, recommending various virtues, such as brotherly love. With learned conversations, new friendships, jokes, and an honorary degree to treasure, Franklin looked back on his weeks in Scotland as "the densest happiness" he had ever experienced in his life. He returned to London to find the British celebrating another kind of triumph. General James Wolfe had won a magnificent victory on the Plains of Abraham, before Quebec, on September 13, 1759. It meant the end of French rule in North America and the imminent close of the Seven Years' War. Almost immediately, politically minded Britons began discussing peace terms. What, they asked, should be done with the rich sugar island of Guadeloupe in the West Indies, captured from the French earlier in the war. At this point in history, the West Indies produced far more wealth for England than did the North American Colonies, and thus generated substantial support in Parliament. Some politicians recommended that Britain return Canada to France in the peace negotiations and retain Guadeloupe. To Franklin this was not only idiocy, it was a callous disregard of America's safety and security. Without the French in Canada to supply the Indians with weapons and ammunition, there was at least a hope that the bloody border wars that had distressed Pennsylvania and neighboring Colonies for generations might finally come to an end. Franklin leaped into the debate over Canada with a series of letters in British newspapers, and finally with a closely reasoned essay, *The Interest of Great Britain Considered*, published in April, 1760. A brief, humorous version of this argument, which probably expressed more of Franklin's real feelings toward the notion of returning Canada, appeared anonymously in William Strahan's paper, *The London Chronicle*.

[London, December 27, 1759]

Mr. Chronicle,

We Britons are a nation of statesmen and politicians; we are privy councellors by birthright; and therefore take it much amiss when we are told by some of your correspondents, "that it is not proper to expose to public view the many good reasons there are for restoring Canada," (*if we reduce it.*)

I have, with great industry, been able to procure a full

account of those reasons, and shall make no secret of them among ourselves. Here they are. Give them to all your readers; that is, to all that can read, in the King's dominions.

1.   We should restore Canada; because an uninterrupted trade with the Indians throughout a vast country, where the communication by water is so easy, would encrease our commerce, *already too great*, and occasion a large additional demand for our manufactures, *already too dear.*

2.   We should restore it, lest, thro' a greater plenty of beaver, broad-brimmed hats become cheaper to that unmannerly sect, the Quakers.

3.   We should restore Canada, that we may *soon* have a new war, and another opportunity of spending two or three millions a year in America; there being great danger of our growing too rich, our European expences not being sufficient to drain our immense treasures.

4.   We should restore it, that we may have occasion constantly to employ, in time of war, a fleet and army in those parts; for otherwise we might be too strong at home.

5.   We should restore it, that the French may, by means of their Indians, carry on, (as they have done for these 100 years past even in times of peace between the two crowns) a constant scalping war against our colonies, and thereby stint their growth; for, otherwise, the children might in time be as tall as their mother.

6.   What tho' the blood of thousands of unarmed English farmers, surprized and assassinated in their fields; of harmless women and children murdered in their beds; doth at length call for vengeance; — what tho' the Canadian measure of iniquity be full, and if ever any country did, that country now certainly does, deserve the judgment of *extirpation:* — yet let not us be the executioners of Divine justice; — it will look as if Englishmen were revengeful.

7.   Our colonies, 'tis true, have exerted themselves beyond their strength, on the expectations we gave them of driving the French from Canada; but tho' we ought to keep faith with our Allies, it is not necessary with our children. That might teach them (against Scripture) to *put their trust in Princes:* Let 'em learn to trust in God.

8.   Should we not restore Canada, it would look as if our statesmen had *courage* as well as our soldiers; but what have statesmen to do with *courage?* Their proper

character is *wisdom.*

9.   What can be *braver,* than to show all Europe we can afford to lavish our best blood as well as our treasure, in conquests we do not intend to keep?...

10.   The French have long since openly declar'd, *"que les Anglois et les François sont incompatible dans cette partie de l'Amerique;"* "that our people and theirs were incompatible in that part of the continent of America:" *"que rien n'etoit plus important à l'etat, que de delivrer leur colonie du facheux voisinage des Anglois;"* "that nothing was of more importance to France, than delivering its colony from the troublesome neighbourhood of the English;"...Now, if we do not fairly leave the French in Canada, till they have a favourable opportunity of putting their *burning* and *ruining* schemes in execution, will it not look as if we were afraid of them?...

I will not dissemble, Mr. Chronicle; that in answer to all these reasons and motives for restoring Canada, I have heard one that appears to have some weight on the other side of the question. It is said, that nations, as well as private persons, should, for their honour's sake, take care to preserve a *consistence of character:* that it has always been the character of the English to fight strongly, and negotiate weakly; generally agreeing to restore, at a peace, what they ought to have kept, and to keep what they had better have restored: then, if it would really, according to the preceding reasons, be prudent and right to restore Canada, we ought, say these objectors, to keep it; otherwise *we shall be inconsistent with ourselves.* I shall not take upon myself to weigh these different reasons, but offer the whole to the consideration of the public. Only permit me to suggest, that there is one method of avoiding fairly all future dispute about the propriety of *keeping* or *restoring* Canada; and that is, *let us never take it.* The French still hold out at Montreal and Trois Rivieres, in hopes of succour from France. Let us be but *a little too late* with our ships in the river St. Laurence, so that the enemy may get their supplies up next spring, as they did the last, with reinforcements sufficient to enable them to recover Quebec....

The following letter to Deborah gives us a glimpse of a Franklin family drama. William Strahan had become more and more insistent that Franklin settle in England. He had urged Deborah to come over

Franklin's essay on the Canada question was published in London.

before some Englishwoman captured her husband. He then made a serious proposal of marriage between his son and Sally.

London, March 5. 1760

I receiv'd the Enclos'd some time since from Mr. Strahan. I afterwards spent an Evening in Conversation with him on the Subject. He was very urgent with me to stay in England and prevail with you to remove hither with Sally. He propos'd several advantageous Schemes to me which appear'd reasonably founded. His Family is a very agreable one; Mrs. Strahan a sensible [and] good Woman, the Children of amiable [char]acters and particularly the young Man, [who is] sober, ingenious and industrious, and a [desirable] Person. In Point of Circumstances [there can] be no Objection, Mr. Strahan being [in so thriving] a Way, as to lay up a Thousand [Pounds] every Year from the Profits of his Business, after maintaining his Family and paying all Charges. I gave him, however, two Reasons why I could not think of removing hither. One, my Affection to Pensilvania, and long established Friendships and other Connections there: The other, your invincible Aversion to crossing the Seas. And without removing hither, I could not think of parting with my Daughter to such a Distance. I thank'd him for the Regard shown us in the Proposal; but gave him no Expectation that I should forward the Letters.

John Baskerville

The opportunity to play a joke on a supposed expert was something that Franklin frequently found irresistible. In this letter to the English printer John Baskerville, whom he had met in Birmingham, Franklin deliciously described one of his most successful gambits. Baskerville's typeface was thicker in the heavy strokes, finer in the light ones, and sharper at the angles than the more familiar Caslon type. Many conservatives declared it difficult to read, and it took many years for Baskerville to win popularity. When he published his Cambridge Bible in August, 1763, Baskerville, conscious of the widespread criticism, included an extract of this letter from Franklin.

Craven-Street, London [1760?]

Dear Sir,

Let me give you a pleasant Instance of the Prejudice some have entertained against your Work. Soon after I returned, discoursing with a Gentleman concerning the Artists of Birmingham, he said you would be a Means of blinding all the Readers in the Nation, for the Strokes of your Letters being too thin and narrow, hurt the Eye,

and he could never read a Line of them without Pain.
I thought, said I, you were going to complain of the
Gloss on the Paper, some object to: No, no, says he, I
have heard that mentioned, but it is not that; 'tis in the
Form and Cut of the Letters themselves; they have not
that natural and easy Proportion between the Height
and Thickness of the Stroke, which makes the common
Printing so much more comfortable to the Eye. You see
this Gentleman was a Connoisseur. In vain I endeavoured to support your *Character* against the Charge; he
knew what he felt, he could see the Reason of it, and
several other Gentlemen among his Friends had made
the same Observation, &c. Yesterday he called to visit
me, when, mischievously bent to try his Judgment, I
stept into my Closet, tore off the Top of Mr. Caslon's
Specimen, and produced it to him as yours brought with
me from Birmingham, saying, I had been examining it
since he spoke to me, and could not for my Life perceive
the Disproportion he mentioned, desiring him to point
it out to me. He readily undertook it, and went over
the several Founts, shewing me every-where what he
thought Instances of that Disproportion; and declared,
that he could not then read the Specimen without feeling very strongly the Pain he had mentioned to me. I
spared him that Time the Confusion of being told, that
these were the Types he had been reading all his Life
with so much Ease to his Eyes; the Types his adored
Newton is printed with, on which he has pored not a
little; nay, the very Types his own Book is printed with,
for he is himself an Author; and yet never discovered
this painful Disproportion in them, till he thought they
were yours.

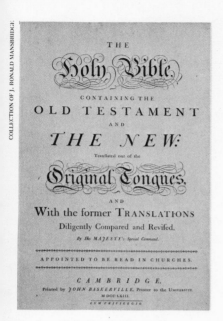

Baskerville's Cambridge Bible

Franklin was a deeply paternal man. He converted
almost every circle in which he moved into a kind of family, with himself
as the father. His life in London was no exception to this pattern. Soon after
his arrival, he and William had rented four rooms at Number 7, Craven
Street, within easy walking distance of the government offices in Whitehall
and the Houses of Parliament. Mrs. Stevenson, his landlady, was a widow,
and her eighteen-year-old daughter Mary, known to the family as Polly, was
an intelligent and sensitive young girl, who soon came to regard Franklin
as her second father. He was delighted when she showed an interest in
science, and this letter was the beginning of a series in which Franklin
attempted to answer her scientific questions.

Cravenstreet, June 11. 1760

Dear Polly,

'Tis a very sensible Question you ask, how the Air can affect the Barometer, when its Opening appears covered with Wood? If indeed it was so closely covered as to admit of no Communication of the outward Air to the Surface of the Mercury, the Change of Weight in the Air could not possibly affect it. But the least Crevice is sufficient for the Purpose; a Pinhole will do the Business. And if you could look behind the Frame to which your Barometer is fixed, you would certainly find some small Opening....

Your Observation on what you have lately read concerning Insects, is very just and solid. Superficial Minds are apt to despise those who make that Part of Creation their Study, as mere Triflers; but certainly the World has been much oblig'd to them. Under the Care and Management of Man, the Labours of the little Silkworm afford Employment and Subsistence to Thousands of Families, and become an immense Article of Commerce. The Bee, too, yields us its delicious Honey, and its Wax useful to a multitude of Purposes. Another Insect, it is said, produces the Cochineal, from whence we have our rich Scarlet Dye. The Usefulness of the Cantharides, or Spanish Flies, in Medicine, is known to all, and Thousands owe their Lives to that Knowledge. By human Industry and Observation, other Properties of other Insects may possibly be hereafter discovered, and of equal Utility. A thorough Acquaintance with the Nature of these little Creatures, may also enable Mankind to prevent the Increase of such as are noxious or secure us against the Mischiefs they occasion....

There is, however, a prudent Moderation to be used in Studies of this kind. The Knowledge of Nature may be ornamental, and it may be useful, but if to attain an Eminence in that, we neglect the Knowledge and Practice of essential Duties, we deserve Reprehension. For there is no Rank in Natural Knowledge of equal Dignity and Importance with that of being a good Parent, a good Child, a good Husband, or Wife, a good Neighbour or Friend, a good Subject or Citizen, that is, in short, a good Christian. Nicholas Gimcrack, therefore, who neglected the Care of his Family, to pursue Butterflies, was a just Object of Ridicule....

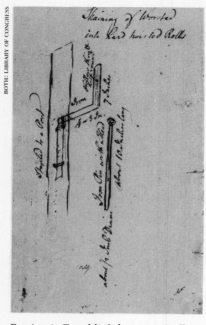

Benjamin Franklin's letters to Polly Stevenson were often scientific and occasionally contained sketches, like this device for "Skeining of Worsted."

In England Franklin busied himself with another invention—the armonica. The idea of a musical instrument made of glasses was not new. By 1761, the instrument had become so popular in London that one of the more skillful professional performers published a set of instructions on how to play it. A friend in the Royal Society introduced the pastime to Franklin, who had inherited from his father a strong interest in music and a modest talent. It did not take him long to find the armonicas then in use very unsatisfactory. The glasses had to be filled with just the right amount of water before each performance, and providing enough glasses to give the instrument a decent range created armonicas so large that it was impossible to play them seated from a single position. In this letter to the Italian scientist and writer Giovanni Battista Beccaria, Franklin told of his improved version of the instrument. It became extremely popular on the Continent, and two of Franklin's protégées, Marianne and Cecilia Davies, gave public concerts across Europe, culminating in Vienna, where they played and sang at the marriage of the Archduchess Amalia to Duke Ferdinand of Parma. Mozart, Beethoven, and several other famous musicians composed music for the armonica. Eventually, however, the instrument got a very bad reputation, because its remarkably sweet and ethereal music was thought to have a depressing effect on the players, even to producing numerous nervous breakdowns.

London, July 13, 1762

Rev. Sir,

I once promised myself the pleasure of seeing you at Turin, but as that is not now likely to happen, being just about returning to my native country, America, I sit down to take leave of you (among others of my European friends that I cannot see) by writing.

I thank you for the honourable mention you have so frequently made of me in your letters to Mr. Collinson and others, for the generous defence you undertook and executed with so much success, of my electrical opinions; and for the valuable present you have made me of your new work, from which I have received great information and pleasure. I wish I could in return entertain you with any thing new of mine on that subject; but I have not lately pursued it. Nor do I know of any one here that is at present much engaged in it.

Perhaps, however, it may be agreeable to you, as you live in a musical country, to have an account of the new instrument lately added here to the great number that charming science was before possessed of: As it is an instrument that seems peculiarly adapted to Italian music, especially that of the soft and plaintive kind, I

Franklin's armonica

will endeavour to give you such a description of it, and of the manner of constructing it, that you, or any of your friends may be enabled to imitate it, if you incline so to do, without being at the expence and trouble of the many experiments I have made in endeavouring to bring it to its present perfection.

You have doubtless heard the sweet tone that is drawn from a drinking glass, by passing a wet finger round its brim. One Mr. Puckeridge, a gentleman from Ireland, was the first who thought of playing tunes, formed of these tones. He collected a number of glasses of different sizes, fixed them near each other on a table, and tuned them by putting into them water, more or less, as each note required. The tones were brought out by passing his fingers round their brims. He was unfortunately burnt here, with his instrument, in a fire which consumed the house he lived in. Mr. E. Delaval, a most ingenious member of our Royal Society, made one in imitation of it, with a better choice and form of glasses, which was the first I saw or heard. Being charmed with the sweetness of its tones, and the music he produced from it, I wished only to see the glasses disposed in a more convenient form, and brought together in a narrower compass, so as to admit of a greater number of tones, and all within reach of hand to a person sitting before the instrument, which I accomplished, after various intermediate trials. . . .

My largest glass is a G a little below the reach of a common voice, and my highest G, including three compleat octaves. To distinguish the glasses the more readily to the eye, I have painted the apparent parts of the glasses within side, every semitone white and the other notes of the octave with the seven prismatic colours, *viz.* C, red; D, orange; E, yellow; F, green; G, blue; A, Indigo; B, purple; and C, red again; so that glasses of the same colour (the white excepted) are always octaves to each other.

This instrument is played upon, by sitting before the middle of the set of glasses as before the keys of a harpsichord, turning them with the foot, and wetting them now and then with a spunge and clean water. The fingers should first be a little soaked in water and quite free from all greasiness; a little fine chalk upon them is sometimes useful, to make them catch the glass and bring out the tone more readily. Both hands are used, by which means different parts are played together. Observe, that the tones

Ticket to the coronation of
George III on September 22, 1761,
which Franklin attended

are best drawn out when the glasses turn *from* the ends of the fingers, not when they turn *to* them.

The advantages of this instrument are, that its tones are incomparably sweet beyond those of any other; that they may be swelled and softened at pleasure by stronger or weaker pressures of the finger, and continued to any length; and that the instrument, being once well tuned, never again wants tuning.

In honour of your musical language, I have borrowed from it the name of this instrument, calling it the Armonica.

By this time, Franklin had received another honorary degree, Doctor of Civil Law from Oxford University. He also completed his negotiations with the Penns. In a compromise, Franklin won the Privy Council's approval for taxing the Proprietors' lands on an equitable basis in return for having agreed to abandon a few other minor points in dispute. By now a new king was on the throne. George III had succeeded his grandfather, George II, on October 25, 1760. William Pitt resigned as Secretary of State, and the Peace Party soon had control of the government. His business almost completed, Franklin made plans to go home. But he stayed long enough to win another victory. William Franklin had by this time obtained his law degree, and his father, through friends that were influential with the new king, obtained for him the Royal Governorship of New Jersey. Although Franklin had tried to arrange a marriage between him and Polly Stevenson, William now married a "West Indian charmer"—Elizabeth Downes, whom he had been courting for a number of years. In the following letters, Franklin said good-bye to Polly Stevenson and to William Strahan, who had become his closest friend in England.

Portsmouth, Augt. 11. 1762

My dear Polly

This is the best Paper I can get at this wretched Inn, but it will convey what is intrusted to it as faithfully as the finest. It will tell my Polly, how much her Friend is afflicted, that he must, perhaps never again, see one for whom he has so sincere an Affection, join'd to so perfect an Esteem; whom he once flatter'd himself might become his own in the tender Relation of a Child; but can now entertain such pleasing hopes no more; Will it tell *how much* he is afflicted? No, it cannot.

Adieu, my dearest Child: I will call you so; Why should I not call you so, since I love you with all the Tenderness, all the Fondness of a Father? Adieu. May the God of all Goodness shower down his choicest Blessings upon you, and make you infinitely Happier than that Event could

175

have made you. Adieu. And wherever I am, believe me to be, with unalterable Affection, my dear Polly, Your sincere Friend

B FRANKLIN

Portsmouth, Monday, Augt. 23. 1762

Dear Sir,

I have been two Nights on board expecting to sail, but the Wind continuing contrary, am just now come on shore again, and have met with your kind Letter of the 20th. I thank you even for the Reproofs it contains, tho' I have not altogether deserved them. I cannot, I assure you, quit even this disagreable Place without Regret, as it carries me still farther from those I love, and from the Opportunities of hearing of their Welfare. The Attraction of *Reason* is at present for the other Side of the Water, but that of *Inclination* will be for this side. You know which usually prevails. I shall probably make but this one Vibration and settle here for ever. Nothing will prevent it, if I can, as I hope I can, prevail with Mrs. F. to accompany me; especially if we have a Peace. I will not tell you, that to be near and with you and yours, is any part of my Inducement: It would look like a Complement extorted from me by your Pretences to Insignificancy. Nor will I own that your Persuasions and Arguments have wrought this Change in my former Resolutions: tho' it is true that they have frequently intruded themselves into my Consideration whether I would or not. I trust, however, that we shall once more see each other and be happy again together, which God, etc.

My Love to Mrs. Strahan, and your amiable and valuable Children. Heaven bless you all, whatever becomes of Your much obliged and affectionate Friend

B FRANKLIN

Chapter 7

Birth of an Ambassador

Franklin returned to Philadelphia with an annoying worry nagging his mind. His enemy, William Smith, now provost of the College of Philadelphia, had spread numerous lies in England about Franklin's loss of popularity in Pennsylvania. This explains the note of triumph in the following letter to William Strahan describing the warm welcome Franklin had met in Philadelphia. Dr. Hawkesworth, mentioned in the opening line, was a writer and editor, who helped his wife run a school at Bromley, Kent; "my little Wife" refers to Strahan's daughter Margaret Penelope, a girl of eleven.

Philada. Dec. 2. 1762

Dear Straney,

As good Dr. Hawkesworth calls you, to whom my best Respects. I got home well the 1st. of November, and had the Happiness to find my little Family perfectly well; and that Dr. Smith's Reports of the Diminution of my Friends were all false. My House has been full of a Succession of them from Morning to Night ever since my Arrival, congratulating me on my Return with the utmost Cordiality and Affection. My Fellow Citizens while I was on the Sea, had, at the annual Election, chosen me unanimously, as they had done every Year while I was in England, to be their Representative in Assembly; and would, they say, if I had not disappointed them by coming privately to Town before they heard of my Landing, have met me with 500 Horse. Excuse my Vanity in writing this to you, who know what has provok'd me to it. My Love to good Mrs. Strahan, and your Children, particularly my little Wife. I shall write more fully per next Opportunity, having now only time to add, that I am, with unchangeable Affection, my dear Friend, Yours sincerely

B FRANKLIN

Back in Philadelphia, Franklin exchanged greetings with two of his favorite female correspondents, Catherine Ray, who had married her second cousin, William Greene, Jr., on April 30, 1758; and Jane Franklin Mecom. Although Franklin did not stay in England for William's wedding to Elizabeth Downes—"the Promotion and Marriage" of his son mentioned by Jane Mecom—he obviously liked his new daughter-in-law. So did William Strahan, who called her "as good a soul as breathes."

Philada: Nov 25th. 1762.

I received your kind congratulations on my return, and thank you cordially. It gives me great pleasure to hear you are married and live happily. You are a good Girl for complying with so essential a duty, and God will bless you. Make my compliments acceptable to your spouse; and fulfil your promise of writing to me; and let me know everything that has happened to you and your friends since my Departure, for I interest myself as much as ever in whatever relates to your Happiness. My best Respects to your Brother and Sister Ward, and Compliments on his advancement to the Government of your Colony; and believe me ever, My dear Caty Your affectionate Friend and humble servant

B FRANKLIN.

Philada. Nov. 25. 1762

Dear Sister,

I thank you for your obliging Letter of the 12th. Instant. My Wife says she will write to you largely by next Post, being at present short of Time. As to the Promotion and Marriage you mention, I shall now only say that the Lady is of so amiable a Character, that the latter gives me more Pleasure than the former, tho' I have no doubt but that he will make as good a Governor as Husband: for he has good Principles and good Dispositions, and I think is not deficient in good Understanding. I am as ever Your affectionate Brother

B FRANKLIN

But Franklin could not forget the happiness he had experienced during his years in England. In this letter to Polly Stevenson, he commented on it in the strongest possible terms.

Philada. March 25. 1763

Your pleasing Favour of Nov. 11 is now before me. It found me as you suppos'd it would, happy with my American Friends and Family about me; and it made me more happy in showing me that I am not yet forgotten by the dear Friends I left in England. And indeed why should I fear they will ever forget me, when I feel so strongly that I shall ever remember them! . . .

Of all the enviable Things England has, I envy it most its People. Why should that petty Island, which compar'd to America is but like a stepping Stone in a Brook, scarce enough of it above Water to keep one's Shoes dry; why, I say, should that little Island, enjoy in almost every Neighbourhood, more sensible, virtuous and elegant Minds, than we can collect in ranging 100 Leagues of our vast Forests.

Early in 1763, William Franklin arrived in Philadelphia with his wife. A few days later father and son journeyed to New Jersey, where William was installed as the province's new governor. In this letter to Strahan, Franklin told of that journey, commented on peace with France, and alluded to the possibility of his returning to England.

Philada. March 28. 1763

I have received your Favours of Oct. 20 and Nov. 1 by my Son who is safely arrived with my new Daughter. I thank you for your Friendly Congratulations on his Promotion. I am just return'd from a Journey I made with him thro' his Government, and had the Pleasure of seeing him every where receiv'd with the utmost Respect and even Affection by all Ranks of People. So that I have great Hopes of his being now comfortably settled.

As to myself, I mention'd to you in a former Letter, that I found my Friends here more numerous and as hearty as ever. It had been industriously reported, that I had lived very extravagantly in England, and wasted a considerable Sum of the Publick Money which I had received out of your Treasury for the Province; but the Assembly, when they came to examine my Accounts and allow me for my Services, found themselves Two Thousand two hundred and fourteen Pounds 10*s*. 7*d*. Sterling in my Debt; to the utter Confusion of the Propagators of that Falshood, and the Surprize of all they had made to believe it. The House accordingly order'd that Sum to be paid me, and that the Speaker

Detail from a 1764 cartoon showing Franklin (left) holding a paper on which is written: "Resolves, ye Proprietaries are knave and tyrant."

should moreover present me with their Thanks for my Fidelity, &c. in transacting their Affairs.

I congratulate you on the glorious Peace your Ministry have made, the most advantageous to Britain, in my Opinion, of any your Annals have recorded. As to the Places left or restor'd to France, I conceive our Strength will now soon increase to so great a degree in North America, that in any future War we may with ease reduce them all; and therefore I look on them as so many Hostages or Pledges of good Behaviour from that perfidious Nation. Your Pamphlets and Papers therefore that are wrote against the Peace with some Plausibility, give one Pleasure, as I hope the French will read them, and be persuaded they have made an excellent Bargain....

I do not forget any of your Reasons for my Return to England. The Hint you add in your last, is good and wise; it could not have been wiser or better if you had drank ever so much Madeira. It is however, impossible for me to execute that Resolution this ensuing Summer, having many Affairs first to arrange; but I trust I shall see you before you look much older.

In the summer of 1763 Franklin turned his attention to the condition of the Post Office. He instituted various improvements in the service, as he made clear in this letter to Anthony Todd, Secretary of the British Post Office.

[Philadelphia, January 16, 1764]
In my last I wrote you that Mr. Foxcroft, my Colleague, was gone to Virginia where and in Maryland some offices are yet unsettled. We are to meet again in April at Annapolis, and then shall send you a full Account of our Doings. I will now only just mention, that we hope in the Spring to expedite the Communication between Boston and New York, as we have already that between New York and Philadelphia, by making the Mails travel by Night as well as by Day, which has never heretofore been done in America. It passes now between Philadelphia and New York, so quick that a Letter can be sent from one place to another, and an Answer received the Day following, which before took a week, and when our Plan is executed between Boston and New York, Letters may be sent and answers received in four Days, which before took a fortnight; and between Philadelphia and Boston in Six days, which before required Three

Weeks. We think this expeditious Communication will greatly encrease the Number of Letters from Philadelphia and Boston by the Packets to Britain.

In spite of peace in Europe, the American frontier remained restless. In this letter to Richard Jackson, the member of Parliament who was now serving as Pennsylvania's agent, Franklin suggested how England might raise money in America in order to support the fourteen battalions the British high command felt it needed to keep the Indians quiet. He then added a succinct narration of an episode that shook Pennsylvania to its foundations. Presbyterian Irish from the township of Paxton murdered a group of peaceful Christian Indians in retaliation for the depredations committed by marauding tribes during the uprising known as Pontiac's War. Franklin condemned the murders in a scorching pamphlet. The frontiersmen reacted by marching on Philadelphia. Franklin hastily organized the Philadelphia militia and then rode out to negotiate a truce with the leaders of the rebels. The opening paragraphs are an interesting indication of Franklin's conservative attitude at this point in his life. "Mr. W." is John Wilkes, the English agitator whose defiance of Parliament and of the laws of libel was roiling London.

"The March of the Paxton Men," a cartoon from 1764, showing Franklin (right) cheering his supporters

Philada. Feb. 11. 1764

I have just received your Favour by the extra Packet of Nov. 26. and am pleas'd to find a just Resentment so general in your House against Mr. W.'s seditious Conduct, and to hear that the present Administration is like to continue.

If Money *must* be raised from us to support 14 Batallions, as you mention, I think your Plan the most advantageous to both the Mother Country and Colonies of any I have seen. A moderate Duty on Foreign Mellasses maybe collected; when a high one could not. The same on foreign Wines; and a Duty not only on Tea, but on all East India Goods might perhaps not be amiss, as they are generally rather Luxuries than Necessaries; and many of your Manchester Manufactures might well supply their Places. The Duty on Negroes I could wish large enough to obstruct their Importation, as they every where prevent the Increase of Whites. But if you lay such Duties as may destroy our Trade with the Foreign Colonies, I think you will greatly hurt your own Interest as well as ours. I need not explain this to you, who will readily see it. The American Fishery, too, should be as little burthened as possible. It is to no purpose to enlarge on these Heads, as probably your Acts are pass'd

In another cartoon of 1764, Franklin (foreground) eyes a group of his Quaker friends, who are expressing their fears of the "Paxton spirit."

before this can reach you.

In my last I mention'd to you the Rioting on our Frontiers, in which 20 peaceable Indians were kill'd, who had long liv'd quietly among us. The Spirit of killing all Indians, Friends and Foes, spread amazingly thro' the whole Country: The Action was almost universally approved of by the common People; and the Rioters thence receiv'd such Encouragement, that they projected coming down to this City, 1000 in Number, arm'd, to destroy 140 Moravian and Quaker Indians, under Protection of the Government. To check this Spirit, and strengthen the Hands of the Government by Changing the Sentiments of the Populace, I wrote the enclos'd Pamphlet, which we had only time to circulate in this City and Neighbourhood, before we heard that the Insurgents were on their March from all Parts. It would perhaps be Vanity in me to imagine so slight a thing could have any extraordinary Effect. But however that may be, there was a sudden and very remarkable Change; and above 1000 of our Citizens took Arms to support the Government in the Protection of those poor Wretches. Near 500 of the Rioters had rendezvous'd at Germantown, and many more were expected; but the Fighting Face we put on made them more willing to hear Reason, and the Gentlemen sent out by the Governor and Council to discourse with them, found it no very difficult Matter to persuade them to disperse and go home quietly. They came from all Parts of our Frontier, and were armed with Rifle Guns and Tomhawks. You may judge what Hurry and Confusion we have been in for this Week past. I was up two Nights running, all Night, with our Governor; and my Rest so broken by Alarms on the other Nights, that the whole Week seems one confus'd Space of Time, without any such Distinction of Days, as that I can readily and certainly say, on such a Day such a thing happened. At present we are pretty quiet, and I hope that Quiet will continue. A Militia Bill is ordered by the House to be brought in, our Want of such a Law appearing on this Occasion to every-body; but whether we shall be able to frame one that will pass, is a Question. The Jealousy of an Addition of Power to the Proprietary Government, which is universally dislik'd here, will prevail with the House not to leave the sole Appointment of the Militia Officers in the Hands of the Governor; and he, I suppose, will insist upon it, and so the Bill will probably fall through; which perhaps is no great Matter, as your 14 Battallions will make all Militias in America needless, as well as put them out of Countenance.

The experience disgusted Franklin and made a collision between him and the proprietary government almost inevitable. The break came when the new proprietary governor refused to keep the agreement that Franklin had made with the Penns in England. The governor insisted that the Proprietors' lands could only be taxed at a rate no higher than the poorest quality land owned by other people. He also insisted that the Penns' town lots be exempted. Franklin and his followers now rammed through the Assembly a petition calling on the king to place Pennsylvania under a royal government. In this letter to Richard Jackson, Franklin declared war.

Philada. March 29. 1764

In my last I inform'd you that the Agreement between the Governor and Assembly was not likely long to continue. The enclos'd Paper will show you that the Breach is wider now than ever. And 'tis thought there will be a general Petition from the Inhabitants to the Crown, to take us under its immediate Government. I send you this early Notice of what is intended that you may prepare Minds for it, as they fall in your Way. If I can have time I will send you a Copy of the Bill we last sent up, and which was refused. But if it goes not by this Vessel, we shall send it via Lisbon in one that sails in a few Days.

Be assured, that we all think it impossible to go on any longer under a Proprietary Government. By the Resolves you will see, that never was greater Unanimity in any Assembly. Enclos'd I send you a Draft of what I think will be pretty nearly the Petition, that you may see the Tenor of it. Note, There was an Agreement between the First Proprietor W. Penn, and the Crown, for the Sale of the Government at £11,000 of which £2,000 was paid him. Note also, that the Crown has a great Sum in the Proprietaries Hands, half the Quitrents of the Lower Counties belonging to the Crown, of which the Proprietaries are Receivers, and I believe have never render'd any Account.

You will endear yourself to us forever, if you can get this Change of Government compleated.

I write in great haste....

THYRSIS, with a Pr*fb*t*rian Nofe. | CORIN, with a Q**k*ronian Nofe.

A 1764 book, The Squabble, A Pastoral Ecologue, *contains this rare caricature of Franklin (right) and criticizes his role in the Paxton case.*

The decision to oust the Proprietors provoked a tremendous political battle in Pennsylvania. They and their followers in turn mustered all their strength to oust Franklin's party from control of the Assembly. Pamphlets flew back and forth, and not a little verbal mud flew with them. Franklin was in the thick of the battle. Five days after the Assembly adjourned, he published explanatory remarks on the Assembly's Resolves and followed this up with a long essay, *Cool Thoughts on the Present Situation of Our Publick Affairs.* The proprietary party fought back with the publication of a speech by one of their leading spokesmen, John Dickinson. The preface to the speech was a panegyric on William Penn in the form of an epitaph. It was cleverly composed of phrases from Assembly documents between the years 1719 and 1756. William Penn's character was, of course, not really in dispute, and Franklin could not resist the opportunity to parody his opponents' efforts to make political capital out of the saintly Quaker founder. In a preface written for the publication of a speech by his political lieutenant Joseph Galloway, Franklin composed this counterepitaph on Penn's sons.

[Philadelphia, August 11, 1764]
Be this a Memorial
Of T⸻ and R⸻ P⸻,
P⸻ of P⸻
Who with Estates immense,
Almost beyond Computation,
When their own Province,
And the whole British Empire
Were engag'd in a bloody and most expensive War,
Begun for the Defence of those Estates,
Could yet meanly desire
To have those very Estates
Totally or Partially
Exempted from Taxation,
While their Fellow-Subjects all around them,
Groan'd
Under the universal Burthen.
To gain this Point,
They refus'd the necessary Laws
For the Defence of their People
And suffer'd their Colony to welter in its Blood,
Rather than abate in the least
Of these their dishonest Pretentions.
The Privileges granted by their Father
Wisely and benevolently
To encourage the first Settlers of the Province.
They,

COOL THOUGHTS

ON THE

PRESENT SITUATION

OF OUR

PUBLIC AFFAIRS.

In a Letter to a Friend in the Country.

PHILADELPHIA:
PRINTED BY W. DUNLAP. M, DCC, LXIV.

Franklin's opponents complained that this pamphlet was "distributed gratis by thousands" in Pennsylvania.

Foolishly and cruelly,
Taking Advantage of public Distress,
Have extorted from the Posterity of those Settlers;
And are daily endeavouring to reduce them
To the most abject Slavery:
Tho' to the Virtue and Industry of those People
In improving their Country,
They owe all that they possess and enjoy.
A striking Instance
Of human Depravity and Ingratitude;
And an irrefragable Proof,
That Wisdom and Goodness
Do not descend with an Inheritance;
But that ineffable Meanness
May be connected with unbounded Fortune.

The fiercely fought election of 1764 had a curious outcome. Franklin and Galloway were both narrowly defeated for reelection, but their party retained firm control of the Assembly. Undaunted, the anti-proprietary party promptly appointed Franklin a special agent to return to London and present their petition to remove the Proprietors and place Pennsylvania under the direct rule of the Crown. Franklin told the story in this brief letter to Richard Jackson.

Detail from a contemporary cartoon depicting Franklin's defeat in the 1764 election; Franklin is portrayed listening to the Devil.

HISTORICAL SOCIETY OF PENNSYLVANIA

Philada. Oct. 11. 1764
I have now only time to cover the enclos'd, and acquaint you that I am no longer in the Assembly. The Proprietary Party by great Industry against great Security carried the Election of this County and City by about 26 Votes against me and Mr. Galloway; the Voters near 4000. They carried (would you think it!) above 1000 Dutch from me, by printing part of my Paper sent to you 12 Years since on Peopling new Countries where I speak of the Palatine *Boors herding* together, which they explain'd that I call'd them a *Herd of Hogs*. This is quite a laughing Matter. But the Majority of the last Assembly remain, and will I believe still be for the Measure of Changing the Proprietary for a Royal Governor. I am, with great Respect Dear Sir, Your most humble Servant

B FRANKLIN

While the Proprietors' followers fumed, three hundred of Franklin's friends escorted him to Chester, where he went aboard the *King of Prussia* on November 7, 1764. As cannons boomed, everyone cheered lustily and sang a parody of "God Save the King:"

185

O LORD our GOD arise,
Scatter our Enemies,
    And make them fall.
Confound their Politicks,
Frustrate such Hypocrites,
Franklin, on Thee we fix,
    GOD Save us all.

The following night, aboard the ship as it anchored farther down the Delaware, Franklin's thoughts turned to his family. His chief concern was his daughter, who he feared would meet with numerous snubs and insults from his political enemies in Philadelphia. In the campaign they had attacked him scurrilously, dredging up the scandal of William's illegitimate birth and accusing Franklin of being a secret enemy of both the Germans and the Quakers. Out of this deep concern he wrote the following wise and tender letter to Sarah Franklin.

Reedy Island Nov. 8. 1764
7 at Night.

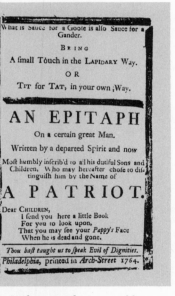

It was in this scurrilous pamphlet that Franklin's enemies dredged up the scandal of William's illegitimacy.

My dear Child, the natural Prudence and goodness of heart that God has blessed you with, make it less necessary for me to be particular in giving you Advice; I shall therefore only say, that the more attentively dutiful and tender you are towards your good Mama, the more you will recommend your self to me; But why shou'd I mention *me,* when you have so much higher a Promise in the Commandment, that such a conduct will recommend you to the favour of God. You know I have many Enemies (all indeed on the Public Account, for I cannot recollect that I have in a private Capacity given just cause of offence to any one whatever) yet they are Enemies and very bitter ones, and you must expect their Enmity will extend in some degree to you, so that your slightest Indiscretions will be magnified into crimes, in order the more sensibly to wound and afflict me. It is therefore the more necessary for you to be extreamly circumspect in all your Behaviour that no Advantage may be given to their Malevolence. Go constantly to Church whoever preaches. The Acts of Devotion in the common Prayer Book, are your principal Business there; and if properly attended to, will do more towards mending the Heart than Sermons generally can do. For they were composed by Men of much greater Piety and Wisdom, than our common Composers of Sermons can pretend to be. And therefore I wish you wou'd never miss the Prayer Days. Yet I do not mean that you shou'd despise Sermons even of the

Preachers you dislike, for the Discourse is often much better than the Man, as sweet and clear Waters come to us thro' very dirty Earth. I am the more particular on this Head, as you seem'd to express a little before I came away some Inclination to leave our Church, which I wou'd not have you do.

For the rest I would only recommend to you in my Absence to acquire those useful Accomplishments Arithmetick, and Bookkeeping. This you might do with Ease, if you wou'd resolve not to see Company on the Hours you set apart for those Studies....

We expect to be at Sea to morrow if this Wind holds, after which I shall have no opportunity of Writing to you till I arrive (if it pleases God that I do arrive) in England. I pray that *his* Blessing may attend you which is of more worth than a Thousand of mine, though they are never wanting. Give my Love to your Brother and Sister, as I cannot now write to them; and remember me affectionately to the young Ladies your Friends, and to our good Neighbours. I am, my dear Sally, Your ever Affectionate Father

B. FRANKLIN

His friends had wished Franklin thirty days' fair wind, and he gratefully reported to Deborah one month later that their wish had come true. He debarked from the *King of Prussia* on December 9, 1764, at Portsmouth and hurried on to London. A few days after he arrived, he dashed off the following note to Polly Stevenson.

[December 12–16, 1764]
I have once more the Pleasure of writing a Line to my dear Polly from Cravenstreet, where I arrived on Monday Evening in about 30 days from Philadelphia. Your good Mama was not at home, and the Maid could not tell where to find her, so I sat me down and waited her Return, when she was a good deal surpriz'd to find me in her Parlour.

Franklin wrote frequently to his wife Deborah, assuring her that he had no intention of staying in London very long. On February 14, 1765, he told her that "a few months I hope will finish affairs here to my wish, and bring me to that retirement and repose with my little family, so suitable to my years, and which I have so long set my heart upon." But London was almost a second home to him by now, and he was soon busily involved in writing and politicking, while he laid the groundwork for his petition to the king. One bit of politics that Franklin did not even bother to mention—at least it does not appear in any of his surviving letters from the early months of 1765—was his involvement with agents of other American Colonies in seeking to dissuade the British government, and the First Minister, George Grenville, in particular, to abandon the plan of raising money in America through a stamp tax on newspapers, legal documents, and numerous other items. In a conference with Franklin and three other agents on February 2, Grenville asked if they knew of a better way of raising the revenue that the British government needed to maintain troops in the border forts and pay the other expenses of the royal government in America. In letters from Pennsylvania the year before, Franklin had commented unfavorably on the idea of a stamp tax, and he now proposed to Grenville a plan for a system of Colonial paper currency under the regulation of Parliament. The users would pay a 6 per cent interest on the money, which would go to the Crown. To bolster his standing with Grenville, and make a better impression, Franklin persuaded Thomas Pownall, former Governor of Massachusetts and a recognized British authority on America, to join him in recommending the plan. With this letter, written on February 12, they submitted a long, detailed draft of how the scheme would work. If Grenville had taken Franklin's advice at this point, the American Revolution might never have taken place. But as Franklin told Joseph Galloway over a year later, Grenville was "besotted with his Stamp Scheme, which he rather chose to carry through."

London Feb. 12. 1765

Sir

We have taken the liberty to enclose and beg leave to submitt to your consideration a measure calculated for supplying the Colonies with a Paper Currency, become absolutely necessary to their Circumstances, by which Measure a certain and very considerable Revenue will arise to the crown.

We are from our Experience and the having been employed in the Public Service in America, intirely confident and certain of the Effect of this measure; And if we shall be so happy as to see it adopted, We are ready to explain the manner of carrying it into Execution—and beg Leave to offerr our services in the Administration and Execution of it on such Terms as Government upon consideration shall find most conducive to the Public Benefit. With the most perfect esteem we have the honour to be Sir Your most Obedient and most humble Servants.

T POWNALL
B FRANKLIN

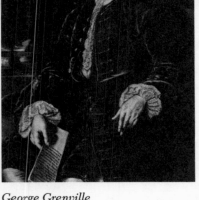

George Grenville

Throughout the first half of 1765, Franklin was optimistic about the chances of unseating the Penns. But the unsettled state of British politics made progress difficult, as he explained in this letter to his old Junto friend, Hugh Roberts. The ministry he mentioned was that headed by George Grenville.

London July 7th. 1765

Your kind Favour of May 20th. by the Hand of our good Friend Mr. Neave, gave me great Pleasure. I find on these Occasions, that Expressions of Steady continued Friendship such as are contain'd in your Letter, tho' but from one or a few honest and sensible Men who have long known us, afford a Satisfaction that far outweighs the clamorous Abuse of 1000 Knaves and Fools.

While I enjoy the Share I have so Long had in the Esteem of my old Friends, the Bird-and Beast-People you mention may peck and snarl and bark at me, as much as they think proper.

There is only some Danger that I should grow too Vain on their Disapprobation....

Our Affairs are at a total Stop here by the Present unsettled State of the Ministry. But will go forward again as soon as that is fix'd. Nothing yet appears that is Discourageing....

I wish you would continue to meet the Junto, notwithstanding that some Effects of our publick Political Misunderstandings may some times Appear there. 'Tis now perhaps one of the *oldest* Clubs, as I think it was formerly one of the *best*, in the Kings Dominions: it wants but about two Years of Forty since it was establish'd; We loved and still Love one another, we are Grown Grey together and yet it is to Early to Part. Let us Sit till the Evening of Life is spent, the Last Hours were allways the most joyous; when we can Stay no Longer 'tis time enough then to bid each other good Night, separate, and go quietly to bed.

Thomas Pownall

News from America soon shook Franklin's optimism. Philadelphia friends sent Franklin at least four different copies of a series of Resolves adopted by the Virginia House of Burgesses at the instance of one of their youngest and most eloquent members, Patrick Henry. The Virginia Resolves rejected Parliament's right to impose such taxes as those of the Stamp Act. In Pennsylvania, the proprietary party used the Stamp Act as a weapon against the Franklin-Galloway plan to remove the Penns. Galloway gloomily told Franklin that "the Prop—y Party and men in power here...

prevail on the People to give every Kind of opposition to the Execution of this Law. To incense their Minds against the King Lords and Commons, and to alienate their Affections from the Mother Country." The opposition to the Stamp Act in other Colonies was no less determined, and in Massachusetts it was tinged with violence. Franklin soon realized that he was in an extremely embarrassing situation. Grenville, in order to make the act more palatable to Americans, had asked Colonial agents to recommend reliable men for the job of stamp commissioners in the various Colonies. For Pennsylvania, Franklin recommended his friend John Hughes. This made it seem to many in Pennsylvania that Franklin not only approved of the act but had actually played a part in helping to pass it. As soon as news of his appointment arrived, Hughes became a target of violent political attacks and threats. He wrote an unhappy letter to Franklin, describing his plight, and Franklin replied in the following cautious terms. The "bill of fees" refers to money Franklin laid out to purchase Hughes's commission. The "petition" is, of course, the plea to remove the Penns. In spite of what he had already heard, Franklin still could not quite believe that the furor over the Stamp Act would or could obscure this issue, so important to him personally.

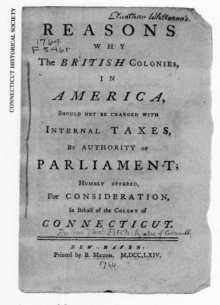

A pamphlet printed in New Haven, Connecticut, in 1764 by Benjamin Mecom, son of Franklin's sister Jane

London, Aug. 9. 1765

Since my last I have received your Favour of June 20. The Account you give me of the Indiscretion of some People with you, concerning the Government here, I do not wonder at. 'Tis of a Piece with the rest of their Conduct. But the Rashness of the Assembly in Virginia is amazing! I hope however that ours will keep within the Bounds of Prudence and Moderation; for that is the only way to lighten or get clear of our Burthens.

As to the Stamp-Act, tho' we purpose doing our Endeavour to get it repeal'd, in which I am sure you would concur with us, yet the Success is uncertain. If it continues, your undertaking to execute it may make you unpopular for a Time, but your Acting with Coolness and Steadiness, and with every Circumstance in your Power of Favour to the People, will by degrees reconcile them. In the meantime, a firm Loyalty to the Crown and faithful Adherence to the Government of this Nation, which it is the Safety as well as Honour of the Colonies to be connected with, will always be the wisest Course for you and I to take, whatever may be the Madness of the Populace or their blind Leaders, who can only bring themselves and Country into Trouble, and draw on greater Burthens by Acts of rebellious Tendency.

In mine of June 29. I sent you the Bill of Fees I had paid, amounting to £5 10s. 0d. Since which I have paid another Demand of £2 4s. 6d. Treasury Fees for a second Warrant, &c. the first not having included the Lower Counties. I now send with this, your Commission, with a Letter from the Secretary of the Stamp Office, with whom you are to correspond.

As to our Petition, the new Secretary of State, General Conway, has appointed next Wednesday to give us an Audience upon it, when I suppose it will be presented. And I have very little doubt of a favourable Progress and advantageous Issue.

Hughes and others were soon writing Franklin letters that brought home to him the seriousness and significance of the American resistance to the Stamp Act. Hughes frankly discussed the possibility of being murdered, and told Franklin how he was "well-arm'd" and "determin'd to stand a Siege" in his Philadelphia home. William Franklin lamented the total lack of directions from the ministry relative to the Stamp Act, and told him that in New York Franklin's old friend Cadwallader Colden, now the acting governor, had moved his son, who was appointed Stamp Commissioner for New York, into New York's fort and had marshaled soldiers and men-of-war to protect the stamps when they arrived. "The Boston Writers have basely spirited up the People there to rise and destroy Mr. Oliver's House, on Account of his being the Stamp Officer, &c.," William added. In this letter to his printing partner, David Hall, Franklin revealed some of the agitation that the crisis was stirring in him. The "quartering clause" refers to an alteration that Franklin had obtained in a bill Parliament had passed earlier in the year, outlining procedures for quartering troops in the Colonies. The original version of the act would have permitted the army to quarter the troops in private homes.

London, Sept. 14. 1765

You tell me "you should have been glad if I could have done anything to prevent the Stamp Act, as nothing could have contributed so much to have *removed the Prejudices* of many of the People against me, who stick not now to say that instead of doing anything to prevent it, I helped to plan it when last in England." To you who know me, I need not defend myself against such base Calumnies, and Time will open the Eyes of others. In the Heat of Party, Abuse is receiv'd greedily, and Vindications coldly. And it is my Opinion, that if I had actually prevented the Stamp Act, (which God knows I did all in my Power to prevent) neither the Malice of the bigotted Abettors of Indian Murder, nor the Malice of the interested Abettors of Proprietary Injustice, would have been in the least abated towards me. Those I have made my Enemies, by exposing their Wickedness and Folly to the World. They are my only Enemies, and they will continue my Enemies, let me do what I will that deserves their Friendship: Otherwise they would have given me some Credit for the Services I did last Winter, in opposing and preventing the Quartering Clause, and obtaining sundry favourable Changes in the Acts of Trade, of which, tho' I do not pretend to the whole Merit, I certainly had a considerable Share: but the Abatement of Postage near 30 per Cent. is, I may say, wholly owing to me, and will save more in the Pockets of Trading People, than all the Stamps they are to pay can amount to: And yet what Effect has that had towards *removing Prejudices?* By your Letter it seems none at all. It shall be my Endeavour, with God's Help, to act uprightly; and if I have the Approbation of the Good and Wise, which I shall certainly have sooner or later, the Enmity of Knaves and Fools will give me very little Concern.

The climax to this stream of bad news from America was a report from Deborah that mobs had threatened her and Sally in the house that Franklin had completed building shortly before he left for England. In a letter she wrote on September 22, 1765, Deborah told her husband how she had stood her ground with the aid of her relations and Franklin's friends. "I sente to aske my Brother to Cume and bring his gun all so so we maid one room into a Magazin. I ordored sum sorte of defens up Stairs such as I Cold manaig my self." On November 9, 1765, Franklin replied in a letter that has unfortunately been torn and worn by the passage of time and is reproduced here with modern interpolations in brackets. "The pious Presbyterian Countryman" was Samuel Smith, a Philadelphia merchant born in New England. The "Test" was the Test Act, which required office-holders in England to swear allegiance to the Church of England.

London, Nov. 9. 1765

Dear Debby,

I received yours and Sally's kind Letters of Sept. 22. and Brother Read's. Also one from our good Neighbour Thomson, and one from Brother Peter; one from Mr. Hall and one from Mr. Parker: All which I pray you to acknowledge for me, with Thanks, as I find I can not have time to write to them by this Packet. I honour much the Spirit and Courage you show'd, and the prudent Preparations you made in that [Time] of Danger. The [Woman?]

deserves a good [House] that [is?] determined [*torn*] to defend it. I hope that Mr. Hughes [recovers?] from that Illness. [*Torn and illegible*] and affectionately [to everyone on?] that List [that] you give me, who were so kind as to visit you [that] Evening. I shall long remember their Kindn[ess. As] to that pious Presbyterian Countryman of mine [whom you] say sets the People a madding, by telling them [that I] plann'd the Stamp Act, and am endeavo[uring to] bring the Test over to America, I thank him he does not charge me (as they do their God) with having plann'd Adam's Fall, and the Damnation of Mankind. It might be affirm'd with equal Truth and Modesty. He certainly was intended for a Wise Man; for he has the wisest Look of any Man I know; and if he would only nod and wink, and could but hold his Tongue, he might deceive an Angel. Let us pity and forget him. I am, my dear Girl, Your ever loving Husband

B FRANKLIN

Protesting the stamp tax, a New Jersey revolutionary paper made use of Franklin's segmented snake.

Franklin now went to work on a full-time campaign to get the Stamp Act repealed. In this letter to William Franklin he gave a vivid picture of his activities and arguments. Lord Rockingham had recently replaced George Grenville as First Minister. Lord Dartmouth was another nobleman sympathetic to America.

London, Novr. 9, 1765

Mr. Cooper, Secretary of the Treasury, is our old Acquaintance, and expresses a hearty Friendship for us both. Enclosed I send you his Billet proposing to make me acquainted with Lord Rockingham. I dine with his Lordship To-morrow.

I had a long Audience on Wednesday with Lord Dartmouth. He was highly recommended to me by Lords Grantham and Bessborough, as a young Man of excellent Understanding and the most amiable Dispositions. They seem'd extremely intent on bringing us together. I had been to pay my Respects to his Lordship on his Appointment to preside at the Board of Trade; but during the Summer he has been much out of Town, so that I had not till now the Opportunity of conversing with him. I found him all they said of him. He even exceeded the Expectations they had raised in me. If he continues in that Department, I foresee much Happiness from it to American Affairs. He enquired kindly after you, and spoke of you handsomely.

I gave it him as my Option, that the general Execution of the Stamp Act would be impracticable without occasioning more Mischief than it was worth, by totally alienating the Affections of the Americans from this Country, and thereby lessening its Commerce. I therefore wish'd that Advantage might be taken of the Address expected over (if express'd, as I hop'd it would be, in humble and dutiful Terms) to suspend the Execution of the Act for a Term of Years, till the Colonies should be more clear of Debt, and better able to bear it, and then drop it on some other decent Pretence, without ever bringing the Question of Right to a Decision. And I strongly recommended either a thorough Union with America, or that Government here would proceed in the old Method of Requisition, by which I was confident more would be obtained in the Way of voluntary Grant, than could probably be got by compulsory Taxes laid by Parliament. That particular Colonies might at Times be backward, but at other Times, when in better Temper, they would make up for that Backwardness, so that on the whole it would be nearly equal. That to send Armies and Fleets to enforce the Act, would not, in my Opinion, answer any good End; That the Inhabitants would probable take every Method to encourage the Soldiers to desert, to which the high Price of Labour would contribute, and the Chance of being never apprehended in so extensive a Country, where the Want of Hands, as well as the Desire of wasting the Strength of an Army come to oppress, would encline every one to conceal Deserters, so that the Officers would probably soon be left alone. That Fleets might indeed easily obstruct their Trade, but withal must ruin great Part of the Trade of Britain; as the Properties of American and British or London Merchants were mix'd in the same Vessels, and no Remittances could be receiv'd here; besides the Danger, by mutual Violences, Excesses and Severities, of creating a deep-rooted Aversion between the two Countries, and laying the Foundation of a future total Separation. I added, that notwithstanding the present Discontents, there still remain'd so much Respect in America for this Country, that Wisdom would do more towards reducing Things to order, than all our Force; And that, if the Address expected from the Congress of the Colonies should be unhappily such as could not be

With its issue of October 31, 1765, The Pennsylvania Journal *stopped publication to protest the purchase of stamps—"*EXPIRING: *In Hopes of a Resurrection to Life again."*

made the Foundation of a Suspension of the Act, in that Case three or four wise and good Men, Personages of some Rank and Dignity, should be sent over to America, with a Royal Commission to enquire into Grievances, hear Complaints, learn the true State of Affairs, giving Expectations of Redress where they found the People really aggriev'd, and endeavouring to convince and reclaim them by Reason, where they found them in the Wrong. That such an Instance of the Considerateness, Moderation and Justice of this Country towards its remote Subjects would contribute more towards securing and perpetuating the Dominion, than all its Force, and be much cheaper. A great deal more I said on our American Affairs; too much to write. His Lordship heard all with great Attention and Patience. As to the Address expected from the Congress, he doubted some Difficulty would arise about receiving it, as it was an irregular Meeting, unauthoriz'd by any American Constitution. I said, I hoped Government here would not be too nice on that Head; That the Mode was indeed new, but to the People there it seem'd necessary, their separate Petitions last Year being rejected. And to refuse hearing Complaints and Redressing Grievances, from Punctilios about Form, had always an ill Effect, and gave great Handle to those turbulent factious Spirits who are ever ready to blow the Coals of Dissension. He thank'd me politely for the Visit, and desired to see me often.

It is true that Inconveniences may arise to Government here by a Repeal of the Act, as it will be deem'd a tacit giving up the Sovereignty of Parliament: And yet I think the Inconveniences of persisting much greater, as I have said above. The present Ministry are truely perplex'd how to act on the Occasion: as, if they relax, their Predecessors will reproach them with giving up the Honour, Dignity, and Power of this Nation. And yet even they, I am told, think they have carry'd Things too far; So that if it were indeed true that I had plann'd the Act (as you say it is reported with you) I believe we should soon hear some of them exculpating themselves by saying I had misled them. I need not tell you that I had not the least Concern in it. It was all cut and dry'd, and every Resolve fram'd at the Treasury ready for the House, before I arriv'd in England, or knew any thing of the Matter; so that if they had given me a Pension on that Account (as

is said by some, I am told) it would have been very dishonest in me to accept of it.

Meanwhile, in the English newspapers, Franklin began
a task that was to occupy him for the next ten years—defending America's
reputation against the volleys of abuse fired at the Colonies by outraged
Britons, who could see no reason why Americans should not pay the same taxes
they paid at home. The following letter attacked a correspondent who, signing
himself Tom Hint, condemned the anti-Stamp Act rioting in New York and
called upon the British army to punish Americans. Franklin did not try very
hard to disguise his identity, signing "F.B." at the close of the letter.

December 20, 1765

To the PRINTER.

I beg room in your impartial paper for a word or two
with your correspondent of Friday Last, who subscribes
himself TOM HINT.

He tells us, that he lived many years in that part of
the world, and is pleased to assert roundly, that "the
most opulent inhabitants of America are of selfish, mean
dispositions, void of public spirit; and that they took
every occasion (during the late war, it seems) of ob-
structing the King's measures, when they in the least
interfered with their particular interests."

It is a heavy charge this: and as I too have lived many
years in that country, I have reason to know that it is a
charge without foundation; and that the very reverse is
true.

I would therefore ask this writer, if he has never
learnt that calumniating even a single person behind
his back, to increase differences between friends, is
unworthy a gentleman; and that stabbing in the dark
is unbecoming a soldier and an officer? Whether he does
not think that calumniating the principal people of
twelve or thirteen colonies, to incite the mother country
to sheath the sword in the bowels of her children, is
not infinitely more wicked? and the doing this under a
feigned name, at three thousand miles distance from the
parties injured, proportionably more mean, base, and
cowardly?

I call upon him, therefore, to name those opulent persons, and point out the instances, putting his own name
openly and fairly to his accusation; or take to himself
in private the conscious shame that belongs to such base-
ness, aggravated by a recollection of the generous hospi-

tality he personally met with in the country he has so unworthily abused.

In Strahan's London *Chronicle,* from February 6 to 8, 1766, Franklin published for the first time his letters to William Shirley, which were graphic proof that America's hostility to taxation without representation had deep roots. Meanwhile, in Parliament, Edmund Burke, the Irish-born private secretary of Lord Rockingham, decided that what the House of Commons needed was information, not more windy rhetoric. He proceeded to arrange for a series of experts on America to testify. One of these was Benjamin Franklin. Knowing the importance of his testimony, because of his worldwide reputation, the supporters of the ministry did their utmost to make it as effective as possible. In the days preceding Franklin's appearance, they conferred with him and worked out a series of questions that they would ask him from the floor. He prepared careful answers to these queries. There would inevitably be questions from the opposition, as well. For these, Franklin would have to depend upon his native wit.

[February 13, 1766]

The EXAMINATION of Doctor BENJAMIN FRANKLIN, before an AUGUST ASSEMBLY, relating to the Repeal of the STAMP ACT, &c.

Q. What is your name, and place of abode?

A. Franklin, of Philadelphia.

Q. Do the Americans pay any considerable taxes among themselves?

A. Certainly many, and very heavy taxes.

Q. What are the present taxes in Pennsylvania, laid by the laws of the colony?

A. There are taxes on all estates real and personal, a poll tax, a tax on all offices, professions, trades and businesses, according to their profits; and excise on all wine, rum, and other spirits; and a duty of Ten Pounds per head on all Negroes imported, with some other duties.

Q. For what purpose are those taxes laid?

A. For the support of the civil and military establishments of the country, and to discharge the heavy debt contracted in the last war.

Q. How long are those taxes to continue?

A. Those for discharging the debt are to continue till 1772, and longer, if the debt should not be then all discharged. The others must always continue.

Q. Was it not expected that the debt would have been sooner discharged?

The only known original example of Franklin's Stamp Act cartoon showing "Britannia" dismembered

FRANKLIN S'OPPOSE AUX TAXES

Contemporary French engraving illustrating Franklin's examination before the House of Commons

A. It was, when the peace was made with France and Spain—But a fresh war breaking out with the Indians, a fresh load of debt was incurred, and the taxes, of course, continued longer by a new law.

Q. Are not all the people very able to pay those taxes?

A. No. The frontier counties, all along the continent, having been frequently ravaged by the enemy, and greatly impoverished, are able to pay very little tax. And therefore, in consideration of their distresses, our late tax laws do expressly favour those counties, excusing the sufferers; and I suppose the same is done in other governments.

Q. Are not you concerned in the management of the Post-Office in America?

A. Yes. I am Deputy Post-Master General of North-America.

Q. Don't you think the distribution of stamps, by post, to all the inhabitants, very practicable, if there was no opposition?

A. The posts only go along the sea coasts; they do not, except in a few instances, go back into the country; and if they did, sending for stamps by post would occasion an expence of postage, amounting, in many cases, to much more than that of the stamps themselves....

Q. From the thinness of the back settlements, would not the stamp-act be extreamly inconvenient to the inhabitants, if executed?

A. To be sure it would; as many of the inhabitants could not get stamps when they had occasion for them, without taking long journeys, and spending perhaps Three or Four Pounds, that the Crown might get Sixpence.

Q. Are not the Colonies, from their circumstances, very able to pay the stamp duty?

A. In my opinion, there is not gold and silver enough in the Colonies to pay the stamp duty for one year.

Q. Don't you know that the money arising from the stamps was all to be laid out in America?

A. I know it is appropriated by the act to the American service; but it will be spent in the conquered Colonies, where the soldiers are, not in the Colonies that pay it....

Q. How many white men do you suppose there are in

North-America?

A. About 300,000, from sixteen to sixty years of age.

Q. What may be the amount of one year's imports into Pennsylvania from Britain?

A. I have been informed that our merchants compute the imports from Britain to be above 500,000 Pounds.

Q. What may be the amount of the produce of your province exported to Britain?

A. It must be small, as we produce little that is wanted in Britain. I suppose it cannot exceed 40,000 Pounds.

Q. How then do you pay the ballance?

A. The Ballance is paid by our produce carried to the West-Indies, and sold in our own islands, or to the French, Spaniards, Danes and Dutch; by the same carried to other colonies in North-America, as to New-England, Nova-Scotia, Newfoundland, Carolina and Georgia; by the same carried to different parts of Europe, as Spain, Portugal and Italy. In all which places we receive either money, bills of exchange, or commodities that suit for remittance to Britain; which, together with all the profits on the industry of our merchants and mariners, arising in those circuitous voyages, and the freights made by their ships, center finally in Britain, to discharge the ballance, and pay for British manufactures continually used in the province, or sold to foreigners by our traders....

Q. Do you think it right that America should be protected by this country, and pay no part of the expence?

A. That is not the case. The Colonies raised, cloathed and paid, during the last war, near 25000 men, and spent many millions.

Q. Were you not reimbursed by parliament?

A. We were only reimbursed what, in your opinion, we had advanced beyond our proportion, or beyond what might reasonably be expected from us; and it was a very small part of what we spent. Pennsylvania, in particular, disbursed about 500,000 Pounds, and the reimbursements, in the whole, did not exceed 60,000 Pounds....

Q. Do not you think the people of America would submit to pay the stamp duty, if it was moderated?

A. No, never, unless compelled by force of arms....

Q. What was the temper of America towards Great-Britain before the year 1763?

A. The best in the world. They submitted willingly to the government of the Crown, and paid, in all their courts, obedience to acts of parliament. Numerous as the people are in the several old provinces, they cost you nothing in forts, citadels, garrisons or armies, to keep them in subjection. They were governed by this country at the expence only of a little pen, ink and paper. They were led by a thread. They had not only a respect, but an affection, for Great-Britain, for its laws, its customs and manners, and even a fondness for its fashions, that greatly increased the commerce. Natives of Britain were always treated with particular regard; to be an Old Englandman was, of itself, a character of some respect, and gave a kind of rank among us.

Q. And what is their temper now?

A. O, very much altered.

Q. Did you ever hear the authority of parliament to make laws for America questioned till lately?

A. The authority of parliament was allowed to be valid in all laws, except such as should lay internal taxes. It was never disputed in laying duties to regulate commerce.

Q. In what proportion hath population increased in America?

A. I think the inhabitants of all the provinces together, taken at a medium, double in about 25 years. But their demand for British manufactures increases much faster, as the consumption is not merely in proportion to their numbers, but grows with the growing abilities of the same numbers to pay for them. In 1723, the whole importation from Britain to Pennsylvania, was but about 15,000 Pounds Sterling; it is now near Half a Million....

Q. What is your opinion of a future tax, imposed on the same principle with that of the stamp-act; how would the Americans receive it?

A. Just as they do this. They would not pay it.

Q. Have you not heard of the resolutions of this house, and of the house of lords, asserting the right of parliament relating to America, including a power to tax

Crude anti-Stamp Act woodcut from The Pennsylvania Journal, *1765*

the people there?

A.   Yes, I have heard of such resolutions.

Q.   What will be the opinion of the Americans on those resolutions?

A.   They will think them unconstitutional, and unjust. . . .

Q.   You say the Colonies have always submitted to external taxes, and object to the right of parliament only in laying internal taxes; now can you shew that there is any kind of difference between the two taxes to the Colony on which they may be laid?

A.   I think the difference is very great. An external tax is a duty laid on commodities imported; that duty is added to the first cost, and other charges on the commodity, and when it is offered to sale, makes a part of the price. If the people do not like it at that price, they refuse it; they are not obliged to pay it. But an internal tax is forced from the people without their consent, if not laid by their own representatives. The stamp-act says, we shall have no commerce, make no exchange of property with each other, neither purchase nor grant, nor recover debts; we shall neither marry, nor make our wills, unless we pay such and such sums, and thus it is intended to extort our money from us, or ruin us by the consequences of refusing to pay it.

Q.   But supposing the external tax or duty to be laid on the necessaries of life imported into your Colony, will not that be the same thing in its effects as an internal tax?

A.   I do not know a single article imported into the Northern Colonies, but what they can either do without, or make themselves. . . .

Q.   Considering the resolutions of parliament, as to the right, do you think, if the stamp-act is repealed, that the North Americans will be satisfied?

A.   I believe they will.

Q.   Why do you think so?

A.   I think the resolutions of right will give them very little concern, if they are never attempted to be carried into practice. The Colonies will probably consider themselves in the same situation, in that respect, with Ireland; they know you claim the same right with regard to Ireland, but you never exercise it. And they may believe you never will exercise it

Example of British stamp used in the Colonies under the Stamp Act

Earthenware teapot, circa 1765, with a decorative protest to the Stamp Act

COLONIAL WILLIAMSBURG COLLECTION

in the Colonies, any more than in Ireland, unless on some very extraordinary occasion.

Q. But who are to be the judges of that extraordinary occasion? Is it not the parliament?

A. Though the parliament may judge of the occasion, the people will think it can never exercise such right, till representatives from the Colonies are admitted into parliament, and that whenever the occasion arises, representatives will be ordered....

Q. Can any thing less than a military force carry the stamp-act into execution?

A. I do not see how a military force can be applied to that purpose.

Q. Why may it not?

A. Suppose a military force sent into America, they will find nobody in arms; what are they then to do? They cannot force a man to take stamps who chooses to do without them. They will not find a rebellion; they may indeed make one.

Q. If the act is not repealed, what do you think will be the consequences?

A. A total loss of the respect and affection the people of America bear to this country, and of all the commerce that depends on that respect and affection.

Q. How can the commerce be affected?

A. You will find, that if the act is not repealed, they will take very little of your manufactures in a short time....

Q. Supposing the stamp-act continued, and enforced, do you imagine that ill humour will induce the Americans to give as much for worse manufactures of their own, and use them, preferably to better of ours?

A. Yes, I think so. People will pay as freely to gratify one passion as another, their resentment as their pride....

Q. If the stamp act should be repealed, would not the Americans think they could oblige the parliament to repeal every external tax law now in force?

A. It is hard to answer questions of what people at such a distance will think.

Q. But what do you imagine they will think were the motives of repealing the act?

A. I suppose they will think that it was repealed from

a conviction of its inexpediency; and they will rely upon it, that while the same inexpediency subsists, you will never attempt to make such another.

Q. What do you mean by its inexpediency?

A. I mean its inexpediency on several accounts; the poverty and inability of those who were to pay the tax; the general discontent it has occasioned; and the impracticability of enforcing it.

Q. If the act should be repealed, and the legislature should shew its resentment to the opposers of the stamp-act, would the Colonies acquiesce in the authority of the legislature? What is your opinion they would do?

A. I don't doubt at all, that if the legislature repeal the stamp-act, the Colonies will acquiesce in the authority. . . .

Q. Do you think . . . that the taking possession of the King's territorial rights, and strengthening the frontiers, is not an American interest?

A. Not particularly, but conjointly a British and an American interest.

Q. You will not deny that the preceding war, the war with Spain, was entered into for the sake of America; was it not occasioned by captures made in the American seas?

A. Yes; captures of ships carrying on the British trade there, with British manufactures.

Q. Was not the late war with the Indians, since the peace with France, a war for America only?

A. Yes; it was more particularly for America than the former, but it was rather a consequence or remains of the former war, the Indians not having been thoroughly pacified, and the Americans bore by much the greatest share of the expence. It was put an end to by the army under General Bouquet; there were not above 300 regulars in that army, and above 1000 Pennsylvanians. . . .

Q. If the stamp-act should be repealed, and an act should pass, ordering the assemblies of the Colonies to indemnify the sufferers by the riots, would they obey it?

A. That is a question I cannot answer.

Q. Suppose the King should require the Colonies to grant a revenue, and the parliament should be against their doing it, do they think they can grant a revenue to the King, without the consent of the parliament of G. Britain?

A. That is a deep question. As to my own opinion, I should think myself at liberty to do it, and should do it, if I liked the occasion....

Q. If the stamp-act should be repealed, and the Crown should make a requisition to the Colonies for a sum of money, would they grant it?

A. I believe they would....

Q. If the stamp-act should be repealed, would it induce the assemblies of America to acknowledge the rights of parliament to tax them, and would they erase their resolutions?

A. No, never.

Q. Is there no means of obliging them to erase those resolutions?

A. None that I know of; they will never do it unless compelled by force of arms.

Q. Is there a power on earth that can force them to erase them?

A. No power, how great soever, can force men to change their opinions....

Q. What used to be the pride of the Americans?

A. To indulge in the fashions and manufactures of Great-Britain.

Q. What is now their pride?

A. To wear their old cloaths over again, till they can make new ones.

It is always fascinating to catch a glimpse of history and its impact on a man almost at the moment it was being made. At two o'clock on the morning of February 22, the committee of the whole House of Commons voted 275 to 167 to repeal the Stamp Act. Only a few hours later, an exultant Franklin dashed off the following letter to his wife Deborah.

London, Feb. 22. 1766

My dear Child,

I am excessively hurried, being every Hour that I am awake either abroad to speak with Members of Parliament or taken up with People coming to me at home, concerning our American Affairs, so that I am much behind-hand in answering my Friends Letters. But tho' I cannot by this Opportunity write to others, I must not omit a Line to you who kindly write me so many. I am well; 'tis all I can say at present, except that I am just now made very happy by a Vote of the Commons for the Repeal of the Stamp Act. Your ever loving Husband

B FRANKLIN

By March 8, the repeal of the Stamp Act had received the royal assent. William Strahan rushed a stenographic copy of Franklin's examination to David Hall in Philadelphia with these expansive words: "To this very examination, more than to anything else, you are indebted to the *speedy* and *total* repeal of this odious law." Strahan may have been laying on the praise a bit thick, to bolster his friend Franklin's reputation. But there is no doubt that Franklin's appearance did play a major role in repealing the Stamp Act, and restoring a state of temporary calm between England and America. As a result, Franklin's political reputation soared to hitherto unknown heights. He was hailed as the savior of America, and the examination was reprinted in Massachusetts, Virginia, and New York, and became required reading throughout the Colonies. Franklin did not allow this abrupt and welcome reversal to go to his head. In this letter to Charles Thomson, he summed up his mature opinion of the tangled skein.

London, Sept. 27. 1766

Dear Friend and Neighbour

I received your very kind Letter of May 20. which came here while I was absent in Germany. The favourable Sentiments you express of my Conduct with regard to the Repeal to the Stamp Act, give me real Pleasure; and I hope in every other matter of publick Concern, so to behave myself as to stand fair in the Opinions of the Wise and Good: What the rest think and say of me will then give me less Concern.

That Part of your Letter which related to the Situation of People's Minds in America before and after the Repeal, was so well exprest, and in my Opinion so proper to be generally read and understood here, that I had it printed in the London Chronicle. I had the Pleasure to find that it did Good in several Instances within my Knowledge.

There are Claimers enow of Merit in obtaining the Repeal. But if I live to see you, I will let you know what an Escape we had in the Beginning of the Affair, and how much we were obliged to what the Profane would call *Luck*, and the Pious *Providence*.

You will give an old Man Leave to say My Love to Mrs. Thomson. With sincere Regard, I am, Your affectionate Friend. . . .

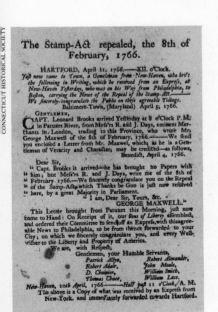

Broadside announcing the repeal of the Stamp Act on February 8, 1766, which did not reach Hartford, Connecticut, until April 11

Franklin knew there was still formidable opposition to America in Parliament. He used his favorite weapon, ridicule, to attack the die-hards in the following newspaper essay. Where it first appeared — sometime in February or March, 1766 — is not known; it was reprinted in the *Pennsylvania Chronicle* for March 16–23, 1767.

[February–March 1766]

To the PRINTER.

It is reported, I know not with what Foundation, that there is an Intention of obliging the Americans to pay for all the Stamps they ought to have used, between the Commencement of the Act, and the Day on which the Repeal takes Place, viz. from the first of November 1765, to the first of May 1766; that this is to make Part of an Act, which is to give Validity to the Writings and Law Proceedings, that contrary to Law have been executed without Stamps, and is to be the Condition on which they are to receive that Validity. Shall we then keep up for a Trifle the Heats and Animosities that have been occasioned by the Stamp-Act? and lose all the Benefit of Harmony and good Understanding between the different Parts of the Empire, which were expected from a generous total Repeal? Is this Pittance likely to be a Whit more easily collected than the whole Duty? Where are Officers to be found who will undertake to collect it? Who is to protect them while they are about it? In my Opinion, it will meet with the same Opposition, and be attended with the same Mischiefs that would have attended an Enforcement of the Act entire.

But I hear, that this is thought necessary, to raise a Fund for defraying the Expence that has been incurred by stamping so much Paper and Parchment for the Use of America, which they have refused to take and turn'd upon our Hands; and that since they are highly favour'd by the Repeal, they cannot with any Face of Decency refuse to make good the Charges we have been at on their Account. The whole Proceeding would put one in Mind of the Frenchman that used to accost English and other Strangers on the Pont-Neuf, with many Compliments, and a red hot Iron in his Hand; *Pray Monsieur Anglois*, says he, *Do me the Favour to let me have the Honour of thrusting this hot Iron into your Backside?* Zoons, what does the Fellow mean! Begone with your Iron, or I'll break your Head! *Nay, Monsieur*, replies he, *if you do not chuse it, I do not insist upon it. But at least,*

To celebrate the repeal of the Stamp Act an obelisk was erected in Boston. This view of one of its sides is a detail from a large etching by Paul Revere and includes representations of Queen Charlotte, King George, and other distinguished patriots.

*you will in Justice have the Goodness to pay me some-
thing for the heating of my Iron.*

F.B.

Only a few weeks after the Stamp Act was repealed,
Parliament reaffirmed that it had no intention of abandoning its traditional
attitude toward the Colonies, by considering a bill renewing England's right
to transport felons to America and extending the right to Scotland. Franklin
drew up this satiric petition, which he permitted Pennsylvania's agent,
Richard Jackson, to pass around to his fellow M.P.'s, unofficially. It "occasion'd some laughing," but the bill passed without debate.

[April 12–15, 1766]

To the honourable the Knights Citizens and Burgesses
of Great Britain in Parliament assembled,
The Petition of BF. Agent for the Province of Pensilvania, Most humbly Sheweth,

That the Transporting of Felons from England to the
Plantations in America, is and hath long been a great
Grievance to the said Plantations in general.

That the said Felons being landed in America, not only
continue their evil Practices, to the Annoyance of his
Majesty's good Subjects there, but contribute greatly
to corrupt the Morals of the Servants and poorer People
among whom they are mixed.

That many of the said Felons escape from the Servi-
tude to which they were destined, into other Colonies,
where their Condition is not known and wandering at
large from one populous Town to another commit many
Burglaries Robberies and Murders, to the great Terror
of the People, and occasioning heavy Charges for the
apprehending and securing such Felons, and bringing
them to Justice.

That your Petitioner humbly conceives the Easing one
Part of the British Dominions of their Felons by burthening another Part with the same Felons, cannot increase
the common Happiness of his Majesty's Subjects; and
that therefore the Trouble and Expence of transporting
them is upon the whole altogether useless.

That your Petitioner nevertheless observes with extream Concern, in the Votes of Friday last, that Leave
is given to bring in a Bill, for extending to Scotland the
Act made in the 4th. Year of the Reign of King George
the First, whereby the aforesaid Grievances are (as he
understands) to be greatly increas'd by allowing Scotland

*A detail from an English cartoon
following the Stamp Act's repeal
shows George Grenville, holding
coffin of "Miss Americ-Stamp," and
other Tory ministers filing behind
him into the family vault.*

also to transport its Felons to America.

Your Petitioner therefore humbly prays, in behalf of Pensilvania and the other Plantations in America that the House wou'd take the Premisses into Consideration, and in their great Wisdom and Goodness repeal all Acts and Clauses of Acts for Transporting of Felons; or if this may not at present be done, that they would at least reject the propos'd Bill for extending of the said Acts to Scotland; or, if it be thought fit to allow of such Extension, that then the said Extension may be carried farther, and the Plantations be also by an equitable Clause in the same Bill permitted to transport their Felons to Scotland.

Already, the Boston runaway, the journeyman printer, the Philadelphia businessman, was quietly assuming the role he had created for himself in the Stamp Act crisis — unofficial ambassador for a yet-unborn American nation. It had been a long journey for Franklin. Looking back across forty crowded years to his youth, he undoubtedly thought that the repeal of the Stamp Act was that "bright point" with which he wished to end his life. He had no way of knowing that the best and most dramatic years were yet to come — with a "point" far brighter than even he dared to imagine.